THE
TALIBAN
SHUFFLE

THE
TALIBAN
SHUFFLE

STRANGE

DAYS IN

AFGHANISTAN

AND PAKISTAN

KIM BARKER

DOUBLEDAY

NEW YORK LONDON TORONTO SYDNEY AUCKLAND

DD
DOUBLEDAY

www.doubleday.com

DOUBLEDAY and the DD colophon are registered trademarks
of Random House, Inc.

Jacket design by Emily Mahon
Jacket photograph by Jared Moosy/Redux
Photo retouching by Benjamin Weisman

LIBRARY OF CONGRESS CATALOGING-IN-PUBLICATION DATA
Barker, Kim, 1970–
The Taliban shuffle : strange days in Afghanistan and Pakistan /
Kim Barker.—1st ed.
p.   cm.
1. Afghan War, 2001—Press coverage. 2. Barker, Kim,
1970– 3. War correspondents—Afghanistan—Biography.
4. War correspondents—Pakistan—Biography. 5. War
correspondents—United States—Biography. 6. Afghanistan—
History—2001– 7. Pakistan—History—21st century. I. Title.
DS371.4135B37 2011
✓958.104'7—dc22   2010024348

ISBN 978-0-385-53331-7

PRINTED IN THE UNITED STATES OF AMERICA

10 9 8 7 6 5 4 3 2 1

First Edition

To the people of Afghanistan and Pakistan,

who are still waiting for the punch line

CONTENTS

THE
TALIBAN
SHUFFLE

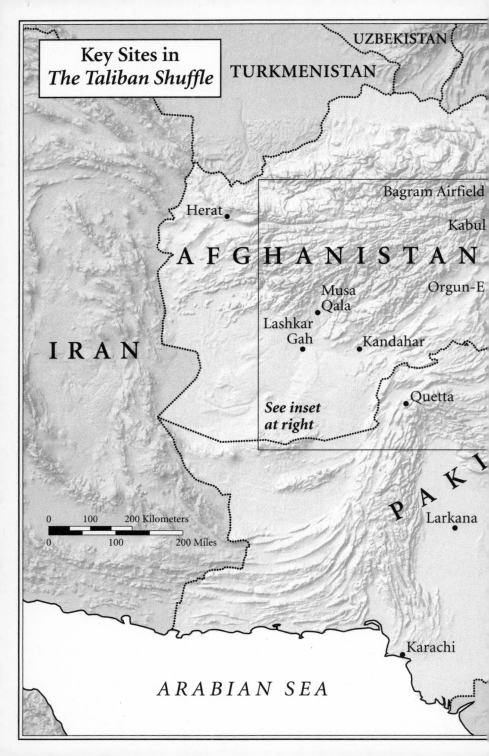

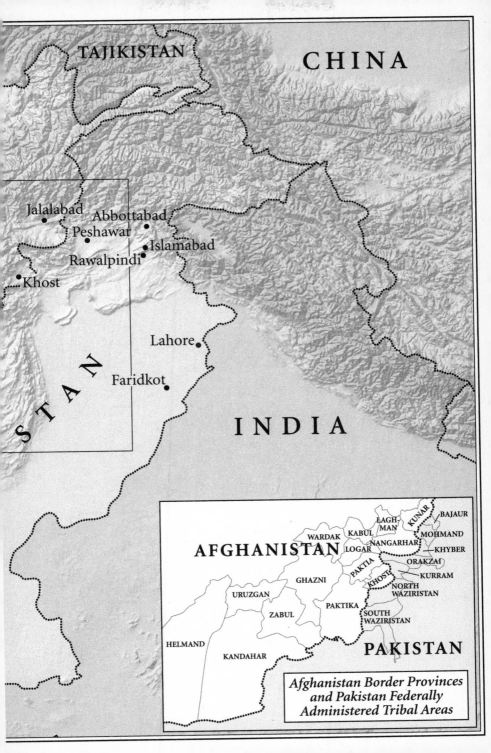

TAJIKISTAN

CHINA

Jalalabad

Abbottabad
Peshawar

Islamabad

Rawalpindi

Khost

STAN

Lahore

Faridkot

INDIA

AFGHANISTAN

LAGH-
MAN
KUNAR
BAJAUR

WARDAK
KABUL
MOHMAND

LOGAR
NANGARHAR
KHYBER

GHAZNI
PAKTIA
ORAKZAI

KHOST
KURRAM

URUZGAN
PAKTIKA
NORTH
WAZIRISTAN

ZABUL
SOUTH
WAZIRISTAN

HELMAND
KANDAHAR
PAKISTAN

*Afghanistan Border Provinces
and Pakistan Federally
Administered Tribal Areas*

PART I **KABUL HIGH**

CHAPTER 1
WELCOME TO THE TERRORDOME

I had always wanted to meet a warlord. So we parked our van on the side of the beige road and walked up to the beige house, past dozens of skinny young soldiers brandishing Kalashnikov assault rifles and wearing mismatched khaki outfits and rope belts hiked high on their waists. Several flaunted kohl eyeliner and tucked yellow flowers behind their ears. Others decorated their rifle butts with stickers of flowers and Indian movie starlets. Male ethnic Pashtuns loved flowers and black eyeliner and anything fluorescent or sparkly, maybe to make up for the beige terrain that stretched forever in Afghanistan, maybe to look pretty.

Outside the front door, my translator Farouq and I took off our shoes before walking inside and sitting cross-legged on the red cushions that lined the walls. The decorations spanned that narrow range between unicorn-loving prepubescent girl and utilitarian disco. Bright, glittery plastic flowers poked out of holes in the white walls. The curtains were riots of color.

We waited. I was slightly nervous about our reception. Once, warlord Pacha Khan Zadran had been a U.S. ally, one of the many Afghan warlords the Americans used to help drive out the Taliban regime for sheltering Osama bin Laden and his minions after the attacks of September 11, 2001. But like a spoiled child, Pacha Khan had rebelled against his benefactors, apparently because no one was paying enough attention to him. First he turned against the fledgling Afghan government, then against his American allies. In an epic battle over a mountain pass, the Americans had just killed the warlord's son. The Pashtun code required revenge, among other things, and now, six days after the battle, here I was, a fairly convenient American, waiting like a present on a pillow in Pacha Khan's house, hoping to find a story edgy enough to make it into my newspaper—not easy considering it was March 2003, and there were other things going on in the world. But Farouq told me not to worry. He had a plan.

Pacha Khan soon marched into the room. He certainly looked the warlord part, wearing a tan salwar kameez, the region's ubiquitous traditional long shirt and baggy pants that resembled pajamas, along with a brown vest, a bandolier of bullets, and a gray-and-black turban. The wrinkles on his face appeared to have been carved out with an ice pick. He resembled a chubby Saddam Hussein. We hopped up to greet him. He motioned us to sit down, welcomed us, and then offered us lunch, an orange oil slick of potatoes and meat that was mostly gristle. I had no choice, given how strictly Afghans and especially Pashtuns viewed hospitality. I dug in, using my hands and a piece of bread as utensils.

But just because Pacha Khan fed us, didn't mean he would agree to an interview. The Pashtun code required him to show us hospitality. It didn't force him to talk to me. Pacha Khan squinted at my getup—a long brown Afghan dress over black pants, an Indian paisley headscarf, and cat-eye glasses. I kept shifting my position—with a bad left knee, a bad right ankle, and a bad back, sitting on the floor was about as comfortable as therapy.

Farouq tried to sell my case in the Pashto language. The warlord had certain questions.

"Where is she from?" Pacha Khan asked, suspiciously.

"Turkey," Farouq responded.

"Is she Muslim?"

"Yes."

"Have her pray for me."

I smiled dumbly, oblivious to the conversation and Farouq's lies.

"She can't," Farouq said, slightly revising his story. "She is a Turkish American. She only knows the prayers in English, not Arabic."

"Hmmm," Pacha Khan grunted, glaring at me. "She is a very bad Muslim."

"She *is* a very bad Muslim," Farouq agreed.

I continued to grin wildly, attempting to charm Pacha Khan.

"Is she scared of me?" he asked.

"What's going on? What's he saying?" I interrupted.

"He wants to know if you're scared of him," Farouq said.

"Oh no," I said. "He seems like a perfectly nice guy. Totally harmless. Very kind."

Farouq nodded and turned to Pacha Khan.

"Of course she is scared of you," Farouq translated. "You are a big and terrifying man. But I told her you were a friend of the *Chicago Tribune*, and I guaranteed her safety."

That satisfied him. Unaware of Farouq's finesse, I proceeded with my questions about Pacha Khan's deteriorating relationship with the Americans. Then I asked if I could have my photograph taken with the warlord, who agreed.

"Make sure you get the flowers," I told Farouq.

In one picture, Pacha Khan peered sideways at me, with an expression suggesting he thought I was the strange one. I snapped Farouq's picture with Pacha Khan as well. Souvenirs in hand, we left. But we still had two more hours of bumpy, unforgiving road south to the town of Khost, an experience similar to being flogged with baseball bats. Farouq taught me the numbers in the Dari language and told me about the real conversation he had with Pacha Khan.

"I don't think it's ethical to say I'm Turkish," I said.

"I don't think it's safe to say you're American. The Americans just killed his son. Trust me. I know Afghans. I know what I'm doing."

I shut my mouth, but I still didn't see what the big deal was. I had glasses. I was obviously harmless. And Pacha Khan seemed more bluster than bullet.

As we wandered around Pacha Khan-istan, calling me naïve was almost a compliment; ignorant was more accurate. This was only my second trip to Afghanistan as a fill-in correspondent for the *Tribune*, and I was only supposed to babysit a war that nobody cared about while everyone else invaded Iraq. With my assumed swagger and misplaced confidence, I was convinced that I could do anything. Meeting a warlord whose son had just been killed by the Americans was nothing but a funny photo opportunity. I felt I was somehow missing out by not being in Iraq, the hitter sidelined for the championship game. Like everyone else, I figured Afghanistan was more of a sideshow than the big show.

Back then, I had no idea what would actually happen. That Pakistan and Afghanistan would ultimately become more all consuming than any relationship I had ever had. That they would slowly fall apart, and that even as they crumbled, chunk by chunk, they would feel more like home than anywhere else. I had no idea that I would find self-awareness in a combat zone, a kind of peace in chaos. My life here wouldn't be about a man or God or some cause. I would fall in love, deeply, but with a story, with a way of life. When everything else was stripped away, my life would be about an addiction, not to drugs, but to a place. I would never feel as alive as when I was here.

Eventually, more than six years down the road, when the addiction overrode everything else, when normalcy seemed inconceivable, I would have to figure out how to get clean and get out. By then, I would not be the same person. I would be unemployed and sleeping at a friend's house in Kabul. Dozens of Afghans and Pakistanis I met along the way would be dead, including one translator. Other friends would be kidnapped. Still other people would disappoint me, sucked into corruption and selfishness precisely when their countries needed them. I would disappoint others. None of us would get it right.

When did everyone mess up? Many times, on all sides, but March 2003 is as good a start as any. From the beginning, the numbers were absurd: Post-conflict Kosovo had one peacekeeper for every forty-eight people. East Timor, one for every eighty-six. Afghanistan, already mired in poverty, drought, and more than two decades of war, with little effective government and a fledgling army that was hardly more than a militia, had just one peacekeeper for every 5,400 people. Then the foreigners cheated on Afghanistan. They went to Iraq.

Had they known anything about the country at all, they would have known that this was a really bad idea. Afghanistan was the so-called Graveyard of Empires, a pitiless mass of hard mountains and desert almost the size of Texas that had successfully repelled invaders like the Brits and the Soviets and seemed amenable only to the unforgiving people born to it. Men learned to fight like they learned to breathe, without even thinking. They fought dogs, they fought cocks. They fought tiny delicate birds that fit in a human hand and lived in a human coat pocket, and they bet on the results. They fought wars for decades until no one seemed to remember quite what they were fighting for. The national sport was essentially a fight, on horseback, over a headless calf or goat. Over the years, whenever Afghan men would tell me that they were tired of fighting, looking weary and creased, I would have only one response: Sure you are.

But now, on this road trip, I didn't worry about any of that. I was like a child, happy with my picture, showing it repeatedly to Farouq, who repeatedly laughed. Hours of bone-crushing road after leaving my first genuine warlord, our driver, Nasir, pulled into Khost and the so-called hotel. It was a second-floor walk-up on Khost's dusty main street, a place that looked as if a gun battle might break out at any second, as if *High Noon* could be filmed at any hour. Khost was a small city just over the border from Pakistan's tribal areas, the semi-autonomous region where insurgents and criminals could roam freely. In Khost, as in the tribal areas, laws were more like helpful hints. Everyone seemed to have a weapon, even the two men sleeping on the hotel balcony, fingers twitching near their triggers. We walked past a room where two Afghan journalists had holed up. They were friends of Farouq, but they gently closed the door on us. I didn't pay much attention. Outside the window in my room, I tried to set up a satellite dish to make a phone call, but the power was out, as usual, and the sun was setting. The satellite phone didn't work. Nothing worked. I grew exasperated.

"Damn it," I announced.

"Kim," Farouq said outside my door.

"This stupid satellite phone won't work. There's no power."

Farouq walked in and tried to get me to focus. "Kim. We need to talk."

"What? When does the stupid power come on?"

"Kim. My two friends, the journalists you just saw, they were both held hostage for four days by Pacha Khan. He threatened to kill them because they worked for the American media, and the Americans killed his son."

This stopped me. "You're kidding me."

Farouq told me that the men had only been freed with the intervention of President Hamid Karzai. I envisioned returning the same grueling way we came, seven hours, most of which passed through Pacha Khan territory.

"Can we drive back to Kabul another way?" I asked.

Farouq thought about it.

"That would take eighteen hours. Through really bad roads and dangerous areas. I think we'll be OK. You're a foreigner. Pacha Khan would be afraid to kidnap you. I just thought you should know. For your story."

Eighteen hours on punishing roads versus seven hours of slightly less punishing roads and the bonus potential of being kidnapped. That was a reality check, one of many I would have. I said I would think about the trip. The next day, we visited a man who had recently been released from the U.S. detention center in Guantánamo Bay,

Cuba. He was a taxi driver and happily showed us his stereo, music, and videos and talked of his love for the movie *Titanic*, proof he wasn't a member of the Taliban, which under the guise of Islam had banned all such frivolities during their five years in power. He was oddly not upset at the Americans, despite being held in Guantánamo for more than a year in what all sides acknowledged had been a mistake. His family welcomed us. I sat in a room with the women, where no strange man, including Farouq, could go. With no translator, we smiled stupidly at one another. The women yanked off my headscarf and marveled at the state of my short brown hair, which resembled a 1970s home permanent gone horribly wrong. One tried unsuccessfully to brush it.

The family invited us to a homecoming party the next day. But I had made a decision. I would listen to Farouq and go back to Kabul through the land of Pacha Khan. No way was I driving eighteen hours on roads that were more like torture devices. As Nasir pulled out of Khost, I decided to feign sickness.

"I'm going to lie down," I told Farouq.

"It's really not necessary," he said.

I lay down in the backseat for what seemed like hours. "Are we there yet?"

Farouq said we were just entering Pacha Khan's stronghold. "There's his truck with the antiaircraft gun."

"What are the men doing?"

"They're waving at us. Why don't you sit up?"

I peeked out the window. The small red pickup truck's windshield was papered in giant mustachioed Pacha Khan stickers and had a large gun somehow strapped to the roof. They waved. I sat up and waved back. We made it to Kabul without further incident. Farouq clearly knew how to handle Afghanistan better than I did.

But the newspaper had no room for my story about Pacha Khan, which was deemed inconsequential compared to Iraq. Almost everything was. So Farouq and I didn't so much work as hang out in the house shared by the *Chicago Tribune* and two other newspapers. Bored, uninspired, dwarfed by the unstoppable search for weapons of mass destruction nearby, Farouq and I played badminton in the backyard, below a trellis of barren grape vines. We had no net, so we just fired the birdie back and forth at each other.

We talked about our lives. The *Tribune*'s regional correspondent, now off covering Iraq, had hired Farouq the year before. His was a typical Afghan story of surviving a series of regimes by any way possible, usually by putting one relative in the ruling regime and one in the opposition. After the Soviets invaded Afghanistan in 1979, Farouq's oldest brother became a pilot under the Communist-backed government. The large extended family shared a house in Kabul, but other villagers from their home province had joined the so-called "mujahedin," or holy fighters, who fought the government with the help of the Americans, Pakistanis, and Saudis. The brother, the pride of the family, died, not in the fighting but in a plane crash along with his wife and children. Farouq was the youngest son in the family, and for days his family hid his brother's death from him. He found out by accident. Afghans have an almost pathological need to avoid being the bearer of bad tidings.

Eventually, the seven main mujahedin groups and their splinters, militias run by powerful warlords like Pacha Khan, pushed out the Soviets in 1989. Peace did not follow. After years of squabbling and a brutal civil war among the militias, the Taliban and its harsh version of Islamic rule arrived in Kabul in 1996. Farouq and his family were all ethnic Pashtuns, like the Taliban, even if in their hearts they were nothing like the Taliban. But they had no choice; like most other Afghans, they kept their heads down and followed the rules. Farouq's female relatives wore blue burqas that turned them into ghosts whenever they left the house. Farouq grew out his beard, although he occasionally got into trouble because his beard just wouldn't grow to the proper length to signify that he was a good Muslim—considered a fistful of beard.

As the Taliban regime spread its reach, Farouq prepared for his future. He became a doctor. He learned anatomy by digging up skeletons in graveyards—the medical students had no other choice. They practiced surgery on the Taliban, repairing wounds earned fighting the militia leftovers now outside the capital, which had coalesced into a group called the Northern Alliance, dominated by ethnic Tajiks from the Panjshir Valley, just north of Kabul.

After living through all this plus the fall of the Taliban regime, Farouq behaved much older than I did. He seemed forty, even though he was only twenty-six. He took care of at least ten relatives, from nieces and nephews to his parents and a disabled sister. Farouq hadn't planned to go into journalism, or to become a "fixer," a foreign journalist's paid best friend, the local who interpreted, guided, and set up interviews. He wanted to be a surgeon. But he would have earned a paltry $100 a month as a doctor. With us, he made $50 a day. All the young English-speaking doctors and medical students had started working with foreign journalists, who probably single-handedly eliminated a generation of doctors in Afghanistan.

Luckily, Farouq, a barrel-chested former weightlifter with a mustache and thick black hair, was a natural journalist. He was intrepid and resourceful. He was eager, probably because he was single, and a single young Afghan man had little in the way of entertainment. It's not like Farouq could date or go to a bar. Kabul had no bars or dates, except for the edible kind. Farouq was also connected to the entire country—related to half, able to convince the other half to talk.

I told Farouq about my own life—kind of. I said I wanted to be a foreign correspondent—kind of. And at thirty-two, I wanted to get married to my serious boyfriend—kind of. Or maybe I wanted to do both. I was still working it out.

At one point, we wandered through the streets of Kabul—cold, gritty, fecal—to try to get some air. Afghans stopped us.

"What is she doing here?" more than one Afghan asked. "Didn't all the foreigners go to Iraq?"

I figured that could be a story, so we interviewed Afghans near the top of TV Mountain, so named because the TV stations had transmitters on top. Kabul was a very literal city: Butcher Street was where the butchers were, where slabs of questionable meat hung, covered with flies. Chicken Street was where chickens used to be sold, but Chicken Street had evolved into the tourist market, where in the 1960s hippies shopped for fur jackets, silver trinkets, and carpets. The market had tentatively reopened after the Taliban fled, selling the same fur jackets and silver trinkets and carpets from thirty years earlier, only to foreign aid workers and soldiers and journalists instead of hippies.

On TV Mountain, the Afghans almost spat out their rage about feeling abandoned. "Believe me—the Americans lost in Afghanistan as soon as they left for Iraq," one man said. Or maybe he said "believe me"—I was learning that this phrase was one of Farouq's trademarks, along with "I'm telling you." I just smiled and nodded. Afghans were as sensitive as a teenage girl about the civil war that happened after the Soviets fled in the late 1980s, when the Americans left the last time around. I wrote a story, but the newspaper had no space. The indignities piled up. My computer keyboard started failing, letter by letter. My satellite phone was broken, and I had no way to get online except for Kabul's Internet cafés. I had to fudge receipts for a new Thuraya satellite phone because we weren't supposed to buy new equipment—all the money was being spent on Iraq. I was starting to really hate that war.

Like any journalist trying to push her way into the newspaper, I figured more action was the answer. Once again, Farouq and I hit the road. We flew to Kandahar, the onetime Taliban stronghold in the south and the second-largest city in Afghanistan, near where the fighting was the worst. We walked onto the tarmac and found our Kandahar driver near a statue that resembled a giant soccer ball. He took us immediately to a boys' school that had just been burned down by members of the Taliban, who destroyed cookies sent by

India and called the headmaster "son of Bush." Then, with the sun sinking and our driver panicking about me wearing glasses in a dicey neighborhood, as glasses were a clear sign I was a foreigner, we drove to our hotel, where my bathroom had been defiled by someone days earlier.

"God, I could use a drink," I muttered, staring at the petrified mess. As far as I knew, Afghanistan was a dry country. I hadn't even tried to find alcohol.

We ate some kebabs. I worked on a story. And then, late at night, I heard a knock at my door. I hesitated to open it, even if it was Farouq. Like every female journalist here, I had suffered problems with overly friendly fixers, mainly in Pakistan, where one translator had pouted for three days because I refused to share a hotel room and a drink or four with him. I opened the door a few inches. It was Farouq, and he was bearing a gift—a bottle of vodka from Uzbekistan.

"I thought you might want this," he said, handing it through the door. "Have a good night."

Then he left, to go tell jokes to Afghan friends in a nearby room or to watch a Mr. Bean movie, both common ways for young men to pass the time here. The vodka was practically undrinkable, but at this point, it was clear—Farouq could do anything, and he was just the right kind of friendly.

The next day, he even found me an Internet café, the first to open in Kandahar. This was a revelation—the Taliban had banned the Internet and any depictions of people, whether in photographs or movies. For the uncensored Internet to be available, especially in Kandahar, represented a real change, definite progress. The café was in a house that looked like a cross between a bordello and a bomb shelter, with thick velvety curtains protecting the privacy of every so-called "cabana" and taped Xs on the windows protecting the customers from any explosions outside. I wondered what the young men of Kandahar spent their time looking at, so Farouq and

I hopped from computer to computer, each cobbled together from old spare parts and, yes, duct tape, checking the lists of favorite websites and the recent surfing history.

"Most of them are about sex," Farouq whispered.

"Most of them are about sex with animals or boys," I corrected, clicking on ultradonkey.com before reaching for my hand sanitizer.

Apparently, freedom had arrived in the south. For now.

CHAPTER 2
MONTANA

flew home to Chicago in late April 2003, just before Bush declared victory in Iraq, and all the other fledgling correspondents also returned to their regular metro reporting gigs. But I could not stay long in the United States—I was already hooked on warlords and bad vodka, my new version of a hot date. Sure, I was in my early thirties. I had a serious boyfriend, an aspiring screenwriter named Chris, and I was on the marriage and baby track. I had good friends and a comfortable life in Chicago. I rode my bike to work, I listened to NPR, I played softball. But my world felt small there, a comfortable habit, an old shoe. Life in Chicago seemed gray compared to the Technicolor jujitsu of Afghanistan. All the other stuff, the marriage and the babies, paled in comparison, paled to the point that they didn't even seem to matter.

This made no sense to my family. I grew up in Montana, where most people graduated high school and never left, where a meal of bull testicles passed for a culinary experience, where my parents scolded me for failing to take proper care of their marijuana plants. We didn't have much money and rarely traveled. The closest I got to overseas was the Great Salt Lake. One year we only celebrated Christmas because Grandpa Halfpap died and left us $750, and because we stole the Christmas tree from our school across the street, after the school dumped it in the alley. (As a bonus, the tinsel was still on it.)

It was probably good that I grew up so sheltered. I was not a brave child. I was convinced that death lurked behind every corner, perhaps the most unlikely future foreign correspondent ever born, the most improbable person to contend with suicide bombs and the real threat of nuclear war. I was scared of the dark, of my dreams, of nuclear weapons, of the Ayatollah Khomeini, who reminded me of Darth Vader. I was a neurotic, everything-o-phobic child, always convinced that any health problem was the dreaded cancer, always worried about stranger-danger.

The peppercorns in cotto salami, and particularly the bluish meat surrounding them, I deemed poisonous and excised with a sharp knife. Halloween candy—a deadly mix of sugar, poison, and razor blades, to be tested first on my brother or our dog. Mushrooms—off-limits, ever since the elephant king in the Babar cartoon died from eating a bad one. Brown pop—it could kill me, even though I had no idea where that thought came from, maybe the Mormon on my softball team. The cloud of ash from Mount Saint Helens—actually nuclear fallout. That bald man down the street—probably a kidnapper or a child molester, I could tell by his shifty eyes. The police asking about the kidnapped girl—probably fake police, or at the very least, police who would take me away from my marijuana-smoking hippie parents. I ran away screaming.

Even when I grew older and slightly braver, my parents had no money for travel. My father may have been an architect, but he was a young rebel, a man who would sooner pay $50 to ship a box of pennies to pay a speeding ticket than just send a check, who when he got upset at a boss would simply quit. We kept moving to more remote places, even to Wyoming, for God's sake, to towns where fewer buildings were being erected, with fewer firms my father could leave. And by the time we rejoined the grid and moved to a suburb of Portland, Oregon, my senior year in high school, I knew what I wanted more than anything else: out. I studied journalism at Northwestern

University outside of Chicago and slogged away on newspaper jobs in various meth-addled industrial towns before landing my dream job at the *Seattle Times*, where for two years I wrote serious stories about the downtrodden and afflicted and won awards for investigative reporting, which sounds pretty good until you realize how prize-filthy journalism is, with awards for topics as specific as the best interpretation of chemistry or the best witty elucidation of the role of institutions in a free society. I even mastered spreadsheets.

But then came the newspaper strike in Seattle and impending financial ruin. I cobbled together rent money by carrying a picket sign, dealing blackjack, and parking cars as a valet—yes, I wore a black bow tie, and true, I was the only non-felon, the only worker with all my teeth, and the only female. Eventually, my co-workers and lack of money started to scare me. I knew I had to find a new job.

I stuck with newspapers, all that I really knew, landing at the *Chicago Tribune* in early 2001, at age thirty, with only two overseas trips to my slender first passport, both in the previous two years. One to Jordan and Egypt, and one to Brazil. When the attacks of September 11, 2001, happened, I was asleep in my bed in Chicago, preparing to work a short day before going to see a live taping of *Jerry Springer*. My roommates pounded on my door to wake me, yelling that nuclear war was imminent, that the Sears Tower was next, and that we had to get out of the city. I flipped on the TV, put on my best suit, and drove to work, the only car heading into downtown Chicago while the highway heading in the opposite direction was a parking lot, jammed with cars trying to flee. I had no choice. As an essential newspaper employee, I had to be at work, tackling the most important stories possible. I spent the day calling gas stations to check the price of gas and interviewing Chicagoans who lived in tall buildings.

Within days, I was assigned to write obits for the victims, up to five a day. But I soon heard that the editors wanted to send more women overseas. I was hardly qualified to go anywhere, even Canada. I had never been to Europe. I spoke only English. I knew little about Al-Qaeda or Osama bin Laden. I knew about as much about Islam as I knew about Christianity, given my hippie infidel upbringing. But I sensed adventure and a way out from the soul-killing task of asking the families of the dead how they felt. I knocked on the door of the top foreign editor and introduced myself.

"I have no kids and no husband, so I'm expendable," I explained.

The boss nodded. Apparently, the newspaper had already realized this. He held up a used envelope with my name scrawled on the back, near the names of two other single women with no children.

"We know who you are," he said. "Get ready to go to Pakistan."

Within four months, I was on a plane, flying into countries I had only read about. Getting overseas was really that easy. Of course, on my first trip overseas, in early 2002, I made countless mistakes. I ordered sushi from the Marriott Hotel in Islamabad, which resembled dorsal fins on a bed of rice and laid me up for days. I sneaked into the forbidden tribal areas of Pakistan with a fixer who seemed more interested in scoring hash than in working and called me "princess" when I complained. And then, when I flew to Kabul the first time, I forgot my cash. That was a major lesson: In a war zone, there are no ATMs.

In the beginning, I was a fill-in correspondent, spending most of my time in Chicago, occasionally dispatched to some random country. I flew to Indonesia to write a vague story about Islam, I covered a devastating earthquake and parliamentary elections in Iran, I spent the invasion of Iraq rambling around Afghanistan with Farouq. But I had caught the bug. What better job could there be than working halfway around the world from my bosses, than being paid to travel? When our South Asia correspondent moved to Italy in early 2004, I applied for her old job, based in India. I took it before even telling my boyfriend about the offer. Not a good sign about the priority of our relationship of almost two years, but Chris still volunteered to move overseas with me later in the year. So my life plan was locked up—I was going to be a swashbuckling foreign correspondent, especially so in South Asia, where at five foot ten, I towered over most of the populace. My boyfriend would perfect his comedy script about killer squirrels.

As soon as I flew into India that June, I called Farouq. He had news: He was getting married. He was not marrying his cousin, as is usually the case in Afghanistan, but his family still picked out his future bride, which is almost always the case in Afghanistan. Luckily, after the two were introduced, they fell for each other.

"You have to come," he told me. "It's a love marriage."

That gave me an excuse to go back, which, after arriving in India, land of quick hands and sharp elbows, I desperately wanted. Even though New Delhi would be my home base, Afghanistan felt more like home than anywhere else in the region. I knew why. Afghanistan seemed familiar. It had jagged blue-and-purple mountains, big skies, and bearded men in pickup trucks stocked with guns and hate for the government. It was like Montana—just on different drugs. So with a list of story ideas and a verbal wedding invite, I flew back to Kabul, now a city of about three or four million, bursting at its muddy seams with returning refugees and foreigners. Farouq and our driver Nasir picked me up in a new SUV—clearly, life was treating Nasir well. Kabul, life was treating like it always did, like a fairy-tale stepchild. Little had changed. I started sneezing immediately, allergic to the one thing Afghanistan produced in abundance: dust.

We drove down the roads, such as they were, bumpy and indifferent, like someone started paving them and then decided "why bother." As usual, I stared out the window as everyone outside stared in at me, both of us watching an equally odd zoo exhibit. The old men wore impossible turbans and had faces etched like a topographical map. Faceless women in dirty blue burqas knocked on our windows, shoving penicillin prescriptions toward us with henna-stained fingers, holding dirty swaddled babies with kohl eyeliner, demanding money. Blue bottles, other journalists called them. It was easy to depersonalize them because these women had no faces, easy to avoid looking at them, to avoid their pleas. But it was tough to ignore the children and the old men, even if we rarely paid out, tough to say no to someone looking you in the eye.

Throughout the capital, evidence of war was still everywhere. The most solid buildings were the squat, rambling concrete apartment complexes and Kafkaesque government ministries left as parting gifts by the Soviets, the tallest of which was the foreboding Ministry of Communications at a mere eighteen stories. Many of the mud buildings were crumbling, and others were pocked with bullet marks or destroyed by rockets. In places, Kabul looked like someone had shaken a giant box of crackers and dumped them out. Traffic lights didn't yet exist. Cops directed traffic around crowded roundabouts. Convoys of foreigner-filled SUVs jockeyed for position with wooden carts pulled by people and donkeys.

Yes, it was good to be back—even if everything in June 2004 was different than before. Farouq could not work with me for a while because he was getting married the next day, which was also his twenty-eighth birthday. The newspaper no longer had a house—we had given that up because the Afghan conflict was no longer seen as big enough to justify the expense. And this overseas gig was no longer a once-in-a-while adventure. Now, I lived here.

Nasir and Farouq dropped me off at a guesthouse, the Gandamack Lodge, named after a famous Afghan battle that the British had lost more than a hundred and sixty years earlier, a sprawling Dr. Seuss–influenced two-story building where one of Osama bin Laden's wives once lived. There was no "Green Zone" in Kabul, no place where all the foreigners lived, protected by walls and men with guns. Instead, foreigners stayed anywhere, in guesthouses like the Gandamack, or in shared houses, which like all Afghan houses were compounds protected by high walls from prying eyes, most likely so women had some privacy. Some foreigners hired security guards. Others didn't.

Farouq, panicked and sweaty over juggling a wedding and me, started making phone calls and eventually found me a fill-in translator, Ajmal Naqshbandi, a sweet, shy, dumpling of a man with a slight mustache, probably because that was all he could grow, who translated every interview like a romantic poem. I liked Ajmal's poetry. I missed Farouq's English skills. Later I would wish I had given Ajmal better advice. I would wish I had told him he was too sensitive for journalists and too brave for his own good, and that news reporting was no profession for a poet.

The next afternoon, Farouq stopped by the Gandamack briefly, and I asked him what I should wear to the wedding. He looked me up and down, at my green baggy Afghan shirt, my baggy black pants, my dusty black tennis shoes.

"What you're wearing is fine," Farouq pronounced.

This was absolutely not true. I showed up that night at the massive wedding hall, where women sat in one large room, men in another, segregated even during a wedding ceremony. None of the Afghan women spoke English. We said hello to one another about fifty times, nodded and smiled, and then said hello some more. They all looked like fairy-tale princesses, with sequin-and-velvet gowns, heavy makeup, and three-tiered hair. My problematic hair had been mashed under a scarf all day. I wore no makeup. Another American woman joined me at a long table—Farouq's former English teacher, who spoke Dari and dressed appropriately. Farouq and his bride came in and sat on a couch in the front of the room of women. She sobbed. He looked grim. No one is supposed to be happy at an Afghan wedding, especially the bride, because she is leaving her family to move in with the groom and his family.

Farouq looked around the room, spotted me, and called me to the stage. Self-conscious in green, I sat with the new couple. I posed for pictures, wondering how the marriage would affect Farouq's plans.

He had wanted to go to medical school in America, and for years friends had tried to help him. But his hoped-for scholarship never panned out. Farouq had stopped talking so much about leaving Afghanistan to study. In one way, this marriage was great—Farouq had a wife, and after twenty-eight years, he deserved something to focus on besides working for everyone else. But I also worried that this marriage could mean the end of Farouq's surgical aspirations, and that he would become like some of the guys I had dated, talking wistfully about plans and goals while working as a waiter to pay the rent.

After dozens of photographs, Farouq and his wife left the stage and the dancing resumed. A few men, the only ones allowed in the women's room besides Farouq and the musicians, videotaped the dancing. Wedding videos are often used by Afghan families to pick prospective brides for single men because, for once, they can actually see what Afghan women look like out of their drab baggy clothes, headscarves, and burqas.

One of the bride's friends adopted me, even though we couldn't understand each other. She had a brown ponytail and wore a man's suit. She touched my knee, grabbed my hand, carefully peeled and cut me pieces of an apple and fed them to me with her fingers, and at one point pulled me toward the dance floor. It felt like a first date with a mime. I did not want to do this, but I relented and started to sway to the Afghan music and its polka-like beat. Then my date left me on the dance floor. Everyone left me on the dance floor. It was like a practical joke, and I was the only person standing, with all the Afghan women clapping and cheering me on, and the few men on bended knee pointing video cameras at me. Just groovy. I was left with a choice: I could sit down, or I could dance like an idiot. I chose the idiot route, jumping up and down like a teenager at a punk-rock concert. By myself. For ten minutes.

And that was how I decided to approach this region. I decided to go all in, for as long as I stayed. I didn't know how long—maybe two years, maybe three, depending on Chris and what happened. My indecision mirrored that of the foreign community, already trying to figure out an exit strategy for Afghanistan and a way out of the quagmire in Iraq.

CHAPTER 3
AMERICAN IDIOT

I soon learned that I rarely had the right clothes, and I rarely knew the right things to say or do. After Farouq finished his wedding duties—no honeymoon, just a lot of traditional family obligations—we ate lunch at the Marco Polo restaurant, a gloomy, fly-spattered hole-in-the-wall with decent meat but no running water in the bathrooms. I launched into a serious conversation, prompted by a book about Islam I had just read and my annoyance with the segregation of the sexes here. Over kebabs, bread, beans, and rice, I lectured Farouq about women in Islam.

"It's all Umar's fault," I said, blaming Islam's second caliph, who lived in the seventh century, for installing certain restrictions on Muslim women.

"No, Kim. He was a good, strong man, and he defended Islam. I am named after Umar, and I can't accept that," Farouq said. Umar had been given the honorary title of "the Farooq," which in Arabic means "the one who distinguishes between right and wrong." Farouq took this stuff seriously. "That's not true," he went on. "Take it back."

But I insisted on my knowledge of Umar and Islam. Farouq narrowed his eyes. Nasir understood very little English, but he looked back and forth between us, hearing in our voices that we were upset.

Nasir chewed a piece of mutton carefully, as if any sudden move would fuel our anger. Farouq, his voice loud but dismissive, went in for the kill.

"Well, I guess it's understandable you would think that. A study just came out by scientists saying that women's brains are smaller than men's. American scientists. So you can't help it."

"Oh my God," I said. "You believe that?"

"Believe me. Yes. Women aren't as smart. There's scientific proof."

"I don't know if I can work with someone who thinks that."

"Fine. I don't need to work for the *Chicago Tribune*. I don't know if I can work with someone who says bad things about Umar."

We stared at each other. And then I realized what I was doing—threatening to fire my lifeline in Afghanistan over a debate about a possible misogynist who lived almost fourteen centuries earlier. Maybe my brain was smaller. I gave in.

"Never mind. Let's just not talk about Umar any more."

But a certain amount of damage had been done. Like all Afghans, Farouq could not ignore such a slight to his honor. I was bumbling around like America, with little awareness of how I was coming across or how my so-called expertise translated on the ground. Farouq told me that I seemed different than when I came to Afghanistan the year before, when we had first met.

"Back then, you were sweet and gentle," he said.

I rolled my eyes. I was never sweet and gentle.

So I left Afghanistan for a while, for Kyrgyzstan, Pakistan, and my theoretical home in India. I returned for Afghanistan's first-ever presidential election, planned for October 2004. By then, the fallout from my behavior was obvious. Farouq tried to book me in the Gandamack, only to find out that I was banned. The Afghan women in charge said I was too much trouble. And that could have been true. When I had stayed there during Farouq's wedding, the laundry had washed my whites with my baggy green wedding shirt, turning all my clothes the color of dishwater. I had complained about the laundry, about the slow Internet, about the fact that all my clothes were misplaced for twenty-four hours. I had complained and complained, even though I was in one of the poorest countries in the world, wracked by decades of war, raising my voice to lecture. "This shirt cost me $70," I explained loudly, holding up a newly tie-dyed Gap blouse. "You have to give me a free night." In Pakistan, such complaints would have worked, maybe because of the hangover from British colonial times, maybe because Westerners were often still treated with deference. In Afghanistan, such complaints won me no friends. Afghanistan had never been successfully colonized, and Afghans tended to seethe quietly toward any uppity foreigner making foreigner-like demands. Especially an American.

"You have to be softer," Farouq told me. "I know my people."

So with the Gandamack, I was out of luck. For the election, I had to stay across the alley at its broken-down stepsister, the Kabul Lodge. I felt like the only kid not picked for a kickball team, close to the other journalists but not one of the other journalists, and I continued to feel like an outsider, continued to wear the wrong clothes.

Nasir, Farouq, and I drove south of Kabul to Logar Province to meet a tribal leader who had just been released from Guantánamo after being held for almost two years. The tribal leader was being welcomed by his tribesmen, but still, in what I interpreted as a gesture of kindness, he walked outside his mud-walled compound to greet us. A burly man with a long gray beard and a turban, he looked at me in the car, shoved a large blue headscarf that matched his eyes through the window, smiled kindly, said something in Pashto, and walked away. (How many headscarves would I accumulate as gifts over the years? Enough to wrap up every female ever born in my family, enough to smother us all.)

"So is he going to talk to us?" I asked Farouq. "What did he say?"

"Don't be offended," Farouq said. " 'Fuck off, farter.' "

Swearing and shoving a scarf through a window was a novel interpretation of the Pashtun code, which required Pashtuns to treat their guests with hospitality, even if their guests were their enemies. But considering how this tribal leader was hustled off by the U.S.

military to Guantánamo, I guess he felt the code no longer applied to Americans.

The adversity continued. Interim president Hamid Karzai's people soon invited me on a campaign trip masquerading as a road opening—while there, I had to move nimbly to avoid a bludgeoning from his American DynCorp security guards, who destroyed pictures snapped by a *New York Times* photographer and knocked the turban off the transportation minister in their attempts to protect Karzai. DynCorp International was one of the burgeoning U.S.-based private military contractors now supplementing our all-volunteer military, which was fracturing with the stress of two wars. In Afghanistan, DynCorp employees guarded Karzai, lived in a makeshift trailer court at the presidential palace, and trained a new presidential guard. I had encountered DynCorp before, kind of, when I was invited to a party thrown at their palace compound. I showed up on the wrong night, the only woman there, except for the half-naked one on a poster inside their makeshift bar and the two Chinese women in miniskirts holding hands with DynCorp contractors as they walked toward their trailers.

Farouq and I also went to a Karzai rally at the Kabul soccer stadium—the same stadium where the Taliban once beheaded alleged criminals and cut off the hands of thieves. The press was funneled into a taped-off pen in the middle of the soccer field, surrounded by Karzai's Afghan security team, who had been trained, of course, by DynCorp. Leaning against the tape, Farouq interviewed an Afghan, who said he was supporting all the candidates, hedging his bets. It was a typical Afghan survival strategy, and Farouq started laughing.

"Why are you laughing?" interrupted a hepped-up, sunglassed Afghan security guard, stepping in front of Farouq. "I will call someone and have you taken away."

Farouq, never one to step down from a confrontation, looked at the man.

"I'm just doing my job."

The Afghan guard swatted my notebook and shoved Farouq.

"I will kill you," he said.

This was how Afghans interpreted DynCorp protocol for dealing with laughing. The guard told us to go away, but we couldn't move. Finally Karzai walked out into the bleachers, talking on his cell phone, and everyone grew quiet, even the Afghan security guard. (In another example of how complicated Afghanistan is, this violent exchange caused Farouq and the security guard to become lifelong friends.) Karzai urged the crowd not to participate in fraud.

"If somebody comes to you and tells you I will give you money to vote for me, if someone uses force to tell you to vote for me, if someone uses power to get you to vote for me, don't vote for me," Karzai announced. "Please."

Over the years, as corruption turned into a cancer around Karzai, I would often think about that comment, but over the years, I would also realize that people rarely paid attention to Karzai.

On the way out of the stadium, a car of Afghans passed us. "Dog washers!" one yelled. That was a favorite epithet for foreigners because, well, a true Afghan would never keep a dog as a pet let alone wash one. Most Afghans, like many conservative Muslims, were suspicious of dogs, believing that angels would not visit a house when dogs were inside.

But regardless of being a stranger in a strange land, a dog washer in a land of cat lovers, for the first time in Kabul, I started to have a social life, largely because of the influx of election workers, do-gooders, and journalists. A new restaurant opened called L'Atmosphère, where foie gras ran $9 and red wine flowed, where there was a pool, a large garden, cats, and rabbits. On some nights, I ate mystery meat at L'Atmosphère. On others, I crept across the alley from the Kabul Lodge to the Gandamack for dinner, braiding my hair to try to look like someone else, slouching to appear shorter, always worried I would be kicked out.

A new friend then invited me to a seminal event—my first Thursday-night Kabul party. Since Friday was the weekly Islamic holiday, Thursday night was the one night everyone had free. Just great—I had nothing to wear. I had only packed black tennis shoes, hiking boots, baggy jeans, baggy black pants, and assorted long Afghan shirts, the shortest of which hit me mid-thigh. So I opened up the metal trunk left by my predecessor, filled with maps, undefined power cords, vague equipment, and assorted leftover clothing. The only item that bore a resemblance to Western clothing was a baggy white T-shirt proclaiming TURKIYE on the front. I put on the T-shirt, jeans, and hiking boots. I looked in the mirror and performed a harsh self-assessment. I would never be described as a beautiful woman, but I could usually pass for cute and occasionally, when viewed in a certain light, even sexy. But I had not really taken care of myself since coming overseas. I hadn't had a haircut in five months, and my split ends and slight curl gave me a frizzy aura. In my chronic hair wars, my gray roots were overtaking my brown ends. I had nothing to cover my under-eye circles, and I had definitely gained weight and acquired a bad complexion due to a diet of kebabs, rice, bread, and oil. On this night, I could perform little magic. I smoothed down my hair into a suitable helmet and put on lip gloss and mascara. At least I could show off my blue eyes.

We were dropped off at the guesthouse Afghan Gardens 1, not to be confused with the recently opened Afghan Gardens 2. I was slightly overwhelmed by the number of people jammed onto the concrete porch, the copious amounts of alcohol. The woman who ran the guesthouse wore a slinky black sleeveless dress. Another woman wore high-heeled boots, a long skirt, a fur-lined jean vest showing cleavage, and lounged on a couch, draped over some male friends. Hundreds of people were there; the U.S. embassy spokeswoman and her immediate boss even showed up. The entire party seemed optimistic about the future of Afghanistan and the impending election. And to celebrate, we drank alcohol and danced until 2 AM to songs like "Kiss" by Prince. By that point, it was agreed—Afghanistan was on a path to recovery, and Hamid Karzai, the well-spoken and well-dressed darling of the West, was the answer. Everyone hoped he would win.

I left the party at some point in the early-morning hours, well after most of the other foreigners had gone home but before the Islamic morning call to prayer. Drunk on red wine and paranoid about how I stacked up against the other women at my first big party, I realized that I needed to pay more attention to my clothes, my hair, my exercise routine, because against all logic, a social life in a war zone seemed entirely plausible. My friend's driver dropped me at the Kabul Lodge, and my friend walked me to my room. He sat on my bed and started talking about motorcycles. I flipped on my laptop and scanned a story draft I had written earlier about a popular radio talk show on unrequited Afghan love. I closed one eye and stared three inches from the computer screen, performing the typical edit of the drunk journalist, concentrating hard on every word but comprehending little, all while wondering why my male friend was still here. After fifteen minutes, I shut down my laptop and stood up. My friend moved in for a kiss. Not a good idea—after all, I had the boyfriend half a world away, and my friend and I had both been drinking. So he left. I took another pass at my story, but the words still made more sense as letters than thoughts. I sent an e-mail to my boyfriend, Chris, who was still planning to move to India in a few months. I fell asleep.

In the morning, I awoke with a hangover fueled by cheap wine and guilt, mixed with a feeling of possibility. My social life had not hit a mud wall in Afghanistan. There were parties, a scene, places to wear little black dresses. There was potential here, even if that potential resembled a cross between a John Hughes high-school movie and Sinclair Lewis's *Main Street*, given the small foreign community and the inevitable cliques, with do-gooders, guns for hire, and journos approximating brains, jocks, and goths. I knew what I needed to do. I needed to go shopping.

Zalmay Khalilzad clearly felt as optimistic, at least about the country. Not only was he the U.S. ambassador here—he also happened to be born and raised in Afghanistan. Khalilzad was not a normal diplomat, not a typical ambassador. Zal, as he was known, liked to get his hands dirty. During the large gatherings to pick an interim president in 2002, Khalilzad, then the Bush regime's representative, had been accused of strong-arming the country's former king into abandoning any political ambitions, paving the way for Karzai's selection. Since then, Zal and Karzai seemed to have become best buddies; they talked on the telephone daily and frequently ate dinner together.

Zal liked control. He rode in the cockpit of the U.S. military C-130 Hercules whenever he traveled. "He likes to watch," his press aide once told me. He didn't just sit in the embassy and announce aid—he flew to the provinces and handed out windup radios to women himself. At meetings between Afghans and Westerners, Khalilzad translated, making sure everyone understood one another. At public events where, for diplomatic reasons, Khalilzad spoke English and used an interpreter, he corrected his interpreter's translations. Zal also fed off the media like a personality feeds off a cult. He threw elaborate press conferences at the U.S. embassy, flashing a wide-angle grin and swept-back graying hair and often calling on reporters by name. Every journalist, from the fledgling Afghan reporter to the Norwegian freelancer, was invited and served sodas and water. Surrounded by attractive young female aides in hip, occasionally tight clothing, dubbed by some as "Zal's Gals," and always slightly late for any event, Khalilzad cultivated the air of a diplomatic rock star. He kept answering questions long after "last question" was called, long after his aides stole glances at their watches. "We have time," Zal would say. "Let them ask more." He always smiled, even when talking about tragedy.

But right before the election, Zal again flirted with controversy, accused of trying to fix it for Karzai, already a shoo-in. The other seventeen wannabe presidents had a better chance of being convicted of a felony than of winning an election—in fact, one later would be accused of murder, and others probably should have been. But Zal was accused of trying to make sure that Karzai won convincingly, of trying to persuade rivals to drop out. By now, Zal had earned himself a new colonial-style nickname: the Viceroy.

Regardless, Zal could not help himself. He seemed to lack a filter, and said whatever he thought whenever he thought it, and did whatever he thought was right, regardless of how it looked. In the embassy, some longtime State Department employees craved the return of a real ambassador, one who would stay in the background and not interfere. Zal didn't care. He had helped shove through a messy Afghan constitution that set up a powerful central government and an even more powerful president, even though the country was used to neither. He had his own wing of advisers outside the typical embassy structure, the Afghan Reconstruction Group, made up of government employees and business executives who took leave from their jobs to help rebuild Afghanistan and charged the taxpayers overtime to do so. They were supposed to be an in-house think tank; they soon became the Pentagon's alternative to the United States Agency for International Development (USAID), the civilian foreign-aid wing of the U.S. government theoretically responsible for development projects. That these advisers were often ill versed in the ways of government and duplicated the roles of State and USAID was a serious problem. In some cases, someone in the Reconstruction Group would be working on an issue, and so would someone in the State Department, and so would someone in USAID, but because of infighting and resentments, the three did not talk to one another, and instead had to go up a chain to a supervisor who would then relay whatever concern down whatever chain was deemed necessary.

I was invited on a trip with Khalilzad to Herat just before the election, while Karzai was out of town. This was the territory of the powerful and popular warlord Ismail Khan, an ethnic Tajik who had been one of the most respected commanders during the anti-Soviet war and had gone on to command a key western faction of the Northern Alliance. After the Taliban fled, Ismail Khan had been named governor of his home province, western Herat, which shared a border with Iran, giving him access to border taxes. Although praised for bringing home electricity, money, and trees, the Afghan equivalent of American political pork, Ismail Khan had also ignored Karzai and the central government, keeping customs money for himself and his private militia. Because of this, Karzai had just removed Ismail Khan as governor, sparking riots and unrest. It was unclear whether he would accept Karzai's request to come to Kabul and work as the federal minister of mines and industries.

The pro-government warlords who had led militias during Afghanistan's wars were Karzai's constant battle. They seemed to operate with impunity. The Americans had backed them in driving out the Taliban in late 2001, handing them money, power, and legitimacy. None had been held accountable for war crimes. Most were more powerful than the president when it came to their ability to summon an army, and most figured they were entitled to their fiefdoms and the spoils of power. Neutering them was Karzai's biggest challenge. But Ismail Khan didn't want to budge from his home. He refused the post in Kabul, and said he would negotiate only with Karzai.

No way would I miss this trip. Warlords always made good copy.

I wore my standard garb for leaving Kabul—a long brown embroidered hippie Afghan dress, black pants, and a black headscarf. Zal's Gals were dressed sharply, as if for an American business lunch. When we walked off the plane, Zal hugged the new governor. He then embarked on his itinerary, meeting students, shaking hands, hugging, and meeting U.S. soldiers of the provincial reconstruction team (PRT), calling them "noble."

"Are we done?" he said to an aide. "What about the civilians of the PRT? I need to thank them."

At the governor's residence, Zal met with Ismail Khan behind closed doors for twenty minutes, and ate lunch with the new governor, before holding court at the inevitable press conference. And there, cameras flashing, with Karzai out of the country, Khalilzad baldly announced that he had done what Karzai had been unable to accomplish—he had convinced Ismail Khan to abandon Herat.

"He will move to Kabul," Khalilzad told the room. "It's good for Afghanistan. It's good for him."

Ismail Khan did move. Zal didn't seem to care how Afghans might interpret this, if they would think that the United States was trying to manipulate the Afghan government, six days before the election. Such a Viceroy! He even threw a press conference the next day to talk up the elections, urging journalists not to be lazy and talking about the ramped-up training of the Afghan army. The man was everywhere.

The next weekend, the sun rose on Election Day with a hangover, smeared and hazy. A harsh wind whipped dust across the capital like fire-powered sandpaper. Standing at the polling stations, it was tough to see, not to mention painful. But Afghans started lining up at 5 AM, eager to be the first to vote. Despite threats of violence, the Taliban failed to disrupt much of anything. And by the end of the election, two things were clear: Lots of Afghans voted because they were excited, and the main people who messed up the election were the foreigners. The UN had devised such a complicated method to ink voters' fingers to prevent double voting, that the ink was mixed up and most of it could be washed off with soap and water, meaning that democracy-minded Afghans could vote as often as they wanted. But at that point, such fraud hardly mattered. It was obvious that Karzai had won overwhelmingly, and that Afghans overwhelmingly believed in him. So did everyone else, for that matter. At least for a little while.

CHAPTER 4

THERE GOES MY GUN

Despite my discovery of the Kabul social scene in late 2004, I couldn't seem to separate work and life because there was no real division. My job was the international equivalent of the police beat, and something was always going boom. On my previous trips overseas, I had to summon short bursts of energy, like a sprinter, but now, six months into this job, I felt like I was running a marathon. As I struggled to pace myself and to hop countries like New Yorkers hopped subways, I realized I was in no way prepared for my boyfriend's impending move. So I told him the truth, or at least most of it—that I was never home in New Delhi, spending most of my time in other parts of India or Afghanistan or Pakistan or Kyrgyzstan. But he didn't listen. After more than two years of dating, he wanted a long-term commitment. I still wasn't sure. It wasn't just the demands of work. As the child of divorce, I was wary of signing a one-year lease on an apartment, let alone pledging lifelong fidelity. And the excitement of Kabul pulled me like a new lover. It felt epic, nudging me toward ending this safe relationship. Part of me was much more interested in enrolling in the crazy adrenaline rush of Kabul High than in settling down.

So I told Chris he probably shouldn't come. The next day, he bought a plane ticket. With a new beard and a couple of grubby bags, he showed up at my Delhi apartment early on a December morning. After six months apart, we tried to reclaim our relationship, buying a plug-in Christmas tree, shopping for gifts near skinny Indian Santa Clauses furiously ringing bells, spending a long weekend at an Indian vacation spot. But even there, I continually checked the Internet. A broken-down revolving restaurant that proudly advertised it didn't charge extra for revolving couldn't distract me from work. Back at the apartment for the holiday, Chris convinced me to take a break.

"It's Christmas," he said. "Try to relax. The world won't blow up."

I reminded him of the year before, when an earthquake devastated a town in Iran the day after Christmas. It had been my first experience covering such a massive disaster.

"There you go," he said. "It could never happen two years in a row."

So the next day, a Sunday, I spent the entire day in pajamas, reading newspapers and a novel, watching movies. That evening, an editor called in a panic.

"I assume you're writing a story about the tsunami."

I uttered the words every editor fears.

"What tsunami?"

And then I was gone again, looking at bodies, flying in an empty plane to Sri Lanka, bouncing between disaster zones, trying to make sense of a natural catastrophe that had wiped away more than 230,000 lives in an instant. So much for the world not blowing up. It always did, when nobody expected it, and often in the week between Christmas and New Year's.

Chris and I tried to keep our relationship moving forward. He occasionally traveled with me on stories in India, although I was usually too busy to spend time with him. He didn't get a job; he didn't even look for one. He didn't work on his screenplay. He talked about studying Buddhism and spent an inordinate amount of time researching liberal conspiracy theories involving Bush, Rumsfeld, and summer camp. I spent more and more time on the road, until finally, while planning a romantic getaway to Paris, I realized I didn't feel romantic in the slightest. That's when I hopped on a plane to a place where Chris would never follow—Kabul. Compared to the reality of dealing with my boyfriend, Afghanistan seemed like a vacation.

I decided to apply for my first "embed," the Pentagon-devised program that attached journalists to military units. Critics called the program a blatant attempt at propaganda. Journalists considered it the only way to cover an obvious part of the story—the troops. And what better diversion from a flailing romance than running away with the U.S. Army?

This posed a challenge—given the intensity in Iraq, where sixty-seven U.S. troops were killed in the fighting in May, any story in Afghanistan, where three U.S. troops were killed the same month, would likely grab little attention. Only about 18,000 U.S. troops had deployed to Afghanistan, mainly doing combat operations, and another 8,000 troops from other countries handled peacekeeping. True, more foreign troops were here than the year before, but the number was still nothing compared to Iraq, with 138,000 U.S. troops and 23,000 from other countries. Afghanistan was the small war, even if many were casting it as the "good war" compared to the badness of Iraq.

But it *was* a small war. That spring of 2005, the Taliban were like mosquitoes, constantly irritating, occasionally fatal. Roadside bombs continued to kill soldiers, but helicopter crashes had proved more dangerous. Sure, the Taliban blew up things in the south, but so far they mostly blew up themselves, and their attempts to use recalcitrant donkeys as suicide bombers only provoked laughter. It was a known fact: Afghans and Pakistanis were probably the worst suicide bombers in the entire spectrum of militants.

A photographer and I flew by helicopter to the Orgun-E base in Paktika to embed with U.S. soldiers. Paktika was almost the size of

New Jersey, an extremely poor province with no paved roads and few schools, a mountainous and desolate wasteland plopped along the border with Pakistan, right across from the mountainous tribal agencies of North and South Waziristan, otherwise known as Terrorist Haven, the vacuums of Pakistani authority where the Taliban held sway. The U.S. philosophy had been explained to me at Bagram Airfield, the largest U.S. military base in Afghanistan—the troops "drained swamps," which meant hunting down militants, while "emboldening local leaders and the population."

As long as I was running away from my problems, I wanted to get out on the front lines, where the swamps were being drained. My goal was a town called Bermel, which the Taliban had seized earlier, cutting off the police chief's head. U.S. and Afghan troops had recaptured the town and were fighting the bad guys nearby. (I later found out that this was known in military parlance as "troops in contact," or TIC, or "tick." I would learn that everything in the military had an acronym. The IED was an improvised explosive device, or a roadside bomb. The BBIED was a body-borne improvised explosive device, otherwise known as a suicide bomber. And the DBIED was a donkey-borne improvised explosive device, otherwise known as a really stupid idea.)

Yes, I wanted to get my war on, because I had no idea what I was talking about, what war was really like. To fill my spare time, and to make sure I didn't have a spare second to think, I even lugged along something to set the mood, a miniseries about war, *Band of Brothers*. I planned to be all war, all the time. But as soon as I stepped off the helicopter and met the base media handler, I figured out I was in the wrong place. It soon became obvious that he was unlikely to send me anywhere.

"When you go to the bathroom at night, be sure to take your photographer," my handler told me. "There are only three other women here."

I wasn't sure who or what, exactly, he was worried about, and I didn't know the proper protocol, so I just smiled and nodded. I knew if he wanted the male photographer to shadow me to the bathroom, we would never be flown to the fighting nearby, close to the border with Pakistan. Every day I asked for a "bird," figuring that if I used military slang, it would help. Every day I was told no. And I could see why—soldiers were actually fighting the Taliban down near Bermel, and as journalists, we were the last priority for the precious air slots available, slightly below mail. So instead, the photographer and I were sent out on trips with a platoon of combat engineers who were so bored that the leader carried copies of *The Complete Guide to Investing in Rental Properties* and *Own Your Own Corporation* with him on patrol.

"Oh, it's going to be a long, boring day," he said at the beginning of one. Then he realized that sounded bad. "That's a good thing."

That day alone, we visited five villages. The soldiers had several missions. To find out about Afghans in army uniforms robbing so-called jingle trucks, the acid-trip trucks from Pakistan that transported most food and supplies in the region and featured fluorescent fantasy paintings and dangly metal chains that clanked together and sounded like "Jingle Bells." To find out about a nearby IED. To find out about an alleged insurgent named "Hamid Wali" or maybe "Mohammad Wali," no one seemed sure—names here frankly as common as Jim or John Wilson. And always, their mission was to win hearts and minds, to convince the Afghans that they were there only to help.

We started by walking around a market in Orgun, where stalls sold everything from pirated DVDs to live chickens. One soldier bought a teapot for $3. A staff sergeant tried to build rapport with the shop owner, who wore a pakol, a traditional hat that resembled a pie with an extra roll of dough on the bottom.

"We're just trying to collect information about a robbery that happened less than a week ago," the staff sergeant told Pakol. "Local nationals in green uniforms robbed a jingle truck on Highway 141."

The optimistically named Highway 141 was a one-lane dirt road. Pakol looked suspicious. "We don't know. We come here early in the morning. We leave here late in the evening. We haven't heard any-thing."

The staff sergeant tried another question.

"IED on the way to Sharana?"

"We don't know about this," Pakol said. Then he waited a beat. "If we see mines or something, we'll let you know." He waited another beat. "But if you want tea, we'll give you tea."

With no objections, Pakol blew out dust from a few cups and poured from a pot boiling on a gas canister. We all sipped green tea.

"Did you come to help us or what?" Pakol asked, after the first cup was gone. That was Afghan tea protocol. Always wait for a cup of tea to ask a serious question. Pakol then ticked off his complaints, the things he wanted the Americans to fix.

"The dust is really bad," he said.

"There's always gonna be something," the staff sergeant replied.

With that, we left the shop. As we trudged along, everyone stared at us, making it difficult to shop. I knew why: Here were men in army uniforms, flak vests, and helmets, twenty-first-century soldiers carrying guns, looking like unbeatable futuristic fighting machines, establishing a perimeter, looking, checking, in the middle of a fif-teenth-century dusty souk. I walked in the middle, wearing a head-scarf beneath my helmet, trying to bridge two cultures. I looked at the translator, a nineteen-year-old kid from Kabul. He had wrapped a scarf around the bottom of his face like a Wild West bandit and put on sunglasses and a baseball cap.

"What's up with the outfit?" I asked him.

"So the people don't know me," he said. "The Afghans here say you are not a Muslim if you work with the Americans."

We left town and drove on. Suddenly someone spotted a suspi-cious white bag in the middle of the road. Our four-vehicle convoy lurched to a slow stop. Sergeant Ben Crowley, a smart aleck who thrived on making everyone laugh, jumped out of his Humvee. He looked through the scope of his rifle at the bag. No wires poked out, nothing indicated bomb. He moved closer, his gun pointed at the bag. I guess I should say the suspense was killing us, but that would be a lie. Boredom was killing us. I hopped out of my Humvee and walked up to Crowley.

"You gonna kill it?" I asked, staring at the bag. Traffic lined up behind our convoy.

"Bag of dirt," Crowley said.

"You locked and loaded?"

"No."

That was our usual exchange, even though soldiers were always supposed to have a round in the chamber, ready to fire. We climbed back into our Humvees and bumped down the ruts that passed for roads at a whopping ten miles an hour, the fastest we could go, making our sad, slow escape into the beige sameness of Paktika. We soon set off on a foot patrol near a mud-walled compound. The soldiers from the Afghan National Army (ANA) went first, in a move to respect the local culture and show that Afghans were taking charge of security. A kid ran inside the compound. Other children started crying.

"I don't want to talk to you," said a boy, crying inside the doorway.

A neighbor, a man, walked over.

"The men aren't here. They went to town."

A little girl started crying. "I'm scared," she said.

For a hearts-and-minds mission, even one designed to embolden local leaders, this one was starting to fall apart. The Americans decided to fall back.

"Why did you guys come here?" the neighbor asked.

"We're leaving," the translator said. "I don't know."

Then he turned to me. "It's so difficult. The people don't want to talk. They are scared. They say, 'We are gonna go to jail.'"

I knew this from Afghans—they feared that once the American

soldiers showed up at a compound, someone would be carted away and locked up for no reason. This rumor had spread after raids had led to detentions in other villages. In this mostly illiterate country where the rural areas had little in the way of media, news still spread largely through rumor, through word of mouth. Many Afghans had also used the Americans to carry out their own personal vendettas, dropping a dime on some rival who had nothing to do with the Taliban, Al-Qaeda, or any of the other insurgent groups who didn't want foreign troops in Afghanistan.

We left. Almost immediately, the Humvee in front of us broke down. It had been in the shop for a broken fuel pump twice that week. Now it was dead again, choked with the dust that coated everything, somehow working its way beneath fingernails, into the corners of mouths, behind ears, without even trying. We tied up the Humvee to tow it. The soldiers swore. Everything here took forever. Everything moved at the pace of a Humvee towed by red tape over a moonscape. It was one step forward, four steps back. Thus impaired, lugging more than five tons of dead weight, we rolled on to the next village, finding a hostile man working near a ditch.

"Who is your president?" asked a sergeant major, testing the man's knowledge.

"Karzai," replied the hostile man, who had muddy feet. He paused. "Why are you here?"

"Ensuring safety and security to the Afghan people," the sergeant major said. He nodded. "The ANA is here today."

Muddy Feet looked at the sergeant major as if he were impaired. Of course he knew who was president. Of course he knew the ANA was there. He was not stupid. He was not blind. And this conversation was not off to a good start.

"We agree President Karzai is our president," Muddy Feet said, somewhat carefully. "We appreciate our ANA soldiers. You're looking for caches? You're going to search for weapons? You should get permission from our government."

Muddy Feet had just tripped a magic switch. He mentioned "caches," as in "caches of weapons."

The sergeant major looked at the translator. "Why did he bring up caches, when we didn't even talk about it?"

The translator shrugged.

"I think you're going to check in our houses," Muddy Feet said, correctly reading the situation. He shook his head. "That's wrong."

A boy in a Scooby-Doo T-shirt walked up and stared at me. The sergeant major and Muddy Feet stared at each other.

"I'm not afraid of you," Muddy Feet said.

"He's hiding something," the sergeant major said to the translator.

An elder walked up. How did I know? He had a turban and a beard, and all the Afghans parted for him deferentially. The sergeant major turned to the man in charge.

"I've got one question for you," the sergeant major said. "One of your village members brought up the word 'cache.' Do you know anything about a cache?"

"I don't know," the elder said. "I came here fifteen days ago from Karachi."

"Oh, Pakistan!" the sergeant major said, as if that made everything clear. "So you can tell me about the Taliban or Al-Qaeda coming across the border."

The elder stared at him. This was awkward. The Afghan soldiers were sent to search Muddy Feet's compound. They did, finding nothing.

"Tea?" the elder asked.

"Sure," a staff sergeant answered before the sergeant major could say anything. "I'm here to socialize. Whatever he wants." He took off his helmet.

"Take care of your helmet," Muddy Feet said. "Someone might steal it."

We all walked inside a nearby compound, into a sitting room

near the front. Mop-haired girls with kohl-lined eyes and bright orange and green dresses poked their heads around a corner to giggle and stare. We dropped onto cushions in a room. All the Americans took off their helmets and body armor and rested them and their weapons against the wall.

"Whenever you want to come here, you can come here," the elder told them.

A boy poured the sweet milky tea from a thermos and quickly handed us each a cup.

"Some questions," the staff sergeant started. "Do you know about any jingle-truck robberies?"

The elder thought, looked at the ceiling. "Whoever did it, they're not Afghans. They might be from another country."

"What about an IED?"

"I don't know, I was not here," the elder said.

"If you have any problems in the village, come to the base," the staff sergeant told the Afghans. They nodded. Sure they would.

Mission accomplished, we stood, and after lacing up our boots at the door, walked out.

"Let's go sing 'Kumbaya,'" the staff sergeant said, before heading back to the base. I was pretty sure he was joking.

Everywhere we went, we heard the same story. No jingle trucks. No IEDs. No one named Wali.

The roads were so bad that convoys could barely go anywhere. It raised an obvious question—three and a half years after the fall of the Taliban, out near a small U.S. military base in a onetime Taliban haven near the border with Pakistan, little had been improved, like roads and power. The soldiers seemed to be marking time, handing out candy and meeting with elders who just talked about how much they needed. The soldiers were forced to double as aid workers, and aid was noticeably absent. Still, I was told it was better than before—these were the first U.S. soldiers many villagers had seen in two years. Just outside the base, a new cobblestone road named "The

Road of the Future" was being built. At about a mile and a half long and with a U.S. price tag of $200,000, it would be the province's first cobblestone road—slight progress, and an indication of how much effort and money was needed for the smallest of improvements in Afghanistan.

The photographer and I spent most of our time sitting inside the forward operating base, called a "FOB," like the other fobbits, the nickname for people who spent all their time inside the wire. I watched all of *Band of Brothers*. I worked out in the gym. I drank a lot of water and went to bed early every night. I actively avoided calling or e-mailing Chris, falling back on the excuse that I was at war, after all. Being here was like being at the Afghan version of a spa, with no liquor, plenty of sleep, little stress, and little Internet access. I didn't have to worry about the daily news. I didn't have to worry about anything.

Mainly I hung out. I talked to the soldiers in my engineering platoon, including Crowley, a North Carolina native who blew apart any soldier stereotype I had. He had earned an anthropology degree, started graduate school in England before running out of money, and joined the army to be able to afford to go back. He was bright and, at twenty-eight, older than the other soldiers. He was cute, with slightly exaggerated ears and a big smile. Like other soldiers here, he complained to me about the difference between Iraq and Afghanistan, about the amorphous process of winning hearts and minds and meeting villagers instead of fighting bad guys. He handed out candy to kids, yanked off his helmet to wiggle his ears, won a game of "bloody knuckles" with an Afghan boy, played "Dixie" on his harmonica, and accidentally tossed a pen into a pile of cow manure when he was trying to give it to a kid. (The kids, predictably, dove into the manure, fighting over the pen.) Crowley was funny.

"Iraq is like a war," Crowley told me. "This is like a summer camp."

And later, he was more serious. "The army doesn't put a lot of effort into us here," Crowley said. "It seems like the military as a whole doesn't care about the welfare of soldiers in Afghanistan. Here, we get a lot more complacent. I don't ever chamber a round in my rifle anymore. Because I know nothing's gonna happen."

How complacent were these troops? They told us we didn't need to wear our body armor and helmets on patrol, that they weren't necessary. Everyone complained about how Afghanistan was a "forgotten war." They even got generic letters about Iraq from troop-supporting strangers back in the United States.

On patrol, I spent time near Crowley because he was so open and easy. Sometimes he talked about his fiancée and his ex-wife. He was leaving the base in a few days for vacation and was getting married in a week. It was an experience I would repeatedly have, where male soldiers, many starved for female company or for a new ear to listen, would tell me things that they shouldn't necessarily have revealed. Divorce, infidelity, loneliness—they would tell me their secrets and watch me take notes. In return, I would give them nothing—no information about my personal life, my past loves, my own flaws. One soldier in Crowley's platoon, always an outcast, always teased for not holding his weapon correctly, sat down with the photographer and me in the mess hall one afternoon and spilled out how he never should have joined the army.

"I'm just not the world's best soldier," the young man said. "If there's a way to mess something up, I manage to find it."

It created a dilemma. I knew that the soldiers might suffer for their indiscretions. But at the same time, some of their indiscretions would be the most powerful stories. With Crowley's fellow soldier, the one who wasn't cut out for the army, I chose not to quote him. It was a judgment call. I didn't want to be responsible for anything bad that might happen.

Being on an embed created other problems, such as being dependent on the very people you wrote about, and naturally wanting them to like you, and wanting the military not to blackball you.

The soldiers took care of us. They sent a translator to the market to buy sunglasses and sweaters for us. They were American like me. They reminded me of Montana. They yelled at Afghan men who tried to take my picture with their cell phones. "What would you do if we tried to take a picture of your women?" one soldier said to a smiling Afghan, who snapped the picture anyway.

Regardless of any of this, I wrote the story that was right in front of me—the "forgotten war," the bored soldiers, feeling left out of the Iraq action, and Crowley, unlocked and unloaded. He left for vacation, to get married, the same day the photographer and I flew back to Bagram Airfield.

The story got a lot of reaction. I realized how carefully everyone read anything about the troops. Through an unspoken agreement, I was expected to leave out the boredom and the fact that Crowley repeatedly was not locked and loaded. I told my critics that I just wrote what I saw. I moved on.

I had no idea what would happen.

CHAPTER 5
ONE WAY OR ANOTHER

I n Kabul that spring of 2005, the lack of war was as obvious as the bikinis at the pool of L'Atmosphère, the restaurant of wicker chairs, glass-topped tables, and absurdly priced wine that had become the equivalent of the sitcom *Cheers* in the Afghan capital. How quiet was it? It was so quiet that an award-winning war correspondent would spend the summer filming a documentary about a Kabul school for female drivers. It was so quiet that the photographer and I rode around in a government bus in Kabul where workers yanked beggars off the street, effectively kidnapping them for a day, holding them in a school and feeding them some gruel before releasing them, a catch-and-release program for the poor. (By now we knew the regular beggars and their acts. The boy with flippers for arms. The girl who wore her blind brother's suit jacket and led him around by his one good arm. Egg Boy, an entrepreneur who sobbed daily next to broken eggs at various intersections, raking in egg money from concerned foreigners.)

It was so quiet that I went to a brothel for fun, so quiet that I knew I should probably fly home to India to spend time with Chris, so quiet that I decided it was a better idea to hang out in the quiet. It was also so quiet that the U.S. ambassador, Zalmay Khalilzad, left Afghanistan for Iraq, his job done in Kabul, a job transfer that would only later seem significant, when the U.S. embassy finally got ambassadors who acted like ambassadors. In a blue tie, dark blue suit, and white shirt, Zal was predictably somber at his last press conference, telling the room that the country was in the fourth kilometer of a ten-kilometer journey. He also said he was not "a potted plant" and was available to help if Afghanistan ever wanted it.

"My time has come to say farewell," he told the standing-room-only crowd. "I will never forget Afghanistan, and I will return."

His show was Oscar-worthy, and I feared he was about to burst into a version of "Don't Cry for Me, Afghanistan." A few Afghan journalists actually seemed close to tears. Their deference toward Zal bordered on worship.

And then, with a wave and a smile that could have powered a small Afghan village, the Viceroy was gone. I didn't know it at the time, but that would be the last large press conference I would ever attend, or be invited to, at the U.S. embassy, because in the future the embassy would stop holding free-for-all events, stop opening its doors so wide. And Zal would be the last U.S. ambassador who talked to Karzai that often.

Because Kabul was so quiet, our team—Farouq, Nasir, the photographer, and me—went to the most decrepit circus on the planet, the Pak-Asia Circus, making its first grand tour from Pakistan. It featured a ripped tent, a tightrope that sagged dangerously close to the ground, and so much more. The big top here was more of a sad raggedy small top. The knife thrower accidentally hit his beautiful female assistant in the thigh, drawing blood, but here in Afghanistan, such minor bloodshed qualified as slapstick comedy. The circus was usually packed, mainly with government workers, even the army, who didn't have to pay for the eighty-cent ticket. Nasir spotted a familiar face in the audience: the *Titanic*-loving taxi driver I had met two years earlier, who at the time said he was treated well at Guantánamo when he was mistakenly picked up and shipped there. Through Farouq, I asked about his life. He shrugged. He drove another taxi between Khost and Kabul, but he never got his first taxi back. He had gone to the circus twenty times in the past month—Kabul had nothing else to do for fun. But his tone had changed. He talked about an old man who recently had been shot dead in a nighttime raid near Khost by U.S. soldiers.

"America is no good," the taxi driver said. "The Americans are no good. They are not treating Afghans right."

Not much to say to that. He shifted his attention to the circus. So did we. A girl bent her feet over her back and used them to light a Pine Light cigarette. A man dressed up as a frog and hopped around. A boy did a headstand on a man's head. A tightrope walker swilled liquid from an Absolut vodka bottle as he stumbled along the low-slung rope. We said goodbye to the taxi driver to interview a man who came to the circus to escape the headache of having two wives. We never saw the taxi driver again.

But we did drive south to Khost, the eastern town that bordered the tribal areas of Pakistan, to visit the family of the dead man he had mentioned—Shayesta Khan, who had been about seventy-five, a village elder with a long white beard. This was the other side of the war from my embed in Paktika, the side of "collateral damage," the U.S. military term for unintentional injury caused while pursuing legitimate targets. Increasingly, such damage was becoming a problem throughout southern and eastern Afghanistan, the areas dominated by the ethnic Pashtuns and home to most insurgent activity. Anger about so-called "civilian casualties" and house raids was starting to bubble up there. Outside Kabul, in the places where public opinion mattered most, the mood toward the United States was shifting. It was not just the hostility displayed by Afghans upset at U.S. soldiers bursting into their compounds. It was the new willingness to believe the worst, even the most outrageous claims, without question. No one yet understood that what mattered in Afghanistan was not reality—it was rumor, the stories that raced from village to village.

The raid on Shayesta Khan's house was nothing like the compound visits I had observed, where the U.S. soldiers drank tea and tried to respect Afghan culture. This was a nighttime, kick-in-the-door, suited-up raid. An informant had allegedly told the U.S. military that bombs were being made in the compound where about sixty members of Shayesta Khan's family lived. Who the informant was, I could never find out, nor could I find any other evidence that the claims were true.

In the early morning hours, U.S. soldiers had broken down the compound's side door, near steps that led to an open area outside Shayesta Khan's bedroom. Family members said they heard shouting, then gunshots. Everything was a blur, and everyone had a different story. The local Afghan intelligence deputy said Shayesta Khan was shot reaching for a shirt. His sons said their father was shot trying to light a gas lantern. In their initial news release, U.S. military officials said an Afghan man was shot after he ignored a warning from an interpreter and a warning shot. The U.S. officials said the man was in the home of a known bomb-maker and kept moving toward a container on a dresser despite warnings, acting "aggressively" and making "threatening actions."

Who knew which version was right? But I learned certain facts— Shayesta Khan was old, and he was partly deaf, and bullet holes and shattered windows indicated that he was shot from outside his window. Afghan officials who had seen the body said Khan was shot several times, on the left side of his head and body. Afghans we met in the province thought he was innocent, a defenseless village elder who liked to throw rocks to make kids laugh. (Yes, that passed for entertainment in these parts. Still no TV.) His older brother, eighty or so, had no teeth, could barely walk, and didn't realize his brother was dead. His younger brother, seventy or so, said God had willed it.

"That was the decision from God," he said, then shrugged.

Part of me wanted to yell at the man and even shake him. I found the blind acceptance of tragedy maddening in this region, the whole idea that God or fate inextricably decided one's life, that free will had nothing to do with it. I had heard that argument from Hindus and Buddhists about the tsunami; I had privately wondered whether God might want people to use their wits to protect themselves, for instance building their homes more than ten feet away from the water's edge. But in some ways, such unquestioning acceptance was probably the only way to get through mind-blowing tragedy. God was the answer; a peaceful afterlife was the only reason to go through the pain of living.

I stood with Farouq, Nasir, and the photographer inside the narrow room where Shayesta Khan once slept, with two lone black-and-white pictures hanging on the wall—one of him and his wife decades earlier, another of his former boss, a military hospital official from the Communist regime. His prized Holy Quran was wrapped in cloth, near the corner where he had often prayed. The room looked scorched, like someone had somehow set fire to the two metal trunks in the opposite corner. Bullet holes punctuated the wall just above Khan's bed.

Farouq looked at the burn marks in the room. He was quiet, which meant he was upset. When he talked loudly or gruffly, that meant he was fine. I had messed that up in the past. "He was an old man," Farouq said. "He was completely innocent. How could this happen?"

Nasir looked at me, as if I had any answer. He always did that, even though he rarely understood me, and he usually just started laughing at anything I said.

"I don't know," I said. "Scared soldiers, the middle of the night, sudden movement. Someone fired. Messed up."

"But how could the Americans mess up like this?" Farouq replied. "They have the technology to see who they are shooting. He was an old man. Someone should go to prison."

The U.S.-led coalition spokesman described Khan's death to me as "an unfortunate incident" but insisted that the soldiers violated no rules. The press release also said soldiers captured three insurgents suspected of being involved with roadside bombs.

And that was it. The military never put out another statement, one that said that all three supposed insurgents were released within days. Or one that said no bomb-making equipment was actually found in the compound. Instead, the soldiers found one "Jihad Against America" pamphlet, one Kalashnikov assault rifle, a 9-mm handgun, and ammunition. It was actually not a significant haul for a compound of sixty people—in fact, such a weapons supply in a country like Afghanistan, where every man was allowed to keep a gun, was the equivalent of bringing a slingshot to a mortar fight.

Khan's death was a kind of breaking point. At a meeting with President Bush, Karzai asked for more coordination between Afghan and U.S. forces on raids. The Afghan defense ministry publicly criticized the U.S. military for the very first time. A wedge had started to form between the Afghan people and the international forces. The implications were obvious, though no one but Afghans seemed to notice them. The Pashtun code was based on honor, hospitality, respect, and, most important, revenge. An entire clan was obligated to take revenge for wrongs. This was eye-for-an-eye justice, or more accurately, a hundred eyes for an eye, which was why tribal disputes tended to last for generations. The Pashtuns had a proverb about a man taking revenge one hundred years after a slight to his ancestor, and fretting that he had acted in haste. Shooting an old Pashtun man in his home, even by mistake, violated a Pashtun's core beliefs. Revenge was compulsory; not taking revenge would brand Khan's male relatives as cowards. Every perceived injustice in the Pashtun code could conceivably create ten more militants. Even if God willed a death, God also willed a fitting revenge. That was the way of this world. Predictably, we would later learn that one of Shayesta Khan's sons ended up in Guantánamo.

We spent three days in Khost before starting the long drive back to Kabul. About halfway up the bumpy mountain pass, on a road that still had not been paved, our SUV started to strain, utter strange noises, and then, horribly, grind to a stop. There we were, more than two hours outside of Khost, stranded halfway up a mountain. Afghanistan had no AAA. This pass had no phone reception.

"This is not good," I said.

"No," Farouq agreed. "This is a bad area. It's known as the Bloody."

"The Bloody?" I repeated. "It's a mountain pass known as the Bloody? Seriously?"

Farouq nodded. "Not because of the Taliban. More because of thieves. Lots of robberies along this pass. It's easy to hide and stop people. Even kill them. That's why it's called the Bloody."

I was carrying $3,000 in cash, my computer, various equipment.

Farouq and Nasir argued. Then they announced their plan: They would pour water into the radiator—a move that had fixed one of our broken-down cars in the past. They would also dump oil in the oil pan. Other vehicles passed us, the men whiplashing when they saw me. I pulled my scarf up to cover my face and shrank into my seat, trying to hide in the middle of the Bloody.

"Not good, not good," I told Farouq. "Call the police in Khost."

"Kim. Calm down. Relax. I'm handling it."

Farouq climbed out of the SUV with the satellite phone, looking for a signal. He reached a police official after calling several friends and asked the police to come help. "Right away," the official said. Farouq then called Dr. Ali, our friend in Kabul, and asked him to start driving toward Khost to meet us.

We sat for half an hour. By coincidence, a police truck lumbered up the road. Farouq flagged it down and argued with the police to help us. Their answer—no. They were busy. He tried to call back the police official, who didn't answer.

"They want money," Farouq told us.

"They have foreigners trapped on a mountain pass called the Bloody, and they want a bribe," I said, stating the obvious. Afghan AAA, after all. "Perfect. How much?"

"Fifty," Farouq said. "And they'll only tow us to the top of the mountain."

"Of course. Fine."

I could hardly blame the police—they made only about $60

to $100 a month, not enough to survive without corruption. The month before, one counter-narcotics cop had complained to me: "Our salary is too little. If you give a hundred bucks a month to a donkey, it will not fart." So we gave the cops $50, and they tied a thick rope between their truck and our front bumper, looping it several times. The police truck strained with us, moving about ten miles an hour up the bumpy roads. Finally, after about ninety minutes, we made it to the top of the pass. The police untied us and waved. We waved back and started coasting down the other slope, fueled only by momentum, sailing around switchbacks and even passing the police truck at one point, Nasir laughing hysterically in the driver's seat, avoiding tapping the brake. Finally, about half a mile after the road flattened out, we rolled to a stop. Nasir's brother and Dr. Ali, in a tiny white car, pulled up in the opposite direction fifteen minutes later. Ali rolled down the window.

"Need a ride?"

That was logistics in Afghanistan—always figuring out a work-around, or anticipating the unexpected, which we should have expected. Most TV crews, aid agencies, and the UN traveled in convoys. Print journalists could never afford that. We gambled.

Back at the Kabul Lodge, sitting in front of my computer and writing about the dead elderly Afghan man, I wondered what my army engineer platoon would have thought about his death. Just one of the bad things that inevitably happened in war, I supposed. I often wondered what happened to those soldiers, and to Crowley, the intelligent smart aleck hoping to go back to graduate school.

I soon found out. Later that summer, the soldiers would tell another reporter that they felt I had betrayed them. After my story ran, Crowley and some of the other soldiers had been moved to a more dangerous base in Sharana, still in Paktika Province but near Kandahar, because of complaining that they had nothing to do in quiet Orgun-E. Crowley had also been busted to kitchen duty, frying up steaks for two weeks.

So that was my own collateral damage, my own unintended consequences. I was not happy that anyone got in trouble, but I soon forgot about it. Only years later would I find out what had happened to Crowley that August, almost three months after I met the platoon and he got married.

One evening in Sharana, Crowley was sent out on a last-minute mission. He was the gunner in the front vehicle, looking for land mines, for bags in the road, for suspicious cars, his eyes always scanning. But it was dusk—too dark to see much, too light for night-vision goggles. Then the explosion. His Humvee was blown up; a medic inside died. The other four men were injured. Crowley lost the lower part of his right leg. His new wife soon left him.

And that was Afghanistan, a country that lulled people into complacency, where hospitality was continually confused with support. When I finally found out what happened to Crowley, my heart hitting my kidneys during a random Google search, I would track him down, filled with guilt. If I hadn't written the story, he wouldn't have been moved. If he hadn't have been moved, he wouldn't have been blown up. Amazingly, he was gracious and kind. Luckily, he had remarried. He had also left the army and gone back to school. "I like to think of it as the best thing that ever happened to me," he told me. "I don't blame you." But that would only make me feel worse.

CHAPTER 6

MARCH OF THE PIGS

C rouched on the dirty pavement, the fortune-teller studied my palm, shook his head, and started talking.

"What's he saying?" I asked.

Dr. Ali, working with me because Farouq was busy with family obligations, shot me a look, somewhere between a smirk and sympathy.

"He says you will have a miserable life. Nothing will ever go right for you. You will always be unhappy. Do you want to hear more?"

"No," I said. "I get it."

I should have known this would be my fortune at the Kabul Zoo. Bored with all the obvious stories before the parliamentary elections in September 2005, I had made a bold move. I had gone to the zoo, planning to use it as an interesting way to tell the history of modern Afghanistan. My hook was Marjan the lion, donated by Germany in 1978, just as a coup by a Marxist party and Soviet sympathizers in the military sparked rumors of a Soviet invasion. Back then, in the zoo's heyday, more than seven hundred animals lived there.

The next year, the Soviets indeed invaded, and Afghanistan became the major chip in the poker game between the Soviets and the West. The CIA, the Saudis, and Pakistani intelligence eventually decided to support the seven major Afghan jihadi parties, sending money and weapons, using Islam as a rallying tool. And by the end of the 1980s, the Soviets left, followed shortly by American pledges of help. The zoo languished.

An uncertain pall fell over the capital. The pro-Soviet government remained nominally in charge, but soon lost control of the countryside. The jihadi parties pushed toward Kabul, finally capturing the city in 1992. Their fragile warlord coalition held for only a short time. Warlords then took positions outside the city, shelling it while trying to kill and intimidate their rivals' supporters. The Kabul Zoo was not immune—walls were knocked down or scarred with bullets. The zoo museum and the restaurant were rocketed.

Fighters from various factions, hungry for meat, soon realized the zoo had a ready supply. They kebabed the crane and the flamingo, roasting them over an open flame as zoo workers watched. They killed the two tigers for their pelts. One day a few fighters wanted to see how many bullets it took to kill an elephant. The answer: forty. Others stole the wooden fences from the zebra enclosure to feed fires. Animals died of starvation, of disease.

The bedlam inside the zoo mirrored what was happening in the city. Ask Afghans when the worst period of time was in Kabul, and they'll never mention the Soviets or the Taliban. They'll talk about this time, the civil war, when chaos and crazy ruled. They'll talk about the warlords.

One afternoon at the zoo, a Pashtun fighter inexplicably jumped into the cage of Marjan, who promptly bit off the man's arm. The man later died. The next day, the man's brother went to the zoo for revenge. He threw a grenade into the lion cage, which sent shrapnel into Marjan's muzzle, destroying one eye and almost blinding him in the other. The lion's face was frozen in an expression somewhere between grief and a Halloween mask, with eyes that appeared to have melted into his nose.

Even then, the indignities were not over.

The Taliban, a Pakistan-supported movement of ethnic Pashtun students from Islamic schools called madrassas, had seized control of much of the south. Spreading fear and the sick kind of security that only fear can deliver, the Taliban marched north and east, finally arriving in Kabul in 1996. The warlords fled. Taliban leaders then declared that Afghans must live by their version of Islam. Women could not go outside without a burqa or a male escort. Men had to pray, grow beards, and cut their hair. No music, no TV, no photographs of people, no gambling on bird or dog fights, no flying kites, no fun. With this new if perverted kind of justice, life calmed down inside the zoo, but only slightly and only after the zoo director proved that a zoo did not violate Islam, a task more difficult than it sounds. Even so, bored young Taliban soldiers beat the bear with sticks and threw snowballs and rocks at the other animals.

Somehow the zoo survived, but just barely. When the Taliban finally fled Kabul in late 2001, after the September 11 attacks and the U.S.-backed invasion, all that remained were a few vultures, owls, wolves, the beaten-down bear, and Marjan, his bones showing through his coat. With his scars and melted face, Marjan became the symbol of all the injuries inflicted on Afghans over decades of war, of all the pain. His picture appeared on the front pages of newspapers worldwide and sparked numerous tributes on the Internet. He was Afghanistan—battered, blind, blurry, but still strong.

Within two months, he fell down dead. The bear followed soon after.

Obviously the international community had to do something. So it threw money at the problem, a reaction it would eventually have to all the crises in the country. All told, Americans donated the bulk of $530,000 raised by top international zoo managers. It was supposed to be more than enough to fix the problems at the Kabul Zoo. It was not. Afghanistan was not just a money pit; it was a money tar pit, a country where money stuck to walls and fingers and never to where it was supposed to stick. And the Chinese didn't exactly help—a phrase that was to be repeated for years to come in almost every sector of government and aid, as China refused to do much in Afghanistan but profit from natural resources such as the country's copper mine. Against the wishes of every other country, the Chinese government decided that the world's worst zoo needed more animals. So it donated two lions, two bears, two pigs, two deer, and one wolf. The pigs, which resembled large Iowa farm pigs more than exotic zoo pigs, soon gave birth to five piglets. Afghanistan did not need pigs, considered dirty in Islam. It was another fine example of the unnecessary aid deemed necessary by somebody not in the country.

By the time I got to the zoo, right before the elections, the Chinese gift had been exposed as the Trojan horse it was. The male Chinese bear had died the year before, after swallowing a plastic bag filled with banana peels and a man's shoe heel. Four pigs then died from rabies after stray dogs jumped into their pen and bit one. (Luckily the other three pigs were elsewhere at the time. Where? Who knows. They were mysterious pigs.) All the animals had to be vaccinated for rabies. Over the summer, the second Chinese bear broke out of her cage, walked down a zoo path, and hopped into the pigpen, which had a low wall apparently notorious among the animals. Two pigs were there—the other, somewhere else. The bear squeezed both pigs to death. Typically, the Afghans wanted to ascribe some sort of romance to the bear's actions. They loved stories of star-crossed lovers, largely because many of them were forced to marry their cousins, whom they did not love in that soul-consuming, fatalistic way made popular by both Indian and Hollywood movies.

"She was lovesick and lonely and she missed her mate," the deputy zoo director told me. "So she broke into the pig cage and tried to hug the two pigs, but she hugged them too hard and they died."

I nodded and took notes. I tried to poke holes in his logic. "But weren't they female pigs?"

"Yeah, so what? When you're lonely, you'll take love from anywhere, a female bear will take it from a female pig, no problem," he said.

In Afghanistan, I would learn that this was too often true. The zoo workers surrounded the wayward lovesick female bear with torches and nudged her back to her cage. This was considered progress—earlier, workers would have just shot her. Facing reality, China announced it would stop donating animals to the Kabul Zoo until living conditions improved, while, of course, doing nothing to improve those conditions. The one surviving pig would be made famous years later by the international swine flu outbreak. Fearing what it might harbor, Afghans would isolate the country's only known domestic pig, which already must have felt isolated enough because everyone thought it was unclean.

By the time Farouq came back to work, the election campaign was in full swing. Covering the election was a little like writing about the zoo—lots of scars, lots of confusion, lots of mysterious pigs. This election was the final step in the transition to full sovereignty outlined in the 2001 Bonn Agreement, the road map for creating an Afghan government that had been hashed out by prominent Afghans—including most major warlords—in Germany during the fall of the Taliban. Many of the country's top warlords were running for parliament, including some who always made the "best of" lists drawn up by various human-rights groups that no one ever listened to, warlords accused of pounding nails into people's heads, of pouring boiling oil over a body after cutting off a head, which Afghans swore would make a headless body dance.

For years, the international community and the Afghans had been toying with what to do about the warlords and past war crimes, pushing the issue around like a large piece of gristle. The UN, the Afghan government, and its backers had theoretically disarmed the illegal militias and defanged the warlords, but no one had been held accountable for anything. This election, in effect, would erase the board of all previous atrocities and eliminate any possibility of holding any of the warlords responsible for their crimes. Then again, maybe it was already too late. The capricious warlord Abdul Rashid Dostum, known for switching sides like a celebrity changing hair color, was the chief of staff to the commander in chief of the armed forces, a lengthy title that was largely ceremonial but that permitted Dostum to do pretty much what he wanted; Ismail Khan was now minister of power and water; several former warlords were also governors. The wing of Islamist party Hezb-i-Islami that claimed to have broken from founder Gulbuddin Hekmatyar backed many candidates for parliament. Meanwhile, Hekmatyar and the rest of Hezb-i-Islami were busy attacking U.S. troops in eastern Afghanistan.

This election was, perhaps, the most confusing ever held anywhere. Somehow, a voter in Kabul was supposed to pick one candidate out of 390. The ballot folded out into seven large pages, and each candidate had a photograph and a symbol, because many Afghans were illiterate. But creativity ran out, and symbols had to be reused. Candidates were identified as different objects, including a pair of scissors, one camel, two camels, three camels, two sets of barbells, mushrooms, two ice-cream cones, three corncobs, two tomatoes, stairs, a turkey, two turkeys, one eye, a pair of eyes, a tire, two tires, three tires—to name a few. The symbols were randomly drawn out of a box.

The journalists struggled to make sense of the election, of the candidates, of the lack of interest back home. For me, the election was complicated by my inability to sleep. The Gandamack had welcomed me back and all was forgiven, especially after I repeatedly apologized for the Laundry Incident. I had loaned one of the Afghan women who ran the place a Pilates exercise DVD; the Afghan front-door guard, who lost one leg when he stepped on a land mine during the civil war, pumped my arm like it would deliver oil when I first returned. The *Washington Post* was there; the *Guardian* was there; the award-winning British TV journalist doing a documentary on female drivers was there; a photographer friend was there; a group of genial security contractors was there. But my personal life intruded. I had not yet ended my relationship with Chris—I wasn't sure why, maybe because I was never home, maybe because I felt guilty, and maybe because, ultimately, I just didn't want to be alone. Yet my boyfriend started sending me paranoid e-mails, or more paranoid than usual. I called him. He sounded paranoid.

"There are men outside, watching me," Chris told me.

"It's India. There are always men outside watching you."

"Yeah, but they also know what I've done. And they're watching your computer."

"What are you talking about?" I asked. "Are you drunk?"

"No. I was. Now I'm fine. I erased all the incriminating files on your computer."

"What files? What are you talking about? You did what?"

"The proof," he said. "They were watching me. They were scanning your computer."

"You erased my computer?"

I was confused. Chris had never displayed any sign of mental illness before. He told me he had put up notes saying "Think of Kim" and "Remember Kim," and that they were the only thing keeping him together. In other words, yellow Post-its were holding him in place. I told him to go to sleep, to get some rest. I called my office manager and asked her to check on him. This was getting messy. Then Chris called the U.S. embassy help line, asking for help. Someone called back and heard my work answering machine; someone else figured out my e-mail address and wrote me, asking what was going on.

"He's a friend," I wrote back, embarrassed to have my personal life enter my professional one. "He's off his medication."

I worried. For months, I had vacillated on whether to break up with Chris, but if anything happened to him, I would never forgive myself. He had never behaved like this before, but he had never spent this much time in India before, never been alone like this. India was a series of challenges wrapped in a mystical blanket covered in an existential quandary. I often thought that all the gods—maybe three, maybe three thousand in Hinduism—made it easier in India for there to be three thousand answers to a question that should have had only one. India was colorful, fabulous, energizing. India was a Chinese finger puzzle. India made you scream at people like a Hollywood diva for the smallest of reasons. India was a crazy football coach. It could break you if it didn't make you stronger.

Chris was broken. He wouldn't leave India without seeing me. I couldn't leave Afghanistan in the middle of an election. I tried to throw myself into work and to avoid thinking or talking about my boyfriend. The guilt I felt had actual weight—I felt the responsibility of him moving halfway around the world for me, of me failing him, of fears about what was happening to him. I cried in front of Farouq and Nasir on a road trip. Farouq worried.

"I just want you to be happy," he told me.

"Too bad I don't have an eligible cousin," I said.

Maybe the fortune-teller was right. An old friend, a photographer I hadn't seen in more than a year, told me that I seemed angry and bitter. Overseas for longer than me and world-weary, she warned me that maybe it was time to move back to the States, that many things were more important than the parliamentary elections in Afghanistan. Night after night, I lay in the Gandamack room that smelled like my childhood because of the wild marijuana plants outside my window. Night after night, I couldn't sleep.

The construction next door didn't help. Work started at 6 AM and often stopped at 1 AM. As with everything else in Afghanistan, no laws regulated noise or construction. Every night the pounding would be our dinner music. Every night the tenants of the Gandamack would try to make it stop.

Sean, the British journalist who was working on a documentary about female Afghan drivers, was particularly annoyed. I had met Sean with Farouq months earlier, in the garden of the Gandamack.

It was a sunny day, and we were sitting outside in the garden beneath a large umbrella. A man approached us, said hello to Farouq, and thanked him for his advice. He was expansive and obnoxious, attractive and repellant, all in one package. He sat down at another table. I introduced myself, slightly defensive, worried about the man's familiarity with Farouq.

"Call me sometime," he said, handing me his phone number. I soon learned that Sean gave everyone his phone number.

I didn't call at first, but I couldn't help running into him everywhere. Sean was a few years older than me, his hair was prematurely gray, his chin was slightly receding, and his nose balanced out his chin. Yet there was something about him. Sean was so funny, he was always the center of attention, the ironic self-deprecating smart aleck with glasses who sat in the corner surrounded by smart attractive women. Sean was Kabul's version of a B-movie star. He was also a war junkie, having done time in Iraq, and that addiction went a long way toward explaining why he was separated from his wife. Sean and I became quick friends. He had taken me on my first social outing to a brothel in Kabul, and he had told me when his friends had decided to drop me off early because I was cramping their style. He told me when he wanted to copy my story about the first traffic light in Kabul, as part of his documentary. In fact, Sean told me pretty much everything, as he told everyone pretty much everything, even when he told something that was supposed to be secret. Everyone knew that Sean was going through a divorce. Everyone knew that Sean really wanted to stay with his wife. And everyone knew that the divorce was pretty much Sean's fault—he was always on the road, bouncing between war zones, an ageless man-child. But of all the people I had met in Kabul so far, few were as good company as Sean.

Now the construction next door stalked our days and nights. The Gandamack was a two-story guesthouse. The new project, allegedly another guesthouse, soon grew taller than the Gandamack, and the construction workers only seemed to stop working to leer at the female guests in the garden. Any silence was a kind of torture, filled with waiting for the pounding to start again. The hallways echoed with combinations of four-letter words I had never before heard. We tried various tactics to stop the banging at a reasonable hour. Someone found out who owned the land—a respected spiritual leader, a man I had interviewed. I called him one night in a panic.

"Please, please, please, can you get them to stop working by eight?" I asked the holy man. "None of us can sleep. None of us can work. I think I'm losing my mind."

I even played the female card. "The construction workers are harassing the women living here. They're looking at us. It's against Islam."

The spiritual leader was kind, conciliatory.

"Don't worry, Kim, I will stop it. I understand. Don't worry. It's no problem."

I got off the phone. "He says he'll stop it," I told the others.

But within an hour, the banging again sounded like war. I was reminded of what I already knew—any time I was told "no problem" in Afghanistan, the problem bit my head off. I again tried calling the spiritual leader, but the phone rang and rang. He never answered.

The next night, at about eleven, Sean pounded on the upstairs door of one of the security contractors, already in bed, not sleeping.

"Can I borrow your gun?" Sean asked the security guy. It's possible Sean was drinking.

The security guy gave him a toy BB assault rifle and a real gun laser. Sean took the gun and aimed it toward the construction workers. He trained the laser sight on a man's chest. It took the other workers seconds to see the red laser point, then a few more seconds to look over at the Gandamack and the window where a crazed Brit clearly was pointing a remarkably real-looking gun at them. That was what finally stopped the pounding—not reasonable talk, not negotiations, not promises, but the threat of violence. Another Afghan lesson learned.

Finally the election was held. The results were predictable—the warlords, drug lords, and fundamentalist Hezb-i-Islami candidates won their seats, along with a smattering of do-gooders, former civil servants, and women, who under the constitution were given one-quarter of the seats. Despite allegations of fraud and illegal militias, the international election-complaints commission could do little. When the commission reversed one of its only decisions to ban a warlord-linked woman from running, one of the commissioners quit.

Even my first warlord, Pacha Khan Zadran, was allowed to run for parliament, despite his recent résumé of running an illegal militia and fighting the Americans before being arrested in Pakistan and jailed for a time. The disarmament commission reported that Pacha Khan had not surrendered all the weapons necessary to run for parliament. But still, the election commission allowed him, under the more-the-merrier warlord free-for-all. He won a seat. Like everyone else, he was now respectable, the past forgiven.

I stayed in Kabul for days after the election, the last visiting journalist in town. I didn't want to go home, didn't want to face Chris and what I knew I had to do. Finally an earthquake threw me out of bed, an earthquake that seemed to last for minutes and threatened to shake the Gandamack into powder. I flew back to India. The quake killed more than eighty thousand people, mostly on the Pakistani side of Kashmir. I spent barely a night with my fragile boyfriend before flying off to cover the earthquake. By the time I came back, Chris knew he needed to go home to Chicago. I also knew it—I couldn't bear the responsibility.

"I think I want to break up," I said as soon as I walked in the front door.

"I know," he said.

Later I told him he needed to leave. Soon.

"But I want to stay for a while," he said. "I want to be here for your birthday."

"Go home for my birthday."

I wasn't trying to be cruel. The best gift he could give me was to get home safe. So I put my ex-boyfriend on a plane, threw away the Post-it notes bearing my name, and tried to forget about the lost files on my computer, which Chris had wiped clean. The next day I ran away again, back to Afghanistan, where life seemed simpler.

CHAPTER 7
MONKEY GONE TO HEAVEN

left India without telling my bosses. They knew I was going to Afghanistan—they just didn't know when. Not only that—I flew into Kabul, and then almost immediately took another flight an hour west to Herat. Why? Yes, I had found a story that I knew my bosses would want, but I also flew there because a man had invited me. I had become interested in Jeremy earlier that month, just as my long-term relationship was falling apart. This potential fling, spurred on by a flurry of e-mails, would never last. We were both on the bounce. I had met Jeremy a few times during the past year at various parties. Over the summer, he and his long-term girlfriend had split. Jeremy was only twenty-nine, and he bore a strong resemblance to every man I had ever dated—he was artsy, handsome, and angsty; he played the bass guitar; he wore corduroy; and he liked the band Postal Service. I told him very little about my breakup. He invited me to Herat for a long weekend. Coincidentally, a weekend that included my thirty-fifth birthday.

On that Thursday, a translator I found through Farouq picked me up at the airport. We started reporting a story on the largest parliamentary vote-winner in the province, which was near Iran and much more developed than most of Afghanistan. The top winner was a woman who won primarily because Afghan men thought the mother of six was hot. After interviewing a few men who had tacked up her election poster like some cheesecake pinup, I went to my hotel to wait for Jeremy to call. He was working on a U.S.-funded agriculture project, delivering wheat seeds to farmers in an attempt to discourage poppy cultivation. The opium trade had sprung back to life after an earlier Taliban crackdown, like a dried-out sponge dropped in water. Jeremy's project was a well-intentioned idea but similar to fighting a hundred-year flood with a sandbag, if the sandbag were given out as a loan and had to be repaid at some point in the future. Jeremy was due back that afternoon from a meeting with farmers in Farah Province. I sat in my room, which was dubbed a "deluxe," apparently because it had four single beds all crammed together, and waited. After an hour, Jeremy called.

"I'm really sorry, there's no way I can get there today," he said. "My talk to the farmers ran long. It's too dangerous to leave this late. My security says we can't go by road."

"Oh. OK, I understand," I said. I did, but I was disappointed. There I sat in Herat, after being invited to town by a guy who wasn't even there. Lame.

"I'll get there tomorrow," he assured me.

Tomorrow was my birthday, but Jeremy didn't know that. I wasn't going to tell him. After all, I had already lied about my age for the first time in my life, without even thinking about it, inexplicably telling him that I was thirty-two. "You don't look it," he had told me.

So it seemed to put far too much weight on this visit to tell Jeremy that I happened to be celebrating my birthday with him. Jeremy did show up that Friday, coming over to my hotel lobby about noon. I skipped down the stairs, wearing a new blue long-sleeved butt-covering loose shirt with baggy black pants and a black headscarf.

"I like your shirt," Jeremy said.

"Thanks," I replied. "It shows off my figure."

We smiled awkwardly at each other and shook hands. This was like seventh grade. We went to see the famed Herat minarets, pockmarked by various artillery. We looked at the rubble surrounding them, including chipped pieces of blue tile that once decorated the minarets. We could not hold hands. We could not hug. I could not spend the night at his place nor stay too long in his room—too embarrassing for him and his staff, since he lived in his office. Everything in Afghanistan was about appearances, even for foreigners. Especially for the women—we were already considered loose and easy, just by our very existence.

Jeremy and I ate dinner at a kebab joint that was shaped like a giant swan. I had been here before, on a trip with Karzai's crew, when we sat on daybeds out back and were entertained by live music and a dancing boy. But now it was too cold for such fun. We ate dinner quietly because everyone was staring at us. We had no booze to help ease the jitters of an actual date.

After dinner, at Jeremy's office, I sat at his co-worker's desk and checked my e-mail. My bank wanted me to call—they were concerned about fraud. So I called. My bank asked for my mother's maiden name. I gave it. Then my bank asked for my date of birth.

"Why do you need that?" I asked, glancing at Jeremy, who was sitting at the next desk.

"For verification," the bank woman said.

"But I'm verified. I told you who I am. I gave you my mother's maiden name. That's enough, right?"

"We need your date of birth. That's the procedure."

"Um, I don't think that's necessary."

Jeremy looked at me, hearing only my side of the conversation, which in all likelihood sounded strange.

"It is," the woman said.

I knew if I said my date of birth, my house of fraudulent age-faking cards would come crashing down. Plus Jeremy would know it was my birthday. He was not stupid. This was an *I Love Lucy* episode. I thought quickly.

"Today," I told her. I waited briefly, as if she were saying something on the other end of the line. "Yes. But a while ago. A long while ago."

"Oh, so it is," the woman said. "I didn't notice that before. Happy birthday. And what was the year?"

"You need that?"

"We need that."

"That's a very good question," I said. "In fact, I think the correct number you're looking for is one, nine, seven, zero."

Smooth. It worked. Jeremy had no idea.

The next day I continued to report my story. At the hot parliament member's aerobics class, various Afghan women dressed in the same everyday long-sleeved shirts and baggy pants they wore underneath their burqas or black abayas. There was no such thing yet as workout gear for women in Afghanistan, although one standout young woman had somehow managed to get her hands on a sweatshirt. The power went out. The exercise routine made the *Sit and Be Fit* workout program for seniors in the United States look extreme.

When I met Jeremy at the end of the day, I heard the news that three bombs had gone off in Delhi, at markets where I had shopped, killing more than sixty people. I was seriously out of position. I called my bosses and told them I was already in Afghanistan. I felt guilty for putting my personal life ahead of work, even slightly. It affected our night—I was distracted by bomb blasts a country away.

I left for Kabul the next day, saying an awkward goodbye.

"Thanks for coming to visit," he said.

"Well, my bosses wanted a story, so it worked out," I replied. Even then, it was difficult to be honest.

We saw each other a week later, as he passed through Kabul on his way out of the country for vacation, for lunch at the Flower Street Café, a sandwich shop that was relatively private. We held hands beneath the table and kissed goodbye quickly in the path leading toward the front gate, pulling away when an Afghan waiter walked past. Neither one of us necessarily wanted anyone else to know that we were attempting to date. Kind of. We spoke in staccato sentences with abrupt punctuation, not wanting to reveal too much, or ask for too much.

"It's been really nice getting to know you," I said.

"Well. You know. I don't want anything serious. I mean—I'm not—you don't think—"

"Of course!" I interrupted. "You know. I just. Well, I don't want anything serious. Obviously. But it's nice, you know."

"Well—yeah. I like hanging out. We'll see what happens."

"Totally. Have a great vacation."

Seventh grade. Kabul was a fishbowl and not conducive to actual dating, even though the foreign women were vastly outnumbered by the foreign men. Our attractiveness rate skyrocketed accordingly. A ten in Kabul became a five as soon as she walked off the plane in Dubai. We were Kabul Cute, we were Mission Pretty. But still, the men here rarely asked the women out on actual dates—in that, Jeremy was an anomaly. Most of the attempts at mating involved bad tongue action and groping near or inside the bathrooms at L'Atmosphère.

We were a function of our environment. For many, life was a pressure cooker, going from home to office to restaurant, rarely being outside, and the only release was liquor, was parties, was dancing to the same soundtrack, week after week—"Hips Don't Lie," "Crazy in Love," "Don't Cha," and "Let's Get Retarded." (In my nightmares, I can still hear that song list, over and over.) By this point, the social scene resembled a cross between a fraternity party and the Hotel California, where the same characters always seemed to stay too long and drink too much, where entertainment occasionally consisted of spelling words on legs with Nair hair-removal cream. The best pool table—or the only one—was at a brothel called Escalades. The disco Coco Cabana had opened a few months earlier but had rapidly turned into a seedy joint featuring alcohol-fueled grope-fests. The Elbow Room resembled a homey ski lodge, featuring a bar and a fireplace; Thai and Italian restaurants promised bad lighting and chilled red wine. A few thousand foreigners lived in Kabul, and even though many of them never went out at night, enough did to justify a dozen thriving businesses. The expatriate scene of Kabul even had its own magazine—*Afghan Scene*—that included articles and pictures of people at various parties, in various states of inebriation. (To be fair, money from magazine sales helped street kids.)

At this point, prostitutes seemed more in danger of taking over Kabul than the Taliban. Brothels came and went—the Lighthouse, the Tree House, Escalades, the Disco Restaurant, Bobo's, Ching Ching (a so-called Chinese "restaurant" that advertised something called "mosic"). These brothels, mostly staffed with women from China or one of the former Soviet republics, had blossomed in Kabul like poppy farms after the Taliban's fall, even though they were theoretically illegal and catered mainly to the security and contractor communities. Enforcement was spotty. A quixotic Afghan lawyer in a cape would raid one brothel. The poor women would then be bundled up and shipped back to their native country, only to be replaced by another brothel in another two-story house with new Chinese women who barely spoke English and did not speak the local languages at all. In some ways, these women in thigh-high boots and fishnet stockings were much like the Taliban-led militants—a flexible cast of characters who would be somehow eliminated and then replaced by others. A ready supply of bodies always existed for war and sex.

Often, the reality of Afghanistan interrupted the fun. A security guy shot up a bar; an attention-seeking journalist tossed a stun grenade at a party, blowing out all the windows. A consultant company threw a dance and trampoline party with camels and actual Afghan nomads—a measure of authenticity, I guess, that had become legendary with Afghan nomads, who spread rumors across the region of a foreigner trampoline orgy. A rooftop party at the Mustafa Hotel the year before had been interrupted by three rockets overhead, but only slightly, as the revelers, one in a pink feather boa, waved their hands in the air and started to cheer. A toga party two months earlier was cut short by a power outage and generator failure. At that party, most people dressed in white sheets, looking regal and even arranging leaves in their hair. Mindful of how it would look to be killed at a toga party in Kabul, I had opted for compromise—I went, but wore jeans and a pink Puma T-shirt, the Afghan equivalent of wearing clean underwear in case you're run over by a bus. My friend, who worked for Human Rights Watch, had declined his invitation. "Human Rights Watch does not do toga parties in Kabul," he said, and he had a point.

The brothels and over-the-top parties were only a symptom of the absurdity that this war had turned into by the fall of 2005. Foreign aid levels were at record lows compared to the money given per capita to the relatively advanced countries of Bosnia and East Timor, but still, billions of new dollars had poured in, which should have accomplished something significant. Yet no one seemed to be coordinating which money went where. There was duplication, repetition. The capital still had little electrical power, maybe a few hours a day, and many roads that were more pothole than pavement. The country still had relatively few international troops, and of those, some, like the Germans, weren't allowed to patrol after dark. (During the day, they traveled around with an ambulance.) The Afghan government seemed about as effective as a student council, and no one in the international community seemed to pay much attention to what was happening across the border in Pakistan.

But newly single and tempted by the excitement, I jumped into the abyss, throwing myself into going out at night, eagerly enrolling in Kabul High. One night, as I sat with security guys at the Gandamack, a new friend called, insisting on dragging me out. The car was full—I hopped in the back, the only woman with four men who seemed like longtime pals because we spoke the same language and that alone bred a sense of familiarity in a country as foreign as Afghanistan. A media consultant, a former U.S. Marine, a carpet expert, a married guy I didn't really know, and me. We drove around, looking for the telltale neon sign, which meant only one thing in Kabul: a brothel. Finally a tiny two-story house had one, a rainbow of neon lights spelling out THE DELICIOUS BARBECUE in cursive neon script. When we knocked on the door, I almost hoped that the women would not answer.

"Wake up, whores!" announced the former marine, who liked to live up to his reputation for being an obnoxious jerk, as he pounded on the screen door.

Eventually the lights inside The Delicious Barbecue flickered on. Three sleepy Chinese women opened the door, and we walked into the narrow two-story building. The furniture in the front room was minimal, a few plastic chairs, a small wooden bar, all bathed in fluorescent lights that flattered no one. Everything here was hard: the concrete floors and walls, the women, even us. I brushed away the hand of a woman who evidently thought I looked like a better deal for the night than my friends. I smiled through my rejection. She shrugged.

We were here to sing. The women started setting up the karaoke machine and handed us some Heinekens, the beer that had somehow cornered the black market in Afghanistan. And then my social life, as usual, was interrupted by a work call.

It was the Taliban. They always called at the worst times.

I tried to postpone the translation with Farouq, but it was no use. He kept talking over me like the steamroller he was, flattening my useless protests and insistence that I did not have a notebook. No matter, Farouq plowed on. I put down my Heineken and stepped outside into the cool evening.

Earlier that day, Taliban leader Mullah Omar, the famously elusive one-eyed cleric who seemed about as likely to be photographed as cold fusion and was often described as "shy" with foreigners, had allegedly authorized an e-mail statement, urging his followers not to end their armed struggle. Farouq had finally reached the Taliban spokesman. I wanted to know whether the alleged Mullah Omar statement was legitimate and whether he was now surfing the Internet. Quickly, so I could go back inside. But Farouq never did anything quickly or halfheartedly.

"Give me the summary," I said. "Please."

Farouq, unforgivingly thorough and professional, was growing tired of me going out late at night and sleeping in late in the morning. He worried about my new adolescence. He most likely resented that he had to work, when he'd rather be with his family, and when I was out behaving like a teenager. By now, Farouq and his wife had a daughter, and his wife was pregnant with a second child. And by now, he had stopped talking about going to America to study medicine.

"No. Kim, it's Eid tomorrow, and I don't want you calling me and asking me for the translation because I will be with my family, so if it's possible, can I just tell you what he said now?"

Eid al-Fitr was one of the most important Islamic holidays of the year, when Muslims gathered to celebrate the end of the holy month of Ramadan. For the past month, Farouq had not smoked, eaten, or drank during daylight hours, which meant he was crabby. He was hardly alone. Work hours at Afghan offices were typically cut to about 8 AM to 1 PM during Ramadan. It was impossible to accomplish anything. Suddenly realizing I should be grateful that Farouq had actually managed this interview on the last day of the fast—and suddenly realizing how inappropriate it was to be at a brothel on such a holiday—I agreed to spend some more time in the cold.

I sat down on the concrete steps leading into the yard. I pulled a pen out of my purse and three crumpled pieces of paper and scribbled notes on the interview. The claim of the Taliban spokesman: The e-mail was real.

So what, I thought. The fact that Mullah Omar was even making such a statement on the eve of the three-day holiday meant that the armed struggle was in trouble. By this point, November 2005, the Taliban seemed to be irrelevant in much of the country, a largely contained force, maybe two to three thousand men at best, mostly along the border between Pakistan and Afghanistan. Sure, roadside bombs occasionally exploded, like the one that had hit Crowley. But they were rare. Any comeback threat was just Taliban propaganda, an attempt to grab some media airtime in a war room where Iraq had sucked up all the oxygen.

From inside The Delicious Barbecue, the singing began. The media consultant belted out "Rhinestone Cowboy," which caused the yard outside to come to life. The scraggly mutt, chained to the tree, pulled at his collar, jangling the chain. And the two pink-faced rhesus monkeys in the tiny cage, which for some reason I only then noticed despite their peculiar monkey smell, started to mate. Loudly. One monkey kept repeating the letter "e"—strangely, in time to the music.

Keeping up my charade of going to sleep would be difficult.

"Farouq. Farouq." He kept talking.

"I have to go." He kept talking.

I told him there were monkeys having sex to "Rhinestone Cowboy," and I just couldn't talk about the Taliban anymore.

That got him to stop translating. "Monkeys having sex?" he said, pausing before reconsidering his question. "Where are you?"

"In the garden."

That satisfied him. After hanging up, I walked back inside.

"I signed you up for 'Like a Virgin,'" the former marine said.

"Funny."

My only previous attempts at karaoke had involved songs by the Violent Femmes and Guns N' Roses—songs, in other words, where being able to carry a melody did not matter. But what the hell, I figured. Here I was, newly single and newly thirty-five, dressed in baggy jeans, a gray Arkansas T-shirt, and an orange hooded sweatshirt. More important, here I was in Afghanistan, where nothing really mattered, where any sense of self-consciousness had been stripped away.

"Like a virgin," I sang. "Touched for the very first time."

For three hours, the Chinese women sat in the plastic chairs against the wall, a jury of blank faces and folded arms that watched us sing, torturing such classics as Bonnie Tyler's "Total Eclipse of the Heart" and Boney M.'s "Daddy Cool." A random Western man occasionally showed up, stepped inside, and went upstairs draped with the woman of his choice. She would return and slump back into her chair after thirty minutes or so. Bored. At one point, several Heinekens into the evening, we pulled the women out of their chairs and tried to make them dance with us. Finally, we got a reaction. They started laughing. After 1 AM, we left to pick up kebabs, the Afghan equivalent of IHOP, before I kissed one of my new friends good night and fell face-first into bed. I was no longer just observing the bad behavior of the foreign community. Within weeks of my breakup, I had fully signed on.

CHAPTER 8
MESSAGE IN A BOTTLE

Many Afghans were not happy with the direction the country was heading, especially conservatives. And in the middle of this disgust, Abdul Jabar Sabit, a windmill-slaying Afghan lawyer, saw an opportunity. As legal adviser for the Interior Ministry, his job description was somewhat vague, so he decided to declare war on alcohol and brothels, to stem the tide of foreign excess. He had launched a one-man anti-vice mission, a pared-down version of the Taliban's Vice and Virtue Ministry, that notorious charm offensive responsible for enforcing the regime's straitjacket-like morality rules. And in so doing, Sabit had seized on the mood of many Afghans, who felt that the Westerners were just too much—too free with their booze, too loose with their morals, and too influential over young Afghans.

Even though alcohol was illegal, the Afghan government had permitted a two-tiered society—one for Afghans, and one for Westerners. Foreigners could buy booze at two major stores that required passports at the door. Restaurants could serve alcohol to foreigners but not to Afghans, which meant most restaurants that served alcohol did not allow Afghans. The contradiction fueled resentment from everyone. Many Afghans viewed alcohol as more pernicious, more Western and un-Islamic, than opium or hashish. More liberal Afghans figured they should be allowed to drink alcohol inside the restaurants, which were, after all, in their country. Every time Sabit announced another booze battle, Farouq would shake his head.

"The price of raisins is going to go up," he would say. Raisin wine was a concoction made popular during Taliban rule, along with antiseptic and Coca-Cola.

I had first met Sabit in the spring of 2005, in the office of the Interior Ministry spokesman. He had left Afghanistan during the late 1970s and landed first in Pakistan, then the United States, where he worked for Voice of America before moving to Canada. He had joined Gulbuddin Hekmatyar's fundamentalist Islamic party, Hezb-i-Islami, back when Hekmatyar was on our side against the Soviets and before he had turned into a renegade. After the Taliban fell, Sabit, a lawyer by training, had come back to Afghanistan, part of the flood of returning Afghans who claimed they wanted to help rebuild their country. He was an ally of Karzai's—kind of— although he complained all the time about Karzai. Then again, Sabit complained about a lot. He was a human volcano, constantly threatening to explode.

Sabit, who was in his sixties, was a bizarre combination, sporting the long white beard of an Islamic fundamentalist and the bespoke gray suit of an English gentleman. He was an ethnic Pashtun, and he looked it, with wild white hair, bright hazel eyes, and exaggerated features—big ears, big fingers. He reminded me of a skinny yet somehow menacing Santa Claus. Sabit had asked where I lived, and after I told him how often I traveled, he grunted. He quoted a Pashtun proverb about never being friends with a traveler. But that didn't stop him from trying. At our first meeting, he invited me to his house to meet his wife, a raven-haired woman about my age. Although she was fluent in at least three languages, including English, and had been working on a doctorate degree in Canada, she was not allowed to work. For appearance's sake. Whenever she went out in public, she wore a black abaya that covered everything but her eyes.

During that first dinner, Sabit had agreed to take me along on a raid of bars and brothels on the coming Friday night. But when Friday rolled around, I had forgotten about our date, and by the time his driver called, I had already downed a glass of red wine. Regardless, I jumped in the backseat of Sabit's SUV, filled with his flunkies. We then picked up Sabit, who on this night wore a long cape-like green coat with purple stripes, similar to the coat favored by Karzai. We went from brothel to bar to restaurant. Everywhere, Sabit was the customer no one wanted. As soon as he knocked on a gate, whoever answered shouted out warnings. But he wouldn't take no for an answer and pushed his way inside, flanked by his minions—and me, of course.

At one dark brothel with bordello-red walls, a Chinese woman had dressed in a fur jacket, fishnet stockings, a white miniskirt, and white boots—a bit of overkill, given the all-encompassing burqas that many Afghan women still wore.

"Look at that," Sabit muttered. The only customer was a Western man, sitting by himself.

At another fully stocked bar, Sabit insulted the Turkish manager.

"You are Muslim, aren't you?" Sabit said. "You aren't allowed to serve this liquor."

"We are Muslim," the man replied. "But this is business."

The night ended in violence, as did so many things in Afghanistan. After we checked on a guesthouse, even inspecting the bedrooms, a cop on the street failed to properly address Sabit and show him enough respect. Sabit yelled and screamed at the man. I hopped in the backseat of the SUV. Sabit continued to yell, and then started punching the younger man repeatedly in the face, the body. I watched through the window.

"You have to help him," his driver told me. "Mr. Sabit is a crazy man. I'm too scared."

"No way," I said. "I'm going nowhere near him."

Sabit climbed into the passenger seat after making sure the ignorant officer was carted off to jail for the night. He adjusted his coat and looked forward.

"Write that in your story, and I'll kill you," he said.

I wasn't stupid. And I knew a good connection when I found one. From then on, whenever we planned an occasional gathering at a brothel or a major party, I would call Sabit and ask him what he was doing. If he planned to go on raids, I planned to stay home. And that's how I knew that The Delicious Barbecue was a safe bet.

But Sabit required a lot of care and feeding, and he was often impossible to please. Even showing slight annoyance with Sabit's demands sent him into months of silence and furious complaints about me to mutual acquaintances. Just after I returned to India, Sabit flew to New Delhi to have surgery for something related to his ability to digest, a procedure he was incredibly explicit about. He demanded that I pick him up at the airport. I spent five hours waiting for him inside the Indian capital's dingy airport before he finally wandered into the lobby, several hours after all the other Afghans. Only then, I found out that the Afghan embassy had also sent a welcome delegation and a car. After Sabit was admitted to the hospital, he expected me to visit every day, a time suck of at least three hours. I was his lifeline in Delhi, the only person he seemed to know, despite the fact that the embassy treated him like royalty. Deferential men with beards always sat in his hospital room.

"You have lived over here long enough," he admonished me from his hospital bed. "You know Afghans. You know the culture. You know you need to come see me."

"I also have to work," I said. "It's kind of the reason I'm here."

"Work. You're always working."

Even the surgery didn't calm him. "This green tea is awful," he complained from his bed. "Bring me some new tea."

Eventually, after helping sort out his tea and his visa, I sent my driver to take Sabit to the airport to fly home. But he was annoyed because I did not ride along. Over the winter, I heard rumors that Sabit was upset with me. "She's a bad friend," he told an official at the U.S. embassy. I called Sabit from India repeatedly, and he repeatedly hung up on me. When he finally answered, he sounded as hurt as a spurned lover.

"I am so angry at you!" he said, more than once. Sabit often talked in exclamation points. "You are a very bad friend!"

But he eventually forgave me. And our uneasy acquaintance had payback. Sabit had turned into my eccentric grandpa. When I arrived in Afghanistan in March 2006, Sabit sent a VIP bus to pick me up. A few days later, he said he wanted to shoot guns with me. He liked guns. Most places I visited him—work, home, a Turkish restaurant—a gun leaned against some wall. He kept guns like other people keep plants. I accepted his invitation, as shooting guns in Afghanistan sounded like a fine diversion from work. Sabit's new driver picked me up one afternoon in March—his driver was actually his secretary, who had been drafted into driving because Sabit had fired seventeen drivers in the previous year. We picked up Sabit from his office. Sabit had two guns with him, a .22 and a Kalashnikov assault rifle. The driver drove the SUV out of Kabul, south for about thirty minutes, toward the edge of Kabul Province and Sabit's home village.

"Watch the road," Sabit told the driver.

"There's a pothole," Sabit told the driver, pointing at a black dot on the beige horizon.

"You're going too fast."

"You're a horrible driver."

"Slow down."

"Speed up!"

"Be careful over the pothole! You're an idiot!"

The driver/secretary said nothing. He knew better.

"Pull the car over," Sabit demanded after one poorly executed pothole. The driver, white-knuckled, thin-lipped, and staring straight ahead, pulled over on the side of the road.

"Get out," Sabit hissed. "I bet Kim could drive better than you."

This was an amazing insult—the idea that a woman could drive better than an Afghan man, let alone a Pashtun Afghan man, was beyond offensive. Only a handful of Afghan women drove, so few that they were celebrities, that Afghan men actually knew personal details about them. But Sabit followed through on his threat.

"Kim. Drive."

"I don't know if that's a good idea. I haven't driven a car in almost two years."

"But you know how to drive, right? It's the same side of the road as the U.S. Just drive. I'm sure you're better than this idiot."

I got out. The driver got out. "I'm not even supposed to be the driver," he whispered, as we walked past each other on the side of the highway. "I'm the secretary."

I jumped into the driver's seat, a watchful Sabit next to me. I hit the gas and pulled back onto the highway.

"Watch the pothole!" Sabit barked. I slowed down. "See, she is a better driver than you," he told his secretary/driver, now slumped in the backseat.

"Turn here," he demanded.

I turned right off the paved road, onto a dirt road, into a large expanse of dirt that Sabit planned to turn into a fruit orchard. Sabit's servants waited for us. This was just outside his home village, an area where Sabit was also a tribal chief. Here, he was king. His servants had laid out carpets in the dirt for us to sit on, along with a pot of green tea and bowls of chewy fruit candies and almonds covered in a sugary paste. The men looked vaguely surprised to see a Western woman step down from the driver's seat. Sabit talked briefly to them.

"I told them that you are a better driver than my real driver!" Sabit told me. His secretary pouted.

Sabit grabbed the guns. I may have grown up in Montana, but I had little experience with weapons. I had fired a .22 only once before, while visiting a friend in Idaho, and I had never shot a Kalashnikov. Yet I had honed my aim on plenty of video games. Sabit told the men to set up targets. They ran out to the ridges of dirt and set up different targets—mostly clumps of dirt.

"I can't tell what the targets are," I said. "They all look like dirt."

"Pay attention!" Sabit said. He ordered his lackeys to put some coins out. We sat cross-legged on the carpets. I leaned down, fired the .22 and hit a few clumps of dirt, which exploded. I was not really aiming, as I could not tell one clump from another.

"You're not bad," Sabit said.

We kept firing. He passed me the Kalashnikov. The kickback bruised my chest, and the first shot missed all the clumps wildly. Bang, bang, bang. Every bullet sent up a puff of dust. This was much more fun than playing video games. I traded guns with Sabit and shot the .22. A man came running up near Sabit's fence, to our right. He started yelling in Pashto. Sabit leaped up and started running toward the man, screaming and waving his Kalashnikov. The man ran away. Sabit turned around and walked back toward me.

"He told me it wasn't safe and it was too loud," he said, laughing. "I threatened to kill him."

Finally, when Sabit's men moved a coin to a ridge about ten yards in front of me, I hit it with the .22. Not a bad shot, but much more impressive if I hadn't been at point-blank range. Sabit decided to leave. "Come on, you're driving."

I managed to get us back to Kabul, where I somehow maneuvered through the free swim that passed for Kabul traffic, merging around traffic circles, avoiding donkey-pulled carts, all while trying to slow down over potholes. I dropped Sabit off and planned a lunch date the next week. His driver/secretary then drove me home. "He's fired every driver he's ever had," the man told me. "Driving for him is just not possible."

I certainly didn't want the gig. In the following days, I focused on my real job. I worked on a story about three Americans jailed twenty months earlier for running an illegal jail for Afghans under the guise of an import-export business. The team, led by a litigious former U.S. soldier named Jack Idema once convicted of fraud in the States, had actually grabbed Afghan men off the street, accused them of being terrorists, and held them in a makeshift prison. Why? I wasn't certain, but I believed that Idema craved the glory and embraced the messianic ideology of the anti-jihad. He was the kind of guy who would write a book and call it *My War* without irony, the kind of guy who thought he would be the one to bring down Osama bin Laden single-handedly, ideally using a piece of duct tape, staples, and other tricks of his tradecraft. Idema was an embarrassment for almost everyone—mainly because many people had bought his story. U.S. forces held one Afghan turned over by Idema for two months. International peacekeeping forces helped Idema carry out three raids on houses where he captured Afghans. Several Afghan officials were videotaped meeting with Idema, who many people assumed was a member of the U.S. special operations forces because he acted and dressed like one. For years, Idema had been a legend on the Kabul scene, so often at the *Star Wars*–like bar in the Mustafa Hotel that a cocktail was named after him, that two bullet holes in the ceiling were supposedly made by him. He was known as "Tora Bora" Jack, for his tales from 2001 and 2002 when he allegedly hunted bin Laden, which won him a starring role in Robin Moore's book *The Hunt for bin Laden*. A lot of sketchy foreigners had flooded Afghanistan, but Idema was one of the sketchiest. He was known for insinuating that he was a spy. He had tried to hire Farouq to work with him, but Farouq was suspicious of Idema's actual mission.

In July 2004, Idema and the two other Americans were arrested, their jail dismantled, their prisoners freed. Idema and a younger former U.S. soldier claimed to be on a sanctioned supersecret U.S. mission, hunting down terrorists. The third American, a TV cameraman, said he was simply filming a documentary on the hunt for Al-Qaeda. The United States denied any connection to the men, other than admitting they were private American citizens. The trial was hardly fair, the translation atrocious, and Idema kept interrupting with various outbursts. At one point, the lawyer for the cameraman asked the prosecutor, "Can you handle the truth?" On the day of sentencing, in September 2004, Idema wore his traditional black sunglasses and khaki outfit and smoked cigarettes near the judge. When told he could not testify because he was not Muslim, Idema demanded to be sworn in on the Holy Quran, which he then kissed. The audience, mainly Afghans, including those Idema had once locked up, applauded and cheered. One former prisoner jumped up, punched his fist in the air, and launched an impromptu audience cheer of "God is great!"

In his testimony, Idema described a world of spies and intrigue, of good guys and bad ones. He talked about his missions, of his efforts to deliver a "package," which was "tradecraft" for a "high-value target." His passport was issued by a "special agency in Washington," which he could not name. One video featured a blacked-out person, whose face could not be shown for "national security reasons." After the men were sentenced, to as long as ten years, Idema suggested he might kill a couple of people before any appeal and mentioned a "bloodbath."

Since then, the Americans had been held at the Pul-i-Charkhi prison, a sprawling concrete-and-brick complex outside of Kabul, scarred by bullets and rockets and filled with two thousand inmates, including Al-Qaeda and Taliban insurgents and drug dealers. The Americans' sentences had already been drastically cut, and they were nearing freedom. But jail had taken a toll on one man. The journalist had attacked guards, converted to Islam, and adopted the name Najib, guards said. He lived in his own cell. Idema, the other American, and their translator lived a comparatively posh life. They had a wing of the prison to themselves, which was furnished with red Oriental carpets and hand-carved sofas—a similarly sized prison wing across the hall held five hundred and fifty inmates. The men also had cell phones, computer access, and frequent contact with whoever ran a website called superpatriots.us. The site supported the men's mission, featured pictures of them inside their "cell," and at one point quoted Idema as saying that he could drink alcohol and had "a laptop, a phone, private bedroom, private bathroom, two houseboys, one water boy, satellite TV with the Playboy Channel," along with other perks.

"They are treated differently than anyone else," acknowledged the general in charge of the jail. "They have carpets, they have phones, they have special food. Not because they are Americans. Because they are our guests."

Keep in mind, the other guests at the jail were kept like dogs at a pound. So for the Afghan jailers, the Americans had become a major hassle, more so than any terrorist. That's why I wanted to revisit their story. Recent prison riots had been described, hour by hour, on the superpatriots site. The website said it had received reports that the journalist had joined the terrorists and was yelling "God is great" with them. At another point, the journalist was described as a hostage.

I managed to jump through all the cumbersome Afghan hoops to get access to the Americans. I walked up the dank, cold stairs with Farouq and a couple of police officials. We stood outside Idema's cell. Idema's soldier sidekick, looking skinny and wearing a "Special Forces" T-shirt, opened the gate a crack. I gave my business card to him, and he took it to Idema, who grumbled that he did not want to talk to me. The younger soldier returned to the door.

"I do apologize," he said.

"If he changes his mind, call me," I said.

I wrote the story anyway, focusing on the riots, the problems of caring for the Americans, and the amazing website, crammed with information and links. Here, I could peruse the Geneva Conventions, order "The Ballad of the Green Berets," see "the top 10 lie-slinging journalists," and read the men's thank-you notes to people for various gifts, including tuna, ramen noodles, Gummi Bears, Slim Jims, blankets, gloves, and Dinty Moore beef stew. And there were warnings. "A whirlwind is coming, and hell is coming with it," the website said, near a picture of Idema with his fists up and the title "Fighting Jack."

The day the story ran, I went to Jeremy's house for an early dinner. He had moved to Kabul, and we had picked up our awkward fling, fueled by nice gestures on his part such as calling to tell me about a suicide attack I hadn't heard about. I liked him, even if he was slightly moody. That night, after a losing game of poker, Jeremy and I went to sleep early. At 3 AM, my phone started ringing. I picked it up and looked at the number, which I didn't recognize, and didn't immediately answer. The ringing stopped before starting again. I reluctantly said hello.

"Who is this?" I asked, feigning gruffness.

"Listen, you little cunt," an American man's voice said.

"Oh good," I said, and hung up.

Idema. Had to be. I had heard he was vindictive. I also knew he had powerful friends. The phone started ringing again. I turned it off and tried to go back to sleep, slightly nervous. I tapped Jeremy. "Hey. I think Jack Idema just called me." He grunted and rolled over. We would break up the next month, out of ambivalence as much as anything else.

Across the city, Farouq's phone then started ringing. Farouq's number was the second on my business card.

"Is Kim there?" the man asked Farouq.

Uncertain of whether this was a rude friend of mine or bosses from Chicago, Farouq opted for a polite response. "No, I'm Farouq, the translator for Kim and the *Chicago Tribune*. She's probably asleep."

"If you ever work for that fucking cunt again, I'll have you thrown in prison," the man explained.

"Is this Jack? Is that Jack?" Farouq said, his anger rising. The caller hung up. Farouq called him back.

"What kind of language is that?" Farouq asked. "Who do you think you are? What kind of a way is that to behave?" Farouq threatened to come to the prison and hurt Idema if he insulted me again. The caller hung up, then turned off his phone. In a fight between a macho Pashtun and a macho American, I knew who would win, every time.

The next afternoon, I drove to the Interior Ministry for my kebab date with Sabit. I was mildly concerned because the caller had seemed slightly unglued. Idema was extremely connected with the Northern Alliance, the Tajik-dominated militia group that had been the last holdout against the Taliban and that now held key positions with the police and in the prison. Idema had contacts with the police and even sent them out from the prison to run errands for him, friends told me. And the police knew where I lived. So I told Sabit about the phone call. Sabit's eyes narrowed.

"Don't worry," he told me. "The police will do nothing to you. Jack can do nothing to you. I won't do anything unless you ask me to, and if you want, I'll stand guard in front of your door all night."

"That's probably not necessary," I told Sabit. "Let's just wait to see what happens."

For days, nothing happened, so I told Sabit to forget about it. The last thing I needed was another confrontation between another angry Pashtun and Idema. Then I found out what Idema had done. I had become a star on superpatriots.us. My mug shot from the *Chicago Tribune* website had been copied and stretched horizontally, making my face look very wide. The picture and my name had been added to the superpatriots' journalist Wall of Shame with the caption "Cub Reporter." And in front of the world, I was accused of sleeping with Farouq. Within months, I would be unceremoniously retired from the wall, and this would all seem quaint, a silly game, any fear of Idema ridiculous. Idema and his buddies would all eventually be released and leave Afghanistan quietly. But Jack was right about one thing—a whirlwind was definitely coming. Hell was riding shotgun.

CHAPTER 9
LET'S GET RADICAL

Years later, whenever anyone asked when the good war became not such a good war, my answer was easy. On May 29, 2006, when a U.S. military truck suffered mechanical failure and plowed into rush-hour traffic in Kabul, killing three Afghans. Peaceful demonstrations quickly turned into antiforeigner riots. Soldiers fired into the crowd. Afghans ransacked buildings with English-language signs, from relief groups to a pizza restaurant. They even set fire to a building they thought was the Escalades brothel, although the brothel was next door. They shouted, "Death to Karzai," and that regional catchphrase, "Death to America," and ran from street to street, asking guards if foreigners lived inside. They almost threw a light-skinned girl into a fire, until she shouted in Dari and they realized she was Afghan. Karzai's political rivals from the Northern Alliance were blamed for stoking the violence, the worst since the Taliban's fall. At least seventeen Afghans were killed in the rioting; despite considerable efforts, no foreigners died. Karzai demonstrated his usual leadership skills, waiting until the riots had almost run their course to broadcast a televised message, urging calm. But even after calm was restored, Afghans stayed angry.

It wasn't necessarily the booze and brothels. It was the growing gap in the country between the haves and have-nots, the corruption, the warlords now in parliament, the drug lords doubling as government officials, the general attitude of the foreigners from aid workers to the international troops, and the fact that no one ever seemed to be held accountable for anything. Even if the level of foreign aid had been low compared to other "post-conflict" countries, billions of dollars had still poured in. Dozens of new gleaming wedding halls and shopping centers dotted the Kabul landscape. Warlords, drug lords, and influential officials had been handed government land for a cut rate in the neighborhood of Shir Pur, where they built gaudy mansions that looked like grade-school decoupage projects gone horribly wrong, gooey confections of pillars, mirrors, colored tiles, and green windows. But construction started only after bulldozers pushed out the poor people who had lived there before, along with their mud huts. Shir Pur, which meant "child of lions," was now referred to as Shir Choor, which meant "looted by lions." The style of architecture was called "narcotecture"; the hulking monstrosities were described as "poppy palaces."

Yet for an average Afghan, life still consisted of a mud hut, an outhouse, and a couple of hours of electricity a day. Renting a decent concrete house in Kabul now cost at least $1,500 a month. Afghan teachers and police officers made between $60 and $125 a month. The only changes most Afghans had seen in Kabul had been negative ones—higher rents and food costs, higher bribes, greater hassles. Traffic jams were regularly caused by convoys of Land Cruisers with dark windows and no license plates, by U.S. soldiers screaming out orders and pointing their guns, by concrete barriers set up by foreign aid groups and companies worried about suicide bombs.

Later, I would see these riots as a major breaking point in Afghanistan, the time when we first saw just how angry some Afghans were, just how ripe the country was for a Taliban comeback, just how leaderless Afghanistan really was. Later, I would see May 2006 as the beginning of the downward spiral.

But now, I just saw the riots as worrying.

I flew to Kabul. My life had turned into this—a bomb, a riot, an earthquake, and then I hopped on a plane. Although I was theoretically the bureau chief in Delhi, my responsibilities included at least six countries, depending on which powder keg was exploding. So my three-bedroom apartment was essentially a layover. I didn't mind. I really didn't like Delhi that much, sprawling broken megacity that it was, where my hot water didn't work and monkeys used the tarps protecting my plants outside like a trampoline. But really, the reason I disliked Delhi was probably more basic—not enough went boom, not enough to create a tight-knit foreign community, not enough to spin a vortex of work and fun, not enough to burn a candle not just at both ends but to light it up with a blowtorch. Delhi was just too normal.

Also, after two years, I felt I was starting to get the hang of this job, to figure it out. In Afghanistan, I knew when to wear a headscarf, when to shake a man's hand, when to take off my glasses, when to shut my mouth. More accurately, I knew when to ask Farouq what to do, and to listen to what he said. I was also getting used to the pace, to juggling all the countries and all the work. I knew that a train crash or a religious stampede that killed seventy-five in India wasn't a story—they happened all the time. I knew that roadside bombs in southern Afghanistan no longer merited a middle-of-the-night house call by Farouq—they were starting to happen all the time. I knew that I couldn't pursue certain stories found in local newspapers, with headlines such as BABIES MARRY PUPPIES, because I had written too many stories about animals and risked getting a reputation. I was also now exercising regularly, regardless of the country, even just doing Pilates in a hotel room. My hair was cut every couple months; my roots matched my ends. In short, I was shaping up.

I had also started mastering certain tricks, like breathing and biting my lip to hold on to my temper, regardless of what went wrong. I had stopped throwing fits over bad laundry and bad Internet. Well, most of the time. An exception was made for the guys who incinerated my pajama bottoms in an Indonesian hotel room, just because I left them on the bathroom floor. I channeled Sabit as I went off on them.

Back in Kabul after the riots, I opted against staying in the Gandamack or another hotel, potential targets for more violence. Instead, I decided to stay at a friend's house, figuring that there, I would be safer. Just after my plane landed, Farouq and I met my British journalist friend Sean for lunch at L'Atmosphère, which would sometimes let its strict no-Afghan policy slide. Farouq was slightly uncomfortable, but in the daytime, no one seemed to care. Sean wanted to talk about the Taliban and related insurgent groups. But Sean, who liked conspiracies and intrigue just as much as the Afghans, figured his phone could be tapped or the trees in L'Atmosphère bugged. So he never referred to the insurgents by name. He called them "Tango" instead.

"Sami thinks he's got a way to meet Tango," Sean told us. Sami was Sean's fixer.

"Tango? Seriously? You need a better code word," I replied.

His documentary the year before about the driving school for Afghan women was the best I had seen about living in the new Afghanistan—and there had been several, primarily shot by Europeans. But this time, Sean wanted to do a documentary on the Taliban. He wanted war. Sean wanted the typical heart of darkness craved by a subspecies of male foreign correspondent, mostly British, all adrenaline junkies, who figured they were wasting time if they weren't dodging bullets. Clearly, the divorce had gone through. His cause to win back his wife was probably not helped by a magazine spread the previous fall, which featured a picture of him in a Kabul brothel, allegedly soliciting a prostitute for sex. Sean had actually been in the brothel helping a photographer friend get pictures of clients, but since she could not convince any real clients to agree to a picture, she used a photograph she slyly snapped of Sean. Sean's face had been blurred, but his profile was unmistakable. When one of his sons saw the magazine spread, he said simply: "Daddy."

Now, shaded by an umbrella in the garden, Sean asked for advice. With few Taliban contacts, I could offer little help. But Farouq had just been with a journalist in Zabul, Uruzgan, and Kandahar, and he knew a lot more, and he was the one Sean had really wanted to see. Farouq verified what Sean and I had been hearing: Like a bad 1980s hair band, complete with long wild locks and black eyeliner, the Taliban had mounted a comeback this spring.

After we finished eating, Sean asked if I would be the point of contact when he went to meet the Taliban in Helmand, in case he disappeared.

"Sure," I said.

"It's unlikely anyone would ever call you," he said.

"Fine."

The confluence of events suddenly seemed ominous. Afghans were growing angrier at the foreigners and the government. The Taliban was spreading its influence in the south. And the Americans were turning over command of the south to NATO, which was made up of some countries far less committed to war than the United States. I knew I had to get serious.

"I want to meet the Taliban," I told Farouq as we left Sean. "Can we?"

"Maybe," he replied. "There are safe ways to do it."

Farouq was growing increasingly concerned about safety. His wife was about to give birth to their second child. He still liked to travel, but he also didn't want to risk anything. I wondered if he would be willing to make the trip we had made three years earlier to visit Pacha Khan. I wondered if he had lost his edge. Three main fixers were known for meeting the Taliban, and Farouq wasn't one of them. Those were Sami, a man named Tahir, and Ajmal Naqshbandi, my fixer when Farouq had gotten married, who was evolving from shy poet to danger boy.

The United States certainly didn't help convince Farouq that any risk was worth it. One night, Farouq drove down the road with a full SUV—his wife, daughter, two sisters-in-law, and mother-in-law.

Near the Ministry of Interior, he saw a line of headlights moving toward him. When he drew closer, he heard a bang near his windshield. He yanked the steering wheel over, braking hard on the side of the road. Then he heard another bang, and another bang. Only then, he realized the line of headlights was a U.S. military convoy. The U.S. soldiers shined heavy lights toward Farouq and started yelling at him. So Farouq turned off his lights and held his breath, silently scared, unwilling to let his family know just how frightened he was. Farouq told me the soldiers laughed at him.

"I think some of the soldiers knew that I was scared, but still they threw more tube lights on me and pushed me more to the side of the street," he said. "American soldiers are scared from leaves, from trees, rocks, and everything in Afghanistan."

I figured I knew what the bangs could be—when a car failed to stop, soldiers sometimes fired warning shots.

But regardless of his feelings, Farouq started planning a trip down south, as I dove into another serious issue. Hamid Karzai was once the sartorially blessed favorite of the West, but no longer. He had proved to be whiny and conflicted, a combination of Woody Allen, Chicken Little, and Jimmy Carter. Ever since Zal had left the year before, Karzai had lost direction, like the victim of a breakup. The new U.S. ambassador seemed adamant about returning normalcy to the relationship—despite the fact that Afghanistan was anything but normal. Karzai had turned into a weather-vane leader, tilting toward whoever saw him last, increasingly paranoid and suspicious, squeezed between the foreigners and the Afghans.

Even calling Karzai the "mayor of Kabul," as many did, was too generous. When he gave the foreigners an ultimatum to remove concrete security barriers in the city, the foreigners ignored him. When Karzai complained about civilian casualties, nothing changed.

Karzai also was blamed for losing control of his brothers. One brother was a parliament member who rarely showed up. Another was publicly linked to the drug trade in southern Afghanistan, even though he denied it. Another was becoming one of the most influential businessmen in Afghanistan, allowed to privatize government companies such as Afghanistan's only cement factory with impunity, allegedly because of his connections to the president and a slush fund of money provided by deposits in the Kabul Bank. If the president couldn't control his brothers, Afghans argued, how could he control the country?

I begged my sources in the presidential palace to arrange an interview with Karzai, even showing up at a key official's office one afternoon. The official was busy watching *The Three Stooges.*

Eventually Karzai let me shadow him for two days, but he wouldn't sit down for an interview. I watched him in meeting after meeting. He was always folksy and cheery and slightly forced. He was in an impossible position. The elders complained of civilian casualties, the police complained of not having enough weapons. Karzai could not promise anything because he could deliver little. Instead, he whined about the foreigners. In one meeting, he sat at the head of a long table with sixty tribal elders from eastern Nangarhar Province, all angry that Karzai had removed the provincial border police commander. Karzai said he would try to help, but that he had to balance the needs of Afghans and the desires of foreigners.

"Do you agree with me?" Karzai asked. The room of turbaned men sat silently, arms folded, some obviously pouting. "Why are you quiet? Do you agree with me? Do you support me?"

"No!" several men shouted, not unless Karzai reversed his decision.

"You are the president," one elder said. "You can do it. You should do it for us. Otherwise we will not support you."

After another lunch, with elders from Uruzgan Province, Karzai showed what he really believed in—Afghan unity. He wanted people to consider themselves Afghans first, not Pashtuns, Tajiks, or the other major ethnic groups of Hazaras and Uzbeks. He called me to the front of the room as a stage prop.

"Ma'am," he said. "Please come up here."

Karzai always called me "ma'am." I don't know that he knew my name. He pointed to four elders from one Uruzgan district and asked me to identify their ethnicity. I was being set up, but I played along. "Pashtun?" I said. This made him happy because he could deliver his punch line. They were Pashtuns and Hazaras, he said, but they were all Afghans, men who lived side by side in peace, sharing the Pashto language.

"That's how good this country was," Karzai said. "That's how we want to make it again."

Performance over, I returned to my seat. But this idea of unity was not enough to save Afghanistan—not when Afghans still referred to themselves largely by ethnic group, not when the Pashtun-dominated Taliban insurgency was making inroads down south, and not when the Tajik-led Northern Alliance was accused of organizing the Kabul riots. No ethnic group held a clear majority in Afghanistan, even though the Pashtuns had run the show for almost three hundred years, a fact that had fueled resentment and rivalries. About 42 percent of Afghans were Pashtuns, mainly in the south, southwest, and east; about 27 percent of Afghans were Tajiks, mainly in the north; about 9 percent were Hazaras, mainly in central Afghanistan; about 9 percent were Uzbeks, mainly in the north; and the rest of the population was spread among smaller ethnic groups like the Aimak, Turkmen, and Baloch. (Those numbers, of course, were hotly disputed, each Afghan ethnic group always claiming a bigger pie piece. There had never been a census.)

To show who was boss, Karzai, a Pashtun, needed to do something more than an Afghan version of *Free to Be . . . You and Me.* He needed to take charge, to stop making excuses, to stop blaming the foreigners for everything. In short, he needed to man up.

Farouq and I decided to get out of Kabul and go to Kandahar, which doubled as the spiritual birthplace of the Taliban and Karzai's home stomping grounds. As I listened to his plans, I realized that Farouq had not lost his edge. His wife, after all, had just given birth to a son, and he was still game for a road trip. He was just being careful—he had seen how quickly Afghanistan had taken a U-turn in the past, as quickly as a donkey outfitted with a suicide vest. Another journalist, my new housemate Tom, decided to come on our trip south. Tom was British, tall, handsome, skinny, with a mop of brown hair, and he dressed in a dandy-like style of thrift store meets Fleet Street. In the winter, he wore hats and scarves. He seemed like he should smoke a pipe and wear corduroy jackets with elbow patches, but he didn't. He seemed like he should be called dashing, but he wasn't. Tom had been around in Afghanistan almost as long as I had, but we had only become friends in the spring, largely through our mutual friend Sean. Whenever they were both in town, Tom and Sean hung out most nights at L'Atmosphère, two wild-and-crazy guys always trying to outdo each other with self-deprecating dating stories in almost always successful attempts to meet women.

This was my first time traveling with Tom. A friend of Farouq, a Pashtun with a giant black beard, agreed to drive us in a beat-up Toyota Corolla taxi. The car made us look like everyone else. Now we needed disguises. Tom and Farouq grew out their beards, to the extent that they could. I packed a black abaya, which made me look like a graduating high-school senior with a matching headscarf, but Farouq said that wasn't enough. I needed a burqa.

"It's weird to have to ask you," Farouq said. "But you and I know the situation here has gotten worse and worse. I feel more comfortable with you wearing a burqa than not."

I shrugged. His call. "You'll buy it for me, right? You can bring one?"

Farouq agreed to pick out a suitable burqa. On a Sunday morning, I put in brown contact lenses to cover my blue eyes and drew on heavy black eyeliner, to look more like an Afghan woman if I decided to pull my burqa back over my head in the car. Tom, meanwhile, dressed in Afghan clothes and put on an embroidered Kandahari-style cap.

"You look strange," Tom told me, wrinkling his nose at my brown eyes.

"You look like a Kandahari dancing boy," I said.

It was an old joke. Although Afghans virulently opposed homosexuality, the segregation of the sexes had led to certain practices, especially in the Pashtun areas. Kandahar was known for older men sexually using teenage boys, usually to show off prestige and power. At weddings, at festive occasions, at male-only parties, dancing boys would often perform, wearing eyeliner and swinging their hips suggestively, before pairing off for the night. The practice was known as *bacha bazi*, or "boy play." A Pashto proverb maintained that women were for breeding, boys for pleasure, but melons for sheer delight. A popular Afghan joke involved the birds of Kandahar, who flew with one wing in circles and used the other to cover their rears.

Farouq soon showed up with a burqa. I could not avoid it—I would soon look like a giant blue badminton shuttlecock. Tom and I climbed in the backseat of the Corolla, and I put the burqa on the seat between us, knowing I didn't need to wear it in Kabul. Near the edge of town, the car broke down. Car mechanics in Afghanistan never inspired trust, as they often worked out of shipping containers and owned only a screwdriver. But somehow, they usually fixed a car quickly. Afghans were geniuses with figuring out how things worked. Once, when our car battery died on a picnic, Farouq jumped the car by connecting a metal ladder and a cord to another car battery, killing no one.

So I assumed the mechanic would only take half an hour. We sat in the Corolla. As usual, everyone outside the car stared in at me. I had an idea: I slipped on the burqa. The top part grabbed tight around my head. A square of mesh covered my eyes. I was able to breathe through the fabric, so I didn't hyperventilate on bad air. Oppressive, I thought. But oddly liberating. I stared at the old men in their turbans and the young boys shoving each other in the market, and they didn't stare back. I was totally invisible.

We soon drove out of Kabul, and on safe stretches of the road, I pulled my burqa back over my head, as local women did, and with my eyeliner and brown contact lenses and the speed of highway traffic, fooled anyone driving past. We drove south to Kandahar on a highway that the Americans had built in 2003—already, the road was falling apart, and entire chunks had crumbled away, due to poor design, poor execution, and really poor asphalt. The Taliban controlled certain parts of the road, but usually just at night. We were stopped once by the police, and slowed down once, near a U.S. military convoy. The U.S. soldiers didn't know I was an American, and treated our team just like any other group of Afghans in a Toyota Corolla. Like a threat.

"You are in the blue prison," said Farouq, a cigarette dangling from his mouth. He had taken a turn driving, flicking his eyes between the rearview mirror and the men on the side of the road.

Once I stepped out of the car in Kandahar, though, I realized that my prison was far from perfect. Farouq had bought the first burqa he found, but it hit me just below the knee, instead of near the ankle. In the front, the burqa only came to my waist. This two-tiered style was apparently fashionable in Kabul, but not in conservative Kandahar. And it was much too short. I quickly figured out I was wearing the Pashtun equivalent of a miniskirt. I also didn't walk right. Afghan women took demure steps. I walked like a man. Checking myself out in my hotel-room mirror, I decided to wear the long black abaya inside Kandahar, and the burqa when we traveled in the car outside the city. At least the hotel room was nicer than my first time in Kandahar. The TV had about two hundred channels, most of them porn. I checked the room computer's Internet history—more porn. That was a good sign, I supposed. Despite the Taliban comeback, Kandahar was still hung up on sex.

But we had to be careful. Just west of Kandahar, in the district of Panjwai, the Canadians had been fighting actual battles with the Taliban, who had ridden into the district center two months earlier, demanding food and shelter. They had shot down a moderate tribal elder as he shopped for groceries, they had gunned down three police officers on patrol. They were like vampires, disappearing during the day, coming out at night, intimidating everyone. Fearing retribution, no one in the south wanted to look like he supported the government. In neighboring Helmand Province, the Taliban had just ambushed and killed thirty-two people—all relatives and friends of a Helmand parliament member, who would be killed three years later by a roadside bomb. Only four men attended a funeral for a pro-government cleric near Kandahar—and two were gravediggers. The Taliban had taken over several remote districts, such as Chora in Uruzgan, where police had only assault rifles and six rockets when the Taliban showed up with mortars and machine guns.

This was still not Iraq, but the insurgency here had finally registered on the international jihadi network. Al-Qaeda's deputy, Ayman al-Zawahiri, would soon call for all Afghans to rise up against foreign forces. The Taliban and their allies were mimicking tactics used in Iraq—more suicide attacks, more sophisticated bombs, more slick propaganda, more beheadings of reconstruction workers. The insurgents here were also smart, winning popularity points with reports of Islamic courts in rural districts that delivered swift justice. These judges contrasted vividly with government judges, who often demanded bribes or took forever to decide a case.

We drove to Panjwai, fully disguised, with an escort provided by tribal elders. We sat with a few elders on cushions on the floor of a community center. They were scared, and they carried pistols. But they liked my new look.

"We like your burqa very much, but only if you wear it in America too," one said.

"It's very short," added another, looking unsure. "Is that what they wear in Kabul?"

We stayed for less than an hour, incredibly rude in Afghanistan. But Farouq feared that word would spread that foreigners were in town.

"We have to go, Kim," Farouq said. Tom and I wanted to stay longer. "Now," Farouq said. Farouq and Tom made a brief foray into the market, and we drove back to Kandahar without incident.

We then went to see Mohammed Akbar Khakrizwal, a tribal elder who lived in a town just outside Kandahar. The area was not safe; I again wore my burqa. He was the former provincial intelligence chief, and the brother of the former police chief in both Kandahar and Kabul, who had been killed in a bombing at a Kandahar mosque the year before. When Khakrizwal saw me, he laughed.

"Oh, what have you done to yourself?" said Khakrizwal, who, like most tribal leaders I knew, sported a bushy dyed black beard the color of shoe polish, a turban, and a tan salwar kameez. "For one hundred years, no one will recognize you like this. No one will touch you."

He invited us to lunch the next day, along with elders from his Pashtun tribe, the Alikozais, known for their dissatisfaction with both the Afghan government and the Taliban. The Alikozais helped illustrate the complexities of the Pashtun tribal system. Khakrizwal repeatedly explained the Pashtuns to us, helping us draw flowcharts with as many caveats as NATO troops. The Pashtuns in southern Afghanistan were divided into two main branches—the Durranis and the Ghilzais. For most of Afghanistan's history as a sovereign nation, when the country was run by a monarchy, some member of the Durranis had ruled. The Taliban, however, had originally derived most support from the Ghilzais—despite being a larger group, they were always less powerful than the Durranis and not necessarily happy about it.

(A caveat: That is a huge oversimplification. It doesn't account for the fact that the Ghilzais were concentrated in the rural areas, where they had little access to the urban power centers and were therefore susceptible to rebellion. It doesn't account for the fluidity of Afghan tribes, for all the clans and tribes that just seemed to go their own way. Plus, decades of war had chewed up a lot of formerly solid tribal markers and pushed out the onetime leaders.)

The Durranis were then divided into two major branches—the dominant Ziraks and the marginal Panjpais, who had typically been seen as troublemakers and who were sometimes even carved out of the Durrani-Ghilzai split. Many Pashtuns in Kandahar were growing upset at the fact that all contracts and money seemed to be funneled through the two most influential clans of the Zirak branch, which together had controlled the monarchy that led Afghanistan for about two hundred and fifty years—the Popalzais, Karzai's clan, and the Barakzais, their sometime allies. The have-nots resented the power of Karzai's brother, Ahmed Wali Karzai, who allegedly ran most business dealings in the south, including drugs. Even though the Alikozais also belonged to the Zirak branch and theoretically backed Karzai's government, they had seen little benefit from the regime, marginalized and removed from key security positions.

Anger over tribal favoritism and corruption by government leaders and power brokers likely fueled the insurgency, causing some frustrated and jobless young men from the Alikozais, from another Zirak tribe called the Achakzais, and from the major Panjpai tribe of the Noorzais to sign up with the Taliban. Some of the Ghilzais, meanwhile, had turned back to the Taliban in Kandahar, but the Durranis also now played a major leadership role in the Taliban. (The Taliban seemed to recognize more than the government how important it was to treat all the prickly Pashtun divisions equally, or, more accurately, that it was important to simply ignore them. It was unclear how long the insurgent rainbow alliance could last—the Achakzais hated the Noorzais, and vice versa, even in the Taliban—but their collective hatred of the foreign troops and the Afghan government probably overrode their own Hatfield-and-McCoy disputes.)

Even then, it was not that simple. Making things more headache-inducing, about half the Popalzais and Barakzais were also supporting the Taliban, Khakrizwal said, part of the endless attempts to hedge bets and exact varieties of payback. (Some of the Barakzais were still upset about the removal of a previous governor, a Barakzai.

And the pro-Taliban Popalzais? Who knows. Maybe drugs, maybe a bad kebab.) Being a member of the same tribe also didn't guarantee loyalty. For instance, the Kandahar governor was a Ghilzai—but everyone in Kandahar saw him as an outsider from Ghazni Province, two provinces away, practically a foreign country. And the tribes could be flexible based on self-interest. Some Noorzais supported Karzai; some were major drug traffickers allied with the Taliban; some were Taliban; some were everything. (The Taliban had banned poppies while in power, but had now started charging drug traffickers to transport drugs, which helped fund jihad, sow instability, and win the support of Afghans who depended on the drug economy for their livelihood.)

So how much did all the Pashtun tribal alliances and divisions matter? A lot—unless something else mattered more.

The Taliban didn't just gain strength because they understood this, or because they exploited tribal jealousies, disillusionment with the local government, and the rising drug trade. Pakistan's top spy agency, the Inter-Services Intelligence Directorate (ISI), had also recruited for the Taliban, Khakrizwal insisted, in the endless ISI attempt to control Afghanistan. Ever since ISI leaders joined the anti-Soviet jihad in the 1980s, they had been reluctant to let go of Afghanistan. The spy agency had continued to meddle, largely to try to create some semblance of a stable, pro-Pakistan government as a hedge against rival India. That's why Pakistan supported the formation of the Taliban in the 1990s, and why many Afghans believed Pakistan was now playing a double game, pretending to support the West in the war against terrorism by rounding up Al-Qaeda leaders, but allowing and helping the Afghan Taliban to regroup, even permitting training camps along the border. Every Afghan official had mentioned this repeatedly and publicly, even Karzai, who most recently had leveled the accusation the month before. Khakrizwal believed that his brother was killed because he didn't listen to ISI warnings that he was too friendly with India. He even had the name of the ISI man who allegedly sanctioned his brother's killing. (Other Afghans believed that Akbar Khakrizwal was killed because he opposed Karzai's brother or because he opposed the drug trade. Or both.)

After Khakrizwal explained this to us as if we were small children, repeatedly and carefully, he complained that he had tried to explain this to the American soldiers and diplomats, repeatedly and carefully, while he was the provincial intelligence chief. He talked about how key ISI men had mastered the Pashtun rivalries and complexities long ago—and how even though some had retired or quit the ISI since the 1980s, they were still involved in manipulating what was happening in Afghanistan. Khakrizwal knew the key Pakistani spies and named them. He had known them for years.

"The main mistake made by the Americans is this—an American general comes here for six months. Then he's replaced," Khakrizwal said. "For four years, I was the head of intelligence in Kandahar. For six months, I'd work on an American—explaining who are friends, who are enemies—then that person was replaced by another American. Finally, my patience was over. I was tired of giving them advice."

For lunch, we met various Alikozai tribal elders, sat on cushions on Khakrizwal's floor, and ate a salad of cucumbers and radishes, a dish of rice mixed with raisins, carrots, and mystery meat, various meat dishes, and okra in oil. Each elder had lost family members in recent months, each feared the Taliban was winning. One elder described vividly how his two sons had been killed eighteen days earlier in a Taliban ambush. Tom and I looked at each other.

"That's an incredibly sad story," Tom said.

"I can't even imagine," I replied.

Khakrizwal soon gave us a challenge.

"Write down this date," he said. "In one year, the situation will be worse than it is today. I'm telling Americans, if they do not bring changes in their policies, they will say, 'My God, Iraq is a heaven compared to here.' "

It was June 13, 2006.

After we finished several rounds of tea, the elders walked us out into the courtyard to say goodbye. I stood in my short burqa, with it pulled back over my head so my face showed. The elder who just lost two sons looked at me strangely and said something in Pashto. The elders cracked up, as did Farouq.

"What did he say?" I asked.

"Tell you later," said Farouq, still laughing.

We climbed into the Toyota Corolla and waved goodbye.

"Come on Farouq, tell me, what did he say?"

"Don't take this the wrong way—it's Kandahar," Farouq said. "He said, 'If you put a turban on that one, she would be a handsome boy.'"

In Kandahar, I could only take that one way.

Two and a half years later, almost everyone we met on this trip would be dead. Khakrizwal would be shot outside the home where he served us lunch. Many other Alikozai leaders would be killed or die, including the tribal chief, who suffered a heart attack shortly after being hit by a roadside bomb. A female supercop, one of the only women in Kandahar who defied the Taliban, would be gunned down as she left for work with her son. The lone survivor: Karzai's brother, the alleged drug trafficker and power broker, who had denied any wrongdoing, saying that the allegations were simply an attempt to discredit his brother. "I am sick and tired of the drug accusation," Ahmed Wali Karzai told me. "It's the same old story. It's to get to the president." But over the years, the allegations would only gain credibility, with various Western officials talking about them like fact. For whatever reason, almost any Afghan who dared to speak publicly about them would mysteriously end up dead.

We soon drove back to Kabul, accomplishing all but one goal. We failed to meet with the Taliban commander from Helmand. Farouq refused to take me out of Kandahar to meet any Taliban officials in the field because he didn't trust them. The Helmand commander said he could not drive to Kandahar to meet us because the Americans had launched a new operation, aimed at flushing out the insurgents. Operation Mountain Thrust featured more than ten thousand international and Afghan troops, the largest operation since the fall of the Taliban. With a name like that, I knew I had to get some.

CHAPTER 10
HELL YES

Sure, Operation Mountain Thrust may have sounded like a porno—English-speakers in the country milked it all they could, drawing out the pronunciation into "mount-and-thrust"—but at least it wasn't Operation Turtle, the even more ridiculously named operation nearby. This mission was seen as crucial, aimed at securing dangerous areas in the south before the United States officially handed them over to various NATO countries, especially since the Taliban was trying to take advantage of that handover. In many cases, the troops were moving into areas they had never before entered, undoubtedly a bit late, almost five years into the war, but who was counting? The war would be won or lost here, in the dangerous and so-far-untamed south. The Canadians had taken over in Kandahar. The British were taking the lead in Helmand, the southern province that bordered Kandahar on the west. The Dutch—the Dutch?—would take Uruzgan, the small province just to the north of Kandahar and east of Helmand. The Romanians would take the lead in Zabul, east of Kandahar and Uruzgan. The United States would shift its primary mission to eastern Afghanistan, but really, it seemed like the Americans hoped to tiptoe out of Afghanistan altogether.

After signing up for another embed, I found myself earmarked for Helmand, ground zero of everything bad in Afghanistan, the heart of both the Taliban and the poppy trade. It hadn't always been this way. Helmand was once the country's breadbasket. The United States had spent so much development money here in the 1960s and 1970s that part of Helmand was dubbed "Little America." But development stalled during the country's wars, and farmers fell back on the region's longtime favorite cash crop, a flower that grew well during droughts and earned top dollar, the poppy, the raw material for opium and heroin. While in power, the Taliban regime had briefly banned farmers from growing poppies—largely to win international recognition, rather than for religious reasons. But in the years since the Taliban fled, poppies had returned to much of Helmand, because even though the government had banned the plant, it had not enforced that ban, and many influential Afghans here profited from the trade. Afghanistan now produced more heroin and opium than anywhere else in the world, and Helmand was the epicenter. Consequently, Helmand was one of the prettiest provinces in Afghanistan. During the spring, fields were splashes of brilliant red, orange, and purple.

Neither NATO nor the United States seemed quite sure how to tackle the drug trade. Allow the opium and heroin to flow, and watch the region sink further into lawlessness. Crack down on the opium farmers, and risk driving them into the arms of the Taliban, now protecting and encouraging the trade.

Until now, few of the international forces had spent much time in Helmand—there were simply not enough troops in the country to adequately cover the south. The major exception was the U.S.-led antiterrorist squad, mostly composed of U.S. special operations forces—the men with beards from elite parts of the military whom we were never supposed to refer to nor talk to while on embeds—and the men with beards from government agencies referred to as "other government agencies," a term that typically included the CIA and other spook-like groups. These men had been operating in Helmand since the beginning of the war, hunting Al-Qaeda and other top terrorists, or so we were told.

As part of Operation Mountain Thrust, the regular U.S. Army was now moving into Helmand to try to secure key parts before officially handing over the province to the British. The army had just opened up new outposts, the major one about three miles from a town called Musa Qala, a stronghold of insurgents, poppy farmers, and drug traffickers.

I had managed to get an embed in Musa Qala, despite what happened with Crowley the summer before. Somehow I had avoided any blacklist. And supposedly I was lucky. Many journalists considered this to be the best embed possible. But I wasn't thrilled. It sounded scary, much scarier than Paktika.

In late June, after days of waiting on the sweltering Kandahar tarmac, I boarded a Chinook helicopter bound for Helmand. I buckled up, along with several soldiers and a new U.S. military translator, an Afghan American who had grown up on the East Coast. He looked uncomfortable in his fatigues, like he was afraid he might wrinkle them.

"What will you be doing?" I asked the man, who had the highest clearance possible because he was an American citizen.

"Working with the special forces, I guess." He slumped in his seat a bit at the idea.

"Wow." I looked at him closer. He didn't look Pashtun. "Are you Pashtun?"

"Uzbek."

"And you grew up in the U.S.?"

He nodded.

"You speak Pashto?"

He shrugged. "Yeah. Enough to get by."

This was not encouraging. His Pashto could have been perfect, but the Afghans in Helmand would not trust an Uzbek or his translation. They would see his very existence as an insult to Pashtuns and an indication of how little the Americans understood. Uzbeks were from the north, known for oppressing the Pashtun minority there. This translator would also be unaware of all the tribal rivalries, of the granular ins and outs that made up every community in Afghanistan, each a universe of petty historic squabbles and alliances that mattered. Besides, speaking enough Pashto to get by was by no means enough Pashto. This was not the first time, nor would it be the last, that I met an Afghan translator who had been dropped into the wrong area.

The helicopter drowned out any hope of more conversation. Our pair of Chinooks took off, flying low over rolling hills. Every time the Chinooks flew the two-hour distance between Kandahar and Helmand, they took a different route over different hills, to avoid possible insurgents. The copilot handed me a headset so I could listen to the banter up front.

"Look. Even the girls are throwing rocks at us," the pilot said, pointing at the hillside below. Indeed, the girls were.

"Everyone throws rocks at us," the copilot answered. We all laughed.

Our helicopters landed outside a tiny base in the middle of the desert, kicking up sand into a swirling cloud of beige as we jolted to the ground. Quickly we climbed out the back, where the sand soon clogged every orifice, my eyes, my nostrils, my ears, my mouth, choking me and erasing the bulk of my senses. I pushed through the beige, following the dark outlines of the translator and other U.S. soldiers, wearing one backpack, carrying another with my right hand, my helmet slipping sideways on my head. I saw shapes of people waiting to board the helicopters back to Kandahar. One shape grabbed me by the flak vest.

"Are you a journalist?" he shouted over the roar of the helicopter.

"Yeah. You're a photographer?" I shouted back, noting his camera.

"I'm a German photographer," he corrected. "This place is hell. Get out while you can."

The shape then turned and ran for the helicopter. I stared after him for a few seconds, wishing I could follow, then, resigned to my fate, pushed through the hot dust fog toward a truck, where I dumped my bags gratefully. We then trudged inside the base. I saw the Uzbek head off with some men with beards. I never saw him again.

"Hell" was a compliment. The temperature here soared higher than 120 degrees. The new base was modest, a few big tents that each slept fifty or so people and kept getting blown down by the winds, which whipped through the camp like a thief, leaving behind a fine dust the consistency of talcum powder. Barbed wire and a ring of HESCOs, large bags filled with sand, protected the camp. Sentries stood on a hill above the camp and in guard towers. In the desert that stretched forever, seeing anyone approach was easy. It was not that obvious what the soldiers were doing out here. Their goal was supposedly to clear the territory of bad guys, hold the territory, and build stuff for Afghans. Yet barely enough soldiers were here to fill a movie theater, let alone clear anything or hold it. And the closest town, again, was three miles away.

The media handler, an affable soldier with thick Mr. Magoo glasses, introduced himself and explained the camp and its rules. He pointed out two large guns on the side of the base, 105-mm howitzers, and told me not to be afraid if I heard loud blasts in the middle of the night—the Americans were firing the howitzers into the desert, letting the Taliban know that they were there. He told me women could use the showers only at certain times, which I promptly forgot. Showering here would be like trying to beat back the Taliban with Karzai pamphlets, as pointless as a pedicure in Kabul. Mr. Magoo showed me the tactical operations center (known as the TOC, pronounced like "talk"), the only place with air-conditioning on the base. Outside, other air conditioners sat unused and dusty, with no generator to power them. The Taliban had just destroyed the base's new large refrigerator unit as it was being driven through Musa Qala, along with containers of Red Bull and Gatorade and many soldiers' personal belongings.

I was told to find a cot. One tent had two rows of green cots, with only a few women takers, and I dropped my bags on an empty one, sending up clouds of dust. I walked outside the tent and looked for water—different bins set up across the base held thousands of bottles of water, all instant-coffee hot from the sun. I carried a bottle back to my cot. An embed was essentially a test of patience. Too eager, and a reporter risked alienating soldiers. Too passive, and a reporter risked sitting around reading leftover thrillers. As I had just arrived, I waited for the soldiers to come to me. It did not take long. They called me "ma'am," and asked where I was from. They showed me how to cool down my bottled water—take a sock, wet it with a splash of the hot water, drop the bottle inside the wet sock, and tie it to a bed frame or tent post near the wind, which was everywhere. The water was lukewarm within minutes.

The soldiers called their new home Camp Hell or worse. Some referred to the nearest large village, Musa Qala, as Taliban Town. The base, its satellite, and the supply route had been attacked every few days. The soldiers were first ambushed outside of Kandahar, as they were leaving to set up the base. A gunner had been shot dead when his convoy was ambushed. A medic, who always carried a picture of his wife and newborn son, was killed when an old land mine exploded. The fighting was the reason I had to wait days in Kandahar for a helicopter ride.

Other militants attacked, but one of the most telling was a lone militant on a motorcycle, later dubbed by my friend Sean as the stupidest Taliban insurgent ever born. Three days after troops arrived, a man rode up on a motorcycle. Guards in the towers tracked him with binoculars for what seemed like a mile, always coming closer, carving an obvious path in the flat desert. The Afghan then stopped and pulled out a mirror from his pocket. He turned the mirror toward the base and flashed it quickly, as if to get the soldiers' attention. Flash, flash. Flash, flash. Flash, flash. He drove a little farther and repeated his performance with the mirror. Attention caught, the U.S. soldiers on guard duty sent out an Afghan army truck to investigate. As the truck sped toward the man, he whipped out a Kalashnikov from under his outfit and began firing at the truck. He barely got a shot off. An Afghan soldier manning a heavy machine gun started firing. And firing. And firing more. He kept firing until his tub of bullets was empty and the motorcycle man had long stopped posing a threat. An American watching the scene unfold decided he had to talk to the Afghan soldier.

"Why did you keep shooting?" he asked the Afghan. "And why did you use all the bullets?"

"The Taliban killed my brother," the Afghan replied, grinning. "I really hate them."

And that showed just how impossible everything was out here. This was a war in which an Afghan militant thought his best option was to attack an American base alone on a motorcycle. And an Afghan soldier thought he was equally wise to unleash all his precious ammunition on a dead man, while Afghan soldiers in other parts of Afghanistan complained of having no weapons and no bullets and were even being killed for lack of ammunition. Figuring out the bigger idiot was tough.

Other Afghans trekked out to the base—but they were all elders, complaining that they did not want the U.S. soldiers to come to their villages anymore because everyone was scared of them and afraid of Taliban retaliation. It was a tough crowd. Hearts and minds were not on offer. A medical convoy tried to give free medical help to the village of Sarbesa. But the elders said the U.S. soldiers scared the women and children and asked the medics to hold their clinic somewhere else.

Unlike on other embeds, the officers here were so strapped, spread so thin, they had no time to worry about what I was doing or writing. They sent me on patrols with guys who had seen their friends die in Afghanistan, into a place that was by no means secure. The soldiers were nervous, which made me nervous. Any car, any person, major panic. Nobody waved. Children did not crowd around the Humvees, asking for pens and candy, as they did in the rest of

Afghanistan. When we drove through a village, the women and children ran away. This was never a good sign.

On one patrol, we visited a clinic built through the U.S. schools-and-clinics program, the pet project of Zal, the former U.S. ambassador. The program was largely considered a debacle. The new buildings came in shoddy, late, and over budget. The lead USAID contractor, the Louis Berger Group of New Jersey, reportedly charged U.S. taxpayers an average of $226,000 for each building—almost five times as much as Afghans and European nonprofit groups had paid for similar buildings. Louis Berger officials told journalists that their buildings took longer to build because they were required to train Afghan contractors to do the work; the buildings cost more because they were earthquake resistant. In reality, most of the money probably got chewed up along the way. USAID contractors like Louis Berger spent a lot of money on highly paid U.S. staff and couldn't supervise projects in difficult areas, increasing the likelihood of fraud. And even though Louis Berger hired Afghan contractors, those companies often subcontracted to someone else, who sometimes subcontracted to someone else. Corners were cut. Many buildings were already falling apart. Some roofs had caved in from heavy snow.

We sat with the elders at their new clinic.

"Do you use it?" an American staff sergeant asked.

"Well . . . we have no medicine," an Afghan answered, then added, almost as an afterthought, "And we have no doctor."

In other words, no, they did not. I went on these missions when the soldiers did them, but sometimes they didn't, and sometimes they didn't invite me, like when it seemed too dangerous. Their mood was the opposite of the mood on my embed the year before, when I wrote primarily about the forgotten war. The men still felt like no one was paying attention to Afghanistan, but here they knew that their enemy was serious, and that someone should have maybe figured that out earlier.

On the base, conditions were so backpacking basic, we were all reduced to the same sexless, miserable, dust-covered robots, amused by fights between camel spiders and scorpions held in cardboard boxes. The soldiers filmed the fights and replayed the highlights, much like they watched videos of their recent firefights. The winner in Ultimate Fighter Afghanistan was a particularly large camel spider, which practically ripped the head off any scorpion found to challenge it.

I was occasionally bored, yet constantly exhausted. I rested in my cot and read my neighbor's bad spy novels involving heroic Americans with names like Jimmy and Ace. I couldn't watch videos or write. I couldn't risk taking my computer out of my backpack, because of the omniscient and omnipresent wind, which carried the dust with it. The wind was always in the room, a participant in every conversation. The dust coated soldiers when they napped for an hour, and by the time the morning came around, all of us looked gray and dead. Not that we could sleep, for the heat, for the wind. Putting in contact lenses every morning was like scraping my corneas with a bunion remover.

One night I escaped to the only dustless place in the whole base, the TOC, to talk to the man in charge about everything that had happened. He was interrupted by a whisper about a TIC in the TOC—in other words, troops in contact that could be monitored in the tactical operations center.

In addition to Musa Qala, a satellite U.S. base had been set up in the north. That evening, the Taliban had attacked a U.S. patrol near there. The troops retaliated, backed by a B-1 bomber. Soldiers then spotted fourteen Afghans fleeing to an alleged known Taliban safe house. A Predator filmed the men running into the house, which was surrounded by mud walls. In the well-lit control room, we all watched the grainy Predator feed of the safe house on a large screen on the wall. The captain I had been interviewing verified the target with the men on the ground. He called his superiors; he was approved. So he told the B-1 bomber to drop a five-hundred-pound bomb. Yes, a five-hundred-pound bomb seemed a bit of overkill for a mud hut, but that was the only ammunition the B-1 had, and the Predator had nothing. On the screen, we watched the bomb hit, sending up a giant plume of smoke. The men cheered briefly. Then the smoke cleared.

The bomb had missed the house by about two hundred and twenty yards, a large gap that no one was able to explain, destroying a patch of trees, perhaps some animals, and hopefully no human beings.

"He missed," the officers in the room said softly, incredulously, almost in unison. A few men put their heads in their hands. Then, slowly, everyone turned their heads toward me, the reporter standing in the room like an elephant. I held up my hands.

"What can you do?" I asked. It was a rhetorical question.

"Somebody's messed up," the captain muttered. Now he had to get approval to drop another bomb, which took hours.

The insurgents stayed in the safe house, allegedly, and this time, when the bomb was dropped, it hit the right target, setting off secondary explosions, likely from ammunition inside.

The Taliban had started seizing on such mistakes, especially in a hostile zone like Helmand Province, where people were more than willing to believe the worst of the U.S. military. It didn't matter that much of Afghanistan was backward, occasionally primitive. Most Afghans seemed to have an almost religious faith in American technology, talking about how U.S. troops could drop a bomb on a two-inch target, and how if they missed, they missed on purpose.

The next day a patrol was sent to the site to inspect the rubble and talk to nearby villagers. The story was the same as elsewhere: No Taliban here. Security is fine. Please leave.

After four days, during which I bathed with gritty wet wipes and figured out the long odds, I got out of Camp Hell. I had seen no real government and little aid that mattered. The United States had set up a tiny base in the middle of Taliban territory and started firing off howitzers every night, a move that probably terrified any Afghans who might have wanted them around. The base wasn't protecting anyone or able to win any hearts or minds. Instead, it stirred up a hornet's nest, with no conceivable way to calm it down, no real alternatives to poppies, no government authority. The United States did not bear all the blame. The lack of resources and troops here was the product of years of outrageous neglect by the entire international coalition.

Soon after I left the Musa Qala outpost, set up at considerable expense by the Americans to pave the way for the British, the British arrived. Almost immediately, the British closed the base, deeming that they needed to actually be with the people in the town of Musa Qala to do an effective counterinsurgency. So the base was moved, but that didn't really work, either. The Taliban constantly fired at the new outpost's landing zone. Worried about being shot down, many helicopters simply turned back to the main British base, Camp Bastion.

With obvious supply problems and no reinforcements, British troops had little hope of dealing with the Musa Qala threat. The Taliban fought hard and dirty. The Brits spread out, fighting in the districts of Garmsir, Sangin, and Gereshk. The Danes relieved the Brits in Musa Qala, but were quickly replaced by the Brits again. So the British commander made a controversial decision in the fall of 2006—again, a few months after I was there—to respect a truce between the weak Afghan government and the tribal elders of Musa Qala, who swore up and down and promised a hundred times over that they would keep the Taliban away. The Taliban allegedly agreed. After the deal held for a month, the British moved out their troops, much to the consternation of the United States. These truces had been tried repeatedly in the tribal areas of Pakistan, had been criticized repeatedly by NATO and Afghan officials, and had failed repeatedly. Nonetheless, this time it would be different, the British maintained.

Months later, in February 2007, the Taliban took over Musa Qala and jailed all tribal leaders who had agreed to the truce. It would be another ten months before NATO could reclaim Taliban Town.

CHAPTER 11
MY NEW HOUSE

The night was not one of those blind-drunk ones at L'Atmosphère, not one when couples kissed sloppily in the bushes or the bathroom, or when people kept drinking until the sameness seemed fun, or when someone fell asleep leaning against a tree, or when a security guy tried to convince women, some successfully, that he was researching *Real World Kabul* for MTV. About midnight, with the crowd winding down, we called a taxi from the leading taxi company that catered to foreigners in Kabul and charged only $5 per stop. These taxis were safe, and they knew every place that foreigners went. Kabul had no addresses, just bad roads and neighborhoods and directions like "the first house on the road with a bunch of sunflowers out front," so every house had a nickname. We piled into the cab.

"Fun House," my housemate said.

I'm not sure who named the house, maybe a driver from the taxi company. A cast of about ten people shifted in and out of the five bedrooms of the Fun House, a low-slung poorly laid out building where one bedroom spilled into another, severely limiting privacy. Lawyers, journalists, UN workers, a human-rights worker, a vague consultant, almost everyone had been in and out of Afghanistan for a long time, since the rockets on the rooftop of the Mustafa,

Jack Idema, the toga party. And everyone else knew the Fun House. I rented a room and charged it to my company, which was much cheaper than staying at the Gandamack and, obviously, much more fun. The friendships we forged here, through adversity, curfews, and lack of power, were the quickest and most intense I had ever made. All of us were on the same acid trip, regardless of whether we grew up in London or Johannesburg or Billings, Montana. We were instant family—just add war.

How fun was the Fun House? So fun that the housemates bet on who would be the first to have sex outside on the daybed, so fun that grown men had been known to wear wigs and perform drunken somersaults in the living room, so fun that my housemate Tom and I procrastinated one afternoon by holding target practice on a melon with a battery-powered BB gun bought at the World of Child toy store down the road.

"I know you can shoot because you're from Montana," said Tom, the British freelance journalist I had traveled with to Kandahar.

I aimed at the melon. I shot Tom in the shin.

In other words, the fun at the Fun House was the kind that interrupted the monotony of life in Afghanistan like a sharp kick to the kneecap. (Tom was fine.) Even as the Taliban gathered strength in the south and the Afghans increasingly seethed against the foreigners, the foreigners in the capital pushed back. Restaurants like L'Atmosphère were in full swing. Thursday-night theme parties and Friday-afternoon barbecues were regular. There was a salsa night, a trivia night, and a fledgling poker night on which contractors would soon shrug off losses of thousands of dollars. It was junior year at Kabul High—a time when we knew all the different players and were no longer gawky freshmen in the wrong clothes but weren't as jaded as we'd eventually become. It was party time, and this was the party summer, the summer of 2006, the Summer of the Fun House. Kabul was an oasis.

Adding to the fun, Sean had also just returned to Kabul from one of his earliest forays to meet Tango, a crapshoot that involved actual Taliban insurgents pointing guns at him and Sami, his fixer. While in Helmand, Sean had called me every few days. At one point, he complained that Sami had abandoned him in his hotel after announcing he just couldn't work with Sean anymore. But Sami returned to Sean like the bad habit he was. Sometimes Sean wouldn't answer his phone when I called, and once, he disappeared for a week. He spoke in whispers. He wouldn't talk about what he was doing, convinced his calls were being monitored, so our conversations were perfunctory and laced with Tango.

"People are listening," he said.

"Oh, like you're so important."

Out for his first Thursday night since coming back, Sean told us his story of meeting Tango. Even though I had heard the story a dozen times, it continued to be entertaining. He knew how to massage a tale. He'd tell it once, watch his audience's reaction, and modify the story the next time, always perfecting his delivery.

None of us wanted the night to end, so we piled out of various taxis, walked into the Fun House garden, and collapsed on cushions on the daybed, a freestanding wooden deck covered in stained brown-and-cream Afghan carpets the texture of burlap. The power was out, as usual, but we lit gas lanterns, poured drinks, and put on music, a mix that featured the song "Crazy" by Gnarls Barkley. Tom and I occasionally shot his BB gun at various targets. At one point, I walked through the darkness of the house, using my phone screen as a flashlight, hunting for the bathroom. The door was open— I walked inside. But Sean was already there, washing his hands.

"Oh, sorry, didn't know you were in here," I said. He turned to me.

"Kim," he said, looking directly at me.

"What?"

"Kim," he repeated in a low voice, and then he started to walk toward me. "My little mathlete." Sean knew that I was math student of the year in high school.

I could see what was happening.

"Oh my God. You're not gonna kiss me, are you?"

"Oh. Yes. I. Am."

As always, Sean knew how to punctuate a sentence. He kissed me.

"I have to go to the bathroom," I said, breaking the spell.

Afterward, I walked out to the daybed. Sean was nowhere to be seen. Then he poked his head out of the kitchen door. "Kim, can you help me?"

I walked into the kitchen. He kissed me there, near the sink and the cabinets. Hardly romantic. Tom walked inside.

"Oh. Sorry," he said, turning abruptly. After kissing me one more time in the kitchen, Sean called the taxi company and went back to his room at the Gandamack, which was a good idea. I kind of liked Sean in that vague way that many women kind of liked Sean. But we all knew Sean still loved his ex-wife, and he loved conflict even more.

I was also trying not to date in Kabul, as Afghanistan resembled Alaska if you were a woman—the odds were good but the goods were odd. Although some foreigners here had found love, I had found dead ends. Most of us were running from something, or running toward adrenaline, adventure junkies who when paired up were as combustible and volcanic as baking soda and vinegar. I was realistic. Most female foreign correspondents I knew were single. Most male correspondents, married or entwined. To do this job right took all my energy. And I was plagued by what-ifs. I was now friends with my awkward fling Jeremy, but what if I dated somebody in this aquarium and it went wrong? What if I traveled too much to sustain any relationship? What if I was a frog in boiling water, as overheated as anyone else who chose this life?

A few days later, just before I left for my first trip to the States in more than two years, Sean and I met for lunch near the pool at L'Atmosphère, a real change of scenery, considering we usually sat in the garden. As a woman, I felt the need to clarify what had happened, talk about it, hash it out, examine our relationship under a microscope, turn it over and poke it until dead.

"So that thing?" I asked.

Sean made his usual English attempt at avoiding confrontation—he looked down, shrugged, mumbled, and stared at his fingernails. I deciphered his meaning.

"Fine," I said. "Friends."

The party was winding down, and the Fun House was starting to seem like a rerun. When I came back from Chicago almost two months later, still suffering the culture shock of sudden immersion in billboards, skyscrapers, and constant noise, Sean regaled me with new romances, but with danger, not women, with stories of going off to meet militants in eastern Afghanistan, allies of Gulbuddin Hekmatyar who had ties to Al-Qaeda. He met with some Afghan militants, but their Arab friends said Sean couldn't come to their camp, and Sami also thought it was a bad idea. Sean had also been pinned down by enemy fire while out with the Afghan army and a few British soldiers in Helmand. Clearly, he was gathering a lot of material for his documentary. He soon left again for Helmand, where he would almost get himself killed. Again. Sean could never get enough, would never get enough.

As if to underscore what was happening, the headlines on Afghanistan seemed as over the top as a teenage primetime drama in its third season. The country produced a record amount of opium and heroin in 2006, and now churned out more drugs than the world's addicts could consume. The UN drugs chief called the drug levels "staggering" and warned that the south was displaying "the ominous hallmarks of incipient collapse," which sounded fairly serious. The UN warnings echoed those of the head of the NATO-led coalition in Afghanistan, who in July had cautioned that Western military forces were "running out of time." The Taliban were also steadily pushing into Ghazni Province, only two hours away. Efforts at cracking down on the Taliban there would have been laughable, if the situation weren't so serious. The notoriously corrupt governor in Ghazni banned travel on motorcycles, the favorite Taliban mode of transport. The Taliban then banned travel by car. Many people in Ghazni just stopped leaving home.

But none of this merited much attention outside Afghanistan, not even when the commander of British forces warned that daily fighting in the south was more intense than in Iraq. NATO and the United States claimed to have killed one thousand Taliban fighters in ten weeks—still, the militants kept coming, an endless army.

And soon they arrived in Kabul. One Friday morning, a new housemate and I sat at our dining-room table, sipping coffee and eating muesli with almost-sour milk. We heard a thump, a low noise that sucked all the other ambient noise into it. My housemate, a UN worker, and I looked at each other.

"Bomb?" he asked.

"Hope not," I said.

But it was. Farouq picked me up, and we sped toward the Massoud traffic circle. The statue honoring Ahmad Shah Massoud, the famous anti-Taliban commander who once led the Northern Alliance but was killed by Al-Qaeda two days before the September 11 attacks, was the centerpiece of one of the ugliest traffic circles in Kabul, although not as bad as the traffic circle featuring a tiny Eiffel Tower near the Sham-e-Paris wedding hall. The Massoud circle surrounded a large monument of two hands reaching up and cradling the earth like a bowling ball, which had nothing to do with the message of Massoud. The suicide bomber had hit a U.S. military convoy near the monument, just outside the U.S. embassy. The target and the timing were probably no coincidence. The next day, the country would honor the fifth anniversary of Massoud's death.

We hopped out of the car and walked quickly toward the bomb site, which had already been roped off. I saw a reporter from the BBC.

"How is it?" I asked.

"Gooey," he replied.

Doctors, journalists, police, soldiers—we all relied on black humor. Still, I was unused to major suicide attacks, and his joke made me cringe. The scene hit me even harder. We watched where we stepped. We interviewed people. Fourteen Afghans and two U.S. soldiers were killed, one a woman. Sergeant First Class Merideth Howard of California was fifty-two, a gunner, and the oldest American woman ever known to be killed in combat.

There had been suicide attacks in Kabul before, but they were relatively new, and they were rare. Despite decades of war, suicide bombs had only come to Afghanistan in 2003—before, most Afghans wouldn't have seen the point in blowing themselves up. Sure, they would fight to the death for a cause. But blowing themselves up on purpose? That took all the sport out of war, and more important, most Afghans thought suicide was cowardly.

This attack gave me nightmares. Merideth Howard was a prime example of the stress that two wars had put on the all-volunteer American military. Because of the need to maintain force levels in Iraq and Afghanistan, U.S. soldiers who thought they were finished serving their country were "stop-lossed," their deployments extended; members of the National Guard, meant to be protecting the country during floods and fires, fought on the front lines; and reservists like Howard were sent to Afghanistan. Howard had joined the U.S. Army Reserve on a whim in 1988. After her medical unit was disbanded in 1996, she was assigned to the Individual Ready Reserve, the home of soldiers with no unit. She had gone to monthly drills but mainly spent her duty hours on military paperwork, aiming to put in twenty years before earning retirement benefits.

But for the first time ever, the military had become so strapped that it started staffing provincial reconstruction teams in Afghanistan with a mixture of navy, air force, National Guard, and Army Reserve soldiers. Many in the reserves were like Howard—members of the Individual Ready Reserve, home also to retired officers and soldiers who had recently left the army. Howard and other older soldiers in her unit, which had arrived in Afghanistan almost five months earlier, called themselves the Gray Brigade. She was supposed to handle paperwork, but quickly found that tedious and volunteered to be a gunner. At five foot four, Howard needed to stand on a wooden box to work the Humvee gun.

I couldn't let her go, maybe because the attack was the first major one I had seen, maybe because Howard, with her gray hair and kind smile, reminded me a bit of my mother, and maybe because the idea of Afghan girls seeing an older woman poking out of a Humvee struck me as too incongruous to easily forget. So I tried to track down the family of the suicide bomber, visiting store after store in one section of Kabul where the bomber had allegedly lived. I failed—Mohammad is an amazingly common first name. Then I tried to know Howard. Farouq drove me out to her base in eastern Laghman Province—security was so lax that we managed to drive onto the middle of the base before anyone stopped us, and even then, no one seemed very concerned. I stayed at the base for three days, finding meaning in Howard's hammer, in an unfinished wooden picture frame she was building, in a video showing her as she failed to squeeze the trigger of an automatic grenade launcher while training. Howard laughed when she realized she forgot to remove the safety.

"That could be the problem," she joked.

Another clip, filmed for a U.S. military video highlighting reconstruction work, showed her serious, standing in an Afghan village, her face pink from the hot sun, just after handing out backpacks to kids. "We have a good relationship with the people here in the village," she said.

My search was pointless. Sometimes there was no answer to "why." I had no choice—I had to take Merideth Howard and the attack and shove it all in a box in the back of my mind. Because there was nothing I could do, and I had to work. This became a coping tactic I would master.

Luckily my attention was soon distracted. Another ominous

force landed in Kabul, determined to shake up the country—Al Jazeera English, a sister station to the Arabic version of CNN. I had heard that they were setting up a bureau in Kabul, and that they had a lot of money. But I didn't know they were hunting for an Afghan correspondent. Farouq found out. He had never been in front of a TV camera before, so he sat at home and practiced talking like a TV correspondent to a video camera on a chair. His wife heard him from behind the door, finally asking if Farouq was crazy, talking to himself.

Farouq was nervous about the audition. So he called Sean, back in town from Helmand, sporting a giant cast on his left index finger from a bullet that had ricocheted off a British .50-caliber machine gun while his convoy was under fire from the Taliban.

"Farouq, I know you're nervous, but when you stand in front of the camera, think of the cameraman and the anchor as the most stupid people you can imagine," Sean told him. "Or that the cameraman is standing in front of you naked."

Farouq told Sean not to tell me about the audition, so Sean immediately called. I could hardly blame Farouq for applying. The job didn't pan out—an Afghan correspondent wasn't hired—but Farouq was soon offered a producer position that paid more than twice what I did. Ever since Nasir disappeared for Tajikistan months earlier, drawn by the promise of easy money in the used-car business, Farouq had charged me only $75 a day to drive and translate when I was in the country, less than any other fixer was making.

"I don't want to leave the *Chicago Tribune*, and I've told Al Jazeera I want to keep working with you, whenever you're in town," Farouq said. "You are my friend, and I won't leave you. But they just pay so much money. I have to think of my family."

Afghanistan without Farouq would be like English without vowels—it wouldn't make sense. So I said I would try to increase his pay, to $125 a day, and said Farouq could work with Al Jazeera when I wasn't in Afghanistan. Then I sold this to my bosses, tough considering the money crunch the newspaper was facing. It would not be the last time that money was an issue, for any of us.

The Fun House soon threw a Halloween party, which also marked my thirty-sixth birthday. Farouq and I made another trip to the World of Child toy store, where I bought a semiautomatic BB rifle and a BB pistol. Wearing shorts, a tank top, and Doc Martens, I was the comic-book character Tank Girl. Farouq made plans to come to the party—for years we had celebrated each other's birthdays, even though birthdays were typically not observed in Afghanistan and many Afghans didn't know their actual age. For his costume, Farouq took the easy route. He dressed as a member of the Taliban, although his turban and matching long shirt and pants could just as easily have qualified him as a Pashtun tribal member in the south. That was the thing about the Taliban—they blended.

More than a hundred people crammed into the house and the yard outside. We had Marilyn Monroe, a pirate, Death, the Quaker Oats guy, Cat Woman, a convincing Kim Jong Il, and a belly dancer, along with various sexy witches. Tom bought all the bandages from various pharmacies in Kabul and wrapped himself like a mummy. We danced in a large group, until Tom started to sweat through his bandages, which produced a stench similar to either an antibiotic ointment gone bad or dead people. A shady Afghan American with an Elvis hairdo showed up at about 2 AM—the month before, he had crashed a barbecue at the Fun House and peddled toothpaste tubes full of cocaine for $150 each, snapped up by many foreigners, who judged it bad cocaine but minty fresh. His was a novel business plan—in a country flooded with marijuana and opiates, this man was importing cocaine. (Eventually he figured out the profitable angle—exporting heroin—and was jailed.)

For Halloween, the Afghan Elvis arrived not with drugs but with an entourage including DJ Besho—whose name meant "DJ Diamond" in Dari—an Afghan rapper who set up an impromptu show in the living room. He cleared the dance floor with his rap, which included shout-outs to Wardak and other Afghan provinces. That effectively ended the party. On their way out the door, a member of the rap entourage pocketed my housemate's cell phone.

Later it seemed as if this Halloween blowout was the last gasp of the kind of freewheeling fraternity-party craziness that had become normal in Kabul. The Fun House would soon break up. The foreigner parties would start to have guest lists for security's sake— and often, Afghans like Farouq weren't included on those lists. As the crisis in the country deepened, the Westerners would segregate themselves and retreat into their compounds, building a separate world in Kabul, free of the hassles of Afghanistan, free of Afghans.

CHAPTER 12
BARELY LEGAL

y eccentric grandpa, the Interior Ministry's Abdul Jabar Sabit, had gone from media shy to overexposed almost overnight. The Don Quixote of Afghanistan had led police and journalists on a raid of Afghan corner shops, confiscating about three thousand cans of beer and six hundred bottles of wine in one afternoon. He was hardly alone in his morality quest. The country was considering creating a new vice and virtue department, harkening back to the days of the Taliban, when special cops patrolled the streets looking for men with short beards and women with obvious ankles. All the noise had the intended effect. The two stores that had sold booze to foreigners announced that they would no longer stock alcohol—a move that would not end the capital's booze supply but would make it much more scarce and expensive. Bottles of Jacob's Creek that sold for under $8 in the U.S. would now fetch at least $40 apiece.

I had kept up an acquaintance with Sabit, but a nervous one. I worried that he would turn on me, like he had turned on his other drivers, and I alternately wondered if he was even more fundamentalist than he outwardly behaved, or if he was possibly a hypocrite.

Sabit now courted the media so incessantly, he seemed to be running for office—and as it turned out, he was. The Brits and the

Americans had been trying to improve the country's justice system, even though neither group was supposed to be involved. In one of the biggest practical jokes ever played on Afghanistan, Italy had been tapped to reform the courts, despite the country's lackluster justice record—in only the most recent example, Italy's prime minister had been accused of bribing judges and tweaking laws to avoid conviction. The Italians' efforts on judicial reform in Afghanistan so far could only be described as impotent.

Unwilling to sit on the sidelines, the Brits and the Americans now sold Sabit as the answer to government corruption. He was being pushed as the best choice for attorney general, the top lawyer in the land, a crucial job. Somehow the Afghan government needed to convince its citizens that criminals would be held accountable, that corruption would not be tolerated, and that an Afghan justice system was more effective than the Taliban's Islamic courts. Like civilian casualties, corruption was turning into a major wedge issue. The Taliban may have been strict, but they did promise law and order, and they weren't for sale. (Most of the time. In Afghanistan, there were always exceptions.)

Sabit was not an entirely new suggestion for attorney general. I had heard about this plan months earlier, from a U.S. embassy official.

"Sabit? Really?" I had asked.

"Sure," the embassy man had said. "He may be an unguided missile, but he's our unguided missile."

And maybe that was true—when Sabit visited Guantánamo Bay, he largely validated what the United States had said about the American detention center there, even as he pushed for some allegedly innocent men to come back home. He had also sounded all the right notes about fighting corruption and following the advice of his benefactors. Yet Sabit faced an interesting paradox. Some people saw him as too conservative, given his morality campaign and past alliance with the fundamentalist Gulbuddin Hekmatyar. Others saw him as a U.S. patsy.

But Karzai nominated Sabit anyway, which meant that Sabit had to appear before the Afghan parliament and convince members to vote for him. This wasn't entirely necessary—Karzai largely ignored the body, and would later even choose to keep his foreign minister when the parliament sacked him. But the affirmation would give Sabit legitimacy. He gave a long speech, talking poignantly about corruption and the need to fight it. The parliament overwhelmingly voted for him.

"You should have seen my speech to them," Sabit told me later. "I won them over. By the end, they all loved me. They were all clapping. Some were crying, they were so impressed."

Typical Sabit self-aggrandizement, and I believed one-third of it, a good rule of thumb for most Afghan officials. Regardless, the wild-haired Pashtun with the long white beard and tailored suits who had taught me to shoot a Kalashnikov and threatened to kill his neighbor became the country's attorney general. He called me over to his new office in the fall of 2006. His desk was heaped with bouquets of fluorescent, glittery fake flowers, and I tossed a box of chocolates into the psychedelic garden, which promptly swallowed it. Dozens of men in turbans and various hats sat in his office, which smelled vaguely of feet.

I sat in the office politely. About a hundred more men waited in the lobby and garden. Sabit held court for an hour in Pashto. At a certain point, I walked out and left my regrets with the secretary, who had been fired as Sabit's driver soon after our shooting expedition.

That became a daily routine—Sabit called me over. I sat in his office, drank a lot of green tea, and ate a few bitter almonds. And then I left, without talking to anyone.

"I'm not coming to see you anymore," I finally told him. "It's pointless. You have no time to tell me what's going on."

"Come for kebabs. I promise, I will make time."

"Fine. One more chance."

This time, we ate kebabs wrapped in bread in his upstairs room. I tried to pump him for information on Karzai and corruption, but he ignored me. What was I getting out of this relationship, anyway? He saw me as a friend first, and as a journalist not at all. I saw him as a government official first, and as an arm's-length friend second. We were not remotely on the same field, let alone playing the same game.

"This journalism thing. How long are you going to keep doing it?" he asked me. "You're a bad friend, always coming in and out of the country. If you weren't a journalist, you could just stay in Kabul."

"But that's my job," I said.

"I have a better job for you. USAID is giving me a public-relations adviser. It pays $100,000 a year. The job is yours, if you want it."

So that's how easy making actual money was here. The salary certainly eclipsed mine, although it was still far less than most of my non-journalist friends earned in Kabul. But I knew I didn't want to leave journalism. I also didn't want Sabit as a boss. He may have been the Americans' unguided missile, but unguided missiles sometimes hit unintended targets. Sabit had offered me such perks before—my own Land Cruiser, a security detail, a driver—and I had always turned him down.

"I'll think about it," I said.

But I didn't. Sabit had become slightly possessive, demanding more and more of my time, calling at all hours. When I talked about friends, he got angry. "I don't want to hear about your other friends," he said, more than once. Still, I tried to hold on to Sabit. He was the attorney general, after all. I had also lost some of my other Afghan contacts, to moves out of the country, to misunderstandings, to the fact that I could never seem to hold up my side of an Afghan relationship, an all-consuming campaign that felt like a full-time job. I still had Farouq and his family, but then again, I paid Farouq. At times I felt like I was consistently failing Afghans, never calling as much as I should, never reciprocating. In short, I was too American. So I wanted to keep my eccentric Afghan grandpa in my life. I wanted to be invited over to his grungy apartment in an old Soviet complex, which smelled like a mix of kebabs and fuel because Sabit had to keep a small generator inside for when the power was out.

One day, he called me.

"Come to my office. I have something exciting to show you."

"On deadline, Sabit. I'm too busy."

"Please. It will only take five minutes."

I reluctantly agreed. We walked upstairs. He showed me a single bed, which etched itself in my mind slowly, a sad thin little mattress on a metal frame. This was a new and disturbing development. I raised an eyebrow and looked at him.

"I have a small apartment here now. You can stay here if you want, any time."

I thanked him.

"Looks like a great bed. Wow. Yeah. Nice. I have to go, thanks for showing it to me."

It occurred to me that I was possibly being stalked by the attorney general of Afghanistan. Another journalist then told me that when she had interviewed Sabit, he had repeatedly talked about me.

"He thinks you love him," she said.

"What?"

"He seems to think you're obsessed with him."

Maybe I was in a romantic relationship with the attorney general of Afghanistan but hadn't realized it. Despite my desire to hold on to the Afghans in my life, I needed to break up. Sabit called one Thursday morning.

"Come to the office," he said.

"I can't. I'm busy."

"You're always busy," he said, instantly angry.

"You know, I don't think I can do your version of friendship."

"I can't do yours," Sabit replied. And then he hung up.

In the next few years, we would talk only once on the phone, when I called him to make sure he was OK after one of his many stunts, which occasionally and unsurprisingly involved fisticuffs.

But I followed his career closely. He soon turned into a media darling, the champion of the underdog, determined to root out corruption. Sabit said he would take on the occupants of Shir Pur, the Kabul neighborhood where all the old warlords and drug lords and influential government officials had been given land by the government. He flew around the country, holding press conferences. Every Afghan I met, when trying to name something positive, mentioned Sabit. He was seen as a bit of hope.

But his first major target—a rival accused of the relatively benign crime of threatening a judge—easily evaded arrest, despite cops surrounding his house. Sabit then accused the Kabul airport police chief of corruption, although the chief was universally considered clean. When I worked on a story about corruption, about all the Afghan officials who had asked for *shirini* (Dari for sweets), a man told me a prosecutor under Sabit had asked for $2,000 to free his nephew. And even when Sabit had legitimate targets, he was often ignored. He arrested corrupt officials in the provinces of Herat, Balkh, and Khost. They were released almost as soon as he left town.

Then Sabit messed up publicly. In the spring of 2007, he picked a fight with Tolo TV, the most powerful TV station in Afghanistan. He charged that the station had misquoted him by saying he had said "system" when he really said "judicial system"—impossible considering that Sabit's statement had been televised, and ridiculous because the distinction hardly mattered. In a typical jackbooted abuse of power, Sabit sent police to surround the TV station and arrest various employees. At least two Tolo workers were beaten up. For Sabit, that was not a smart move, considering that Tolo had some very influential Western friends, not to mention pushy journalists. Tolo reporters then dug into Sabit's life, finding out that despite his avowed hatred of corruption, he had somehow secured a nice plot of land behind a hospital in Wazir Akbar Khan, one of Kabul's most exclusive neighborhoods, through connections to the Kabul city government. Other journalists interviewed brothel and restaurant owners claiming they were asked for kickbacks. Some said the most significant change under Sabit was an increase in bribe amounts.

Sabit was his own worst enemy. He had earlier given a TV interview where he had called one of the top religious men in the country a "donkey pussy," a common epithet in Afghanistan. Tolo started playing the clip of Sabit saying "donkey pussy" incessantly—inserting it into the satirical TV show *Danger Bell.* Weeks later, Sabit picked a fight with a Northern Alliance warlord, one described by an Afghan in a 2003 Human Rights Watch report as a "maniac" and "dangerous." On the way to a spot where Afghans picnicked on Friday afternoons, Sabit jumped out of his car during a traffic jam. He was typically angry and blustery, yelling at people, telling them where to go. The warlord drove up with his family, and the two men somehow got into a fight. Sabit was beaten with rifle butts. Although he wasn't seriously injured, the attack showed his power, or lack of it. Police were sent out to the Panjshir Valley to arrest the warlord, but his militia quickly sent them home. Everyone said they were sorry and moved on.

Despite our falling out, I didn't relish Sabit's humiliation. It implied that Afghanistan was dangerously fragile—not because the Taliban was so strong but because the government was so weak. Karzai just kept bending. When anyone challenged him, he folded. And his handling of various crises indicated that he cared more about the foreigners than the Afghans, which made him even more unpopular.

One such crisis involved Ajmal Naqshbandi, the poet of a translator who had helped me when Farouq got married. He was the Afghan everyone talked about, the example of the lack of justice, of the compromises Karzai made. Since I had worked with him three years earlier, he had grown as a journalist, dangerously so. Ajmal had repeatedly traveled to risky parts of the east, developing sources with insurgents there, and he was crazy enough to meet them face-to-face. I saw Ajmal occasionally when he worked with friends or waved from a passing car. Sometimes we ate at the pizza restaurant and guesthouse run by his family.

But that March, Ajmal had taken an Italian journalist to meet the Taliban in Helmand Province. The two men were immediately kidnapped; their Afghan driver's throat was slashed in front of them. The Taliban made their ransom demands. After two weeks, in exchange for five high-level Taliban prisoners and possibly money, the Italian journalist was released. Ajmal was also supposed to be freed—but the Taliban kept him, maybe to make the Karzai government look bad. Three weeks later, after several dramatic appeals by Ajmal, his throat was slit.

At the time I was in Pakistan. As soon as I could get to Afghanistan, Farouq, a few Afghan journalists, and I went to visit Ajmal's family. His new wife, now a widow, was about to give birth. His mother had heart problems. His father could barely talk. His brother looked just like him. The entire family seemed colorless, drained of all emotion. We sat against cushions on the wall and paid our respects before walking out to Ajmal's grave, near his family's home. I stood there, looking at the colorful flags poking out of the dirt, surrounded by these Afghan journalists, men I knew would give their lives for me without even thinking.

And that was it. Two fixers—Sami and Tahir—would still meet the Taliban, would still drive anywhere. But I made a decision. From then on, I had no interest in taking Farouq to Kandahar or Khost. I had no interest in trying to meet the Taliban in person, except in prison.

"If we were kidnapped, you know I would never leave you," I told Farouq as we walked back to our car.

"I know, Kim."

"What am I even talking about? I'm never going to make you meet the Taliban. I'm a crap journalist."

He laughed. Some journalists felt that they could only tell the story of Afghanistan if they met the insurgents, if they spent time with them, and maybe they were right. But I wasn't that reporter, maybe because I was more of a chicken. The price tag on foreigners had also just jumped dramatically. If an Italian could be traded for five Taliban prisoners, including a top commander's brother, what would the next foreign victim go for? And who would the ransom money be used to kill? No story was worth it. We talked to the Taliban over the phone, by e-mail, or, with one savvy spokesman, instant chat. For me, that was enough. I didn't want to risk either of our lives for this war, which at this point seemed doomed.

Adding to my doubts about the present course was the fact that NATO seemed tone-deaf to criticism, especially to any complaints about civilian casualties. All the different countries seemed to have different myopic goals. For Canadians, the war was simply in Kandahar; for the British, the war was Helmand; for the Dutch, Uruzgan. People joked that the three provinces should be renamed Canadahar, Helmandshire, and Uruzdam. Rather than coordinating with central command, each country seemed to do what it pleased. This was obviously dangerous. A Canadian success, if not coordinated across provincial lines, could mean danger for either the Dutch or the Brits. The safety of the troops seemed to be paramount—not the mission. (Maybe because the mission was unclear.) In Helmand, the British troops even briefly broadcast a radio advertisement, telling Afghans that neither foreign troops nor the Afghan army were eradicating poppies. The cynical takeaway: If you want to attack anyone for cutting down your poppies, attack the Afghan police. Not us.

When I tried to talk to a NATO official about these issues, he dismissed me and told me that the radio ad wasn't a story. Weeks later at L'Atmosphère, I told the same official about a civilian casualty allegation involving a young Hazara salt-factory worker shot in his side after NATO troops responded to a suicide attack in Kabul. Neighbors and Afghan police said overzealous NATO forces shot the Hazara man and others—something that had happened in the past after similar attacks. The Hazara man even had an X-ray showing the bullet, which he couldn't afford to remove.

"My idea is this," I told the NATO man, leaning on the bar. "You take the guy and give him the surgery. Then you compare the bullet with bullets used by NATO. You'd know either way. And you'd get all this goodwill, regardless of what you find out, because you took out the bullet."

He just looked at me.

"You know, I used to think you were smart," he said. "But you're really just naïve."

Clearly, for a while at least, I had to put Afghanistan on hold. As a journalist, I shouldn't have been offering suggestions to NATO. I shouldn't have been taking any of this so personally. I shouldn't have been so angry at NATO, or at that Italian journalist, who pumped his arms in the air when he flew back to Rome, while his fixer, Ajmal, sat with the Taliban, waiting to die.

Pakistan beckoned. I knew one thing about the other side of the border: I would never, ever fall in love with that country. There, I could definitely be impartial.

PART II **WHACK-A-STAN**

CHAPTER 13
UNDER PRESSURE

Thousands of people blocked the road, swallowing the SUV in front of us. They climbed on the roof, pelted rose petals at the windshield, and tried to shake or kiss the hand of the man in sunglasses sitting calmly in the passenger seat. Some touched the car reverently, like a shrine. I knew I couldn't just watch this from behind a car window. I had to get out and feel the love.

Wearing a black headscarf and a long red Pakistani top over jeans, I waded through the crowd to the vehicle carrying the most popular man in Pakistan. Iftikhar Mohammed Chaudhry was an unlikely hero, with a tendency to mumble, a prickly ego, and a lazy eye. President Pervez Musharraf, the mustachioed military ruler known for his swashbuckling promises to round up the country's miscreants, had recently suspended Chaudhry as the country's chief justice, largely because Musharraf feared that Chaudhry could block his impending attempt to be reelected president while remaining army chief. But Chaudhry had refused to go away quietly, becoming the first top official in Pakistan to object when Musharraf demanded a resignation. Now Chaudhry was a celebrity, the focal point for the fact that most Pakistanis wanted to throttle Musharraf and permanently end military rule. Anywhere Chaudhry set foot in the spring of 2007 quickly turned into a cross between a political rally and a concert.

Standing near the Chaudhry-mobile, I took notes—on the rose petals, the men shouting they would die for Chaudhry, the nearby goat sacrifice. And then someone grabbed my butt, squeezing a chunk of it. I spun around, but all the men, a good head shorter than me, stared ahead blankly. Pakistan, where even the tiny men seemed to have nuclear arms. Sometimes I hated it here.

"Who did that?" I demanded.

Of course, no one answered.

I turned back around and returned to taking notes. But again—someone grabbed my butt. We performed the same ritual, of me turning around, of them pretending neither me nor my butt existed.

"Fuck off," I announced, but everyone ignored me.

This time when I turned back around, I held my left hand down by my side. I pretended that I was paying attention to all the cheering, sacrificing, and tossing of rose petals. I waited.

Soon someone pinched me. But this time I managed to grab the offending hand. I spun around. The man, who stood about five feet tall and appeared close to fifty, waved his one free hand in front of him, looked up, and pleaded, "No, no, no."

I punched him in the face.

"Don't you have sisters, mothers?" I said, looking at the other men.

Sometimes that argument actually worked.

In Afghanistan, this never happened. Men occasionally grazed a hip, or walked too close, or maybe tried a single pinch. But nothing in Afghanistan ever turned into an ass-grabbing free-for-all. In Pakistan, the quality of one's rear didn't matter, nor did a woman's attractiveness. An ass grab was about humiliation and, of course, the feeling of some men in the country that Western women needed sex like oxygen, and that if a Pakistani man just happened to put himself in her path or pinch her when the sex urge came on, he'd get lucky. I blamed Hollywood.

That was hardly the only difference between the two countries.

In Afghanistan, almost everything was on the surface. Warlords may have been corrupt, but they often admitted their corruption with a smile. Police may have demanded bribes, but they asked on street corners. Karzai may have been ineffective, but he let you watch. The spy agency may have tapped your phones, but no one followed you around. I had Farouq in Afghanistan. I understood Afghanistan, as best I could.

But Pakistan was a series of contradictions tied up in a double game. The country was born out of violence, in the wrenching partition of Pakistan from India in 1947 after the British granted the subcontinent independence. In the migration of Hindus to India and Muslims to East and West Pakistan, nearly a million people were killed, mostly by sectarian mobs. Pakistan's founder, Muhammad Ali Jinnah—a moderate who believed that a united India would have marginalized Muslims—was unclear whether he wanted a secular state or an Islamic one. He said things that could be interpreted both ways: "I do not know what the ultimate shape of this constitution is going to be, but I am sure that it will be of a democratic type, embodying the essential principles of Islam." Whatever that meant. Jinnah may well have had the country's future all mapped out in his head, but he died of tuberculosis and lung cancer just over a year after Pakistan was founded, leaving Pakistanis to debate for generations to come whether he wanted the country's national motto to be "Faith, Unity, Discipline" or "Unity, Faith, Discipline." For many, this was not just semantics—it indicated which precept was to be most important in Pakistan, and hinted at the identity crisis over secularism and Islam that would soon eat at the soul of the nation.

After Jinnah died, it was all downhill. The international community allowed almost half the prize jewel of Kashmir, home to a Muslim majority and precious water supplies, to stay in India, a decision that would turn into the regional bugaboo, sparking wars and shadow wars and cementing Pakistan's national identity as the perennial victim of India. Partition left other, less-obvious wounds.

Pakistan now had only one institution with any sense of stability, training, and memory: the army. And so army leaders, watching incompetent civilians squabble over power and democracy, would feel compelled to step in, over and over. Every military coup would squash civilian institutions and any hope of civil society. Pakistan was supposed to be ruled by a parliamentary democracy with Islam as the state religion and guiding principle for the nation's laws; in truth, Pakistan would be ruled by the seat of its pants, by the military and its associated intelligence agencies, either through a direct military coup, or, when demands for elected leadership grew too loud, through elections with military string-pulling in the background.

Meanwhile, neighboring India, led by the dynasty of the Nehru family, leaders who in the formative years of the country never seemed to die, had been left with most of the subcontinent's people, land, natural resources, roads, and institutions. Democracy took hold, largely because everyone kept voting for the Nehrus' Congress Party and its sense of stability. India had its own growing pains. But they were nothing like Pakistan's.

Bad feelings festered, fed by continual squabbling over Kashmir. Then East Pakistan revolted. And like a mean big brother, India supported the breakaway nation, which became Bangladesh in 1971. Demoralized, depressed, and depleted, West Pakistan—now simply Pakistan—turned to a new hero to lead it forward, a civilian, Zulfikar Ali Bhutto, who had launched the Pakistan Peoples Party and helped identify a major national priority: a nuclear bomb, to counter India. His rule was eventually marred by complaints of corruption, murder, and dictatorial tendencies, familiar complaints about most Pakistani leaders. Bhutto had named an obsequious, compliant army chief in an effort to avoid a coup, and like the other obedient army chiefs, eventually General Zia ul-Haq seized control of Pakistan, saying he was compelled to do so for the good of the nation. Bhutto was hanged in 1979 in a naked abdication of justice. In death, he became the country's most popular leader.

Through all the instability, Pakistan could usually count on one friend: the United States. Sure, the U.S. money ebbed and flowed, depending on events, but Pakistan always knew where the United States stood in the long-running India-Pakistan dispute. America saw India as a Soviet sympathizer, as a red nation in the cold war. (India saw itself as nonaligned, but no matter.) America could count on Pakistan to be virulently anti-Soviet. And as a bonus, with Pakistan the United States often had to deal with just one strongman, a military dictator, to get things done.

Living up to Pakistan's anti-Soviet potential, after the Soviets invaded neighboring Afghanistan in late 1979, General Zia quickly recovered from a U.S. rebuke for hanging his predecessor and signed up for the great CIA-Saudi-Islamist plan to drive out the Communists. Not only did Pakistan see Communism as bad and the Soviet Union as a threat; the country also feared being hemmed in by yet another neighbor sympathetic to India. The indoctrination started. Camps trained Afghans, then Pakistanis, and eventually anyone with a brain cell to fight. Throughout the 1980s, the United States sent textbooks to the Pakistan tribal areas, aiming to teach Afghan refugee children English using the language of jihad, and math using drawings of guns, bullets, soldiers, and mines, thus preparing a generation to fight the Soviet invaders. Shortly after the Soviets finally left Afghanistan in 1989, the United States left as well, abandoning the textbooks and the camps. Pakistan had to clean up the mess. Not only that—the United States banned most economic and military assistance to Pakistan because of its pursuit of a nuclear weapon. A generation of the Pakistani military would miss out on American training and influence, as the Islamists continued to gain favor. And meanwhile, with the collapse of the Soviet empire, America would start flirting much more with India, the world's largest democracy and a giant potential market.

With a new sense of international isolation and the death of General Zia in a suspicious plane crash that may or may not have involved a case of exploding mangos, Pakistan refocused in the late 1980s. In theory, the civilians had taken charge, and the young, charismatic, beautiful Benazir Bhutto, the Harvard-educated daughter of Zulfikar, now ran the country. But behind the scenes, the military and the country's intelligence agencies sidelined her. Some jihadi fighters were directed into a shadow war in Indian-controlled Kashmir, while others kept fighting in Afghanistan until the pro-Soviet government finally collapsed. For a decade Pakistan's leadership was tossed like a football between different civilian leaders accused of corruption—from Bhutto to then military lackey Nawaz Sharif, back to Bhutto, then back to Sharif, who finally delivered that nuclear weapon.

In 1999, another obedient army chief decided it was his turn to run Pakistan. Pervez Musharraf, promoted by Sharif, deposed Sharif. As both president and army chief, Musharraf soon grew popular for a rebounding economy he had nothing much to do with, and for slightly more liberal policies, at least in the cities. After the September 11 attacks, the love affair with America reignited. The Bush administration repeatedly praised Musharraf as a key partner in the war on terror, a bulwark against Islamic extremists.

But by the time I arrived in Pakistan this trip, he had lost considerable popularity, largely because of his professed support for America, his refusal to step down as army chief, and his aggressive megalomania. The removal of the country's chief justice in March 2007 was close to the final straw. In the West, especially in the Bush administration, Musharraf still enjoyed almost universal support. But some senior officials had started to doubt Pakistan's actual intentions. They privately worried that Musharraf and the country's powerful intelligence agencies were playing a double game—taking Western money and hunting Al-Qaeda, while doing little against their old friends, the Taliban. There was a running joke that whenever a finger-wagging U.S. official visited Islamabad and berated officials to do more, the number-three leader of Al-Qaeda would suddenly be killed or captured somewhere in the tribal areas. (Not only a joke; this happened several times.) The numbers backed the doubters—although more than seven hundred Al-Qaeda suspects had allegedly been arrested in Pakistan, few senior Taliban leaders had been captured. Several top militants had mysteriously escaped custody or been released.

The contradictions created by sixty years of obfuscation in Pakistan played out on a daily basis, in the continual whiplash between secularism and extremism, the contorted attempts to hold this fracturing nation together with Scotch tape and honeyed tongues. Islamic clerics forced me to wear a black abaya showing only my eyes, but then privately asked to see my face and hair. One province banned females on billboards, but a subversive drag queen ran one of the country's top talk shows. The tribal areas—officially the Federally Administered Tribal Areas, seven tribal agencies and six frontier regions—were theoretically part of Pakistan, but the laws of Pakistan didn't apply. Islamic militants roamed freely there, but very un-Islamic drugs were sold along the roads, advertised with animal pelts. Alcohol was illegal for Muslims, but most Pakistani men I knew tossed back Johnnie Walker Black Label like eighteen-year-olds at their first college party. The Pakistani military and the three major intelligence agencies, referred to simply as "the agencies," had run the country directly or indirectly for its entire existence and helped form powerful militant groups, which they now disavowed. And, in a particularly brilliant contradiction, Pakistan was still run by a military dictator, who despite seizing power almost eight years earlier and holding on to it through sham elections, had somehow convinced the West that he was setting up a democracy.

A mother and son holding hands at the Karachi airport summed up Pakistan for me. She wore a black abaya and heavy eyeliner. He wore jeans and a T-shirt proclaiming NO MONEY, NO HONEY.

Given my new penchant for punching at rallies, I knew Pakistan had shortened my fuse. What little restraint I had acquired elsewhere had evaporated, largely over issues of personal space. (I was still a Montanan at heart—preferring few people, lots of open range, and boundary lines meant to be respected.) But I knew I needed to dive into the country. I had to stop resisting Pakistan's pull, because Afghanistan and Pakistan fed into each other, and I needed to understand how. It would not be easy. Reporting a story here was like trying to find a specific needle in a stack of needles using a needle, an endless attempt at sorting through anonymous quotes from anonymous intelligence sources and anonymous diplomats. Most terrorist plots in the West traced somehow back to Pakistan—as many as three-quarters, according to some estimates. After a plot was linked to someone in Pakistan, journalists like myself predictably converged on the alleged militant's home village in the middle of nowhere, where the most powerful spy agency, the Inter-Services Intelligence Directorate (ISI), tried to convince us that what we had been told was wrong, and that this was not the village we were looking for, and that there was no way any terrorist would ever come from Pakistan. Wrong town, wrong country. We weren't allowed to go to the tribal areas where many militants had supposedly trained, we weren't supposed to roam free, and we were told that this was all for our safety. The subterfuge here was an art that had been institutionalized.

I blamed India. Everyone here did. To understand Pakistan, India was the key. Why did Pakistan direct its militant groups toward disputed Kashmir instead of disbanding them after the Soviet Union left Afghanistan? India. Why did Pakistan support the Taliban regime in Afghanistan? India. Why did Pakistan develop a nuclear weapon? India. Why did Musharraf support the country's homegrown militant groups even as he arrested Al-Qaeda's alleged number three at any given time? India. And why did Pakistan continually give me such a crappy visa? India.

Being based in New Delhi did not help my attempts to cover Pakistan. India-based journalists were usually given two-week visas.

We were only supposed to go to Islamabad, Lahore, or Karachi, and we were automatically assumed to be spies. As soon as I checked into a hotel, the ISI knew where I was. My phone was tapped. The driver from the Marriott Hotel reported back whom I had talked to and what I had said. Or so I was told. Covering Pakistan was an excuse to let my paranoia run wild. It was like starring in *The Benny Hill Show*, trying to run slightly faster than that creepy old man. If Pakistan had a soundtrack, it would be "Flight of the Bumblebee." If it suffered from a psychological disorder, it would be bipolar.

But the chief-justice controversy was a relatively easy way to dig into Pakistan—obvious, messy, and important. This spat between the judiciary and the presidency was the biggest threat Musharraf had ever faced, bigger than the assassination attempts, the Islamic extremists, the squabbling with Pakistan's neighbors. It could influence the country's presidential elections and the country's future. It was that big.

After the suspended chief justice Chaudhry refused to step down, the lawyers nationwide rose to defend him, saying that the country needed rule of law and the judiciary needed to be independent from the messed-up executive branch. Wearing their uniforms of black suits and white shirts, the lawyers held demonstrations, picking fights with police, who retaliated with tear gas. Some lawyers beat a supposed spy with their shoes right in front of me, even ripping off his tie. Momentum built. Lawyer protests grew into anti-Musharraf protests. Every few days, people met in Islamabad, shouting catchy slogans such as "Go Musharraf go," which meant he should step down, not run for a touchdown, and, my personal favorite, "Musharraf doggie, son of Bush."

Chaudhry's legal team decided to take the chief justice on the road, on a speaking tour to various cities. But the goal was not speeches, as Chaudhry was no orator. The goal was a forever journey, a slow ride. Like all political campaigns in Pakistan, these road trips aimed to yank people out onto the streets to prevent the chief justice's vehicle from moving much at all. The team's top lawyer even drove, at times slower than he probably needed to, and always with the goal of creating drama. Lawyers vied to ride on top of the Chaudhry-mobile, a white 1994 Mitsubishi Pajero on its last wheels. The roof was dented and covered with black shoe marks from the lawyers who had stood there. The sunroof was broken. The running boards had been removed to prevent too many fans from hitching a ride.

In two months, Chaudhry had given six speeches. Each road trip was slower and longer than the one before because of the crowds and occasional stops for spontaneous lawyer speeches. It took about nine hours to drive the hundred miles from Islamabad to Peshawar, and twenty-six hours to drive the hundred and seventy miles from Islamabad to Lahore.

Musharraf wanted none of this. In the seaport of Karachi, Chaudhry's speech was preempted by riots and gun battles sparked mainly by a thug-led pro-Musharraf party—at least forty-one people were killed. TV stations were eventually stopped from broadcasting the road trips live. Hundreds of Musharraf's political opponents were rounded up. Public gatherings of more than five people in Islamabad needed government approval. Musharraf appeared increasingly under siege, paranoid and suspicious. He railed against members of his ruling coalition for failing to support him.

"I bluntly say you always leave me alone in time of trial and tribulation," said Musharraf, a fan of colonial-era English like much of the elite.

The chief justice's team then decided to take the show to the town of Abbottabad, in the North-West Frontier Province. Like every other journalist, I begged to ride in the suspended chief justice's car. I was told no—he did not do ride-alongs, or interviews, or any meetings with the media. A few of us did the next best thing— we rode in the vehicle just behind the Chaudhry-mobile, with the wife of Chaudhry's top lawyer. My good friend Tammy, a glamorous

Pakistani lawyer and talk-show host prone to heat stroke, diamond bling, and citrus-scented facial wipes, was close to the lawyer's family. In Pakistan, such connections were the only way to cut through the British red-tape hangover.

Unfortunately I had gotten out to stretch my legs. So now, just after punching an older man with a comb-over, yards away from the chief justice, I watched a window roll down on his vehicle.

"Is something wrong?" shouted one of the lawyers inside.

"Yeah, something's wrong. These guys keep grabbing me."

He sighed and whispered something to lawyers outside the Pajero. Half a dozen then walked over to me, surrounding my rear flank, trying to protect it. But they were as effective as the country's legal system. The hands kept poking holes in their defenses. I kept spinning around, screaming, gesturing like I was conducting an orchestra on speed, randomly catching hands mid-pinch and then hitting the offenders.

I was creating a scene. This time, the door of the Pajero popped open.

"Kim. Get in," the lawyer said.

This was unexpected. Every journalist I knew had been trying to get inside this vehicle for months. None had. But somehow, where skills, talent, and perseverance had failed, my unremarkable ass had delivered. I climbed into the backseat as another lawyer jumped out of the vehicle to make room for me. I sat quietly.

"Just sit there. Don't say a word," the top lawyer told me, glaring at me in the rearview mirror. "You can stay in here through the worst of the crowds. Do not talk to the chief justice. Do not try to interview the chief justice."

I waited for a beat.

"But what if the chief justice wants to talk to me?"

Chaudhry laughed. I was in. And pretty soon, Tammy and another friend were in the car as well, because once I had breached the car, the others couldn't be kept out. Especially Tammy, who as a minor celebrity had a Wonder Woman ability to make men talk, even without the lasso. As soon as the top lawyer stepped out of the SUV to make a speech, the chief justice, his minder gone, started gushing to Tammy.

"I'm quite happy, you yourself can imagine," Chaudhry said, adding that he felt "wonderful." He said he never would have imagined such a scene before being suspended. "Never, being a judge and a lawyer. Never."

The top lawyer stepped back into the SUV, looking suspiciously from the judge to the backseat. All of us sat quietly.

At points the convoy reached speeds of sixty miles per hour. But whenever we hit a town, or even an intersection, crowds swarmed, bringing traffic to a standstill. People ran through the maze of cars, clutching handfuls of rose petals, trying to find Chaudhry, whom they called "chief." At times it seemed like the SUV would be buried in petals or people. Supporters pounded on the windows so insistently that it occasionally felt like a zombie movie. They shook the vehicle. Stickers and posters showed Chaudhry superimposed over crowds of thousands like a political leader, or Chaudhry and the words "My Hero." Our soundtrack veered between cheering crowds and loudspeakers, blaring a new hit song that repetitively asked army chief Musharraf, "Hey, man, why don't you take off your uniform?"

We reached Abbottabad at a ludicrous 11 PM—driving seventy miles in fourteen hours, meaning an average speed of five miles an hour. A crowd of ten thousand people, mainly lawyers in their black suits and white shirts, had waited in front of a stage since the afternoon. Rebellion was everywhere. A moderator announced that the head of the youth wing of Musharraf's ruling party had quit to join the chief justice's movement. The mayor of Abbottabad, a military town, gave Chaudhry a key to the city. The head of the courts for the province said the government had asked him to stay away from the rally, but he decided to come anyway.

Onstage various people gave speeches, but the highlight of the night was definitely the lawyers, who sporadically burst into dancing conga lines, tossing rose petals in the air. This felt like a party, but no one was drunk.

Chaudhry finally took the stage at 2 AM. He looked at his notes, gave five minutes of thank-yous, and said he would make no political statements. Instead he put on his glasses and diligently read a fifteen-minute speech about the value of an independent judiciary and the equality of law. He looked down at his notes and occasionally seemed close to whispering. He reminded me of Andy Kaufman's character Latka on the sitcom *Taxi,* avoiding the hand-waving theatrics essential to any popular Pakistani speaker.

It didn't matter. The crowd roared.

This had been the longest day I had ever spent in Pakistan. It felt like one of the longest days of my life. But despite the assault on my rear flank, I had never had more fun here. Never before had I actually felt that strange rising-up sensation in my chest about Pakistan—not indigestion but hope. After Afghanistan, I had vowed not to get too attached to a country. And here I was, falling in love again. I was such a chick, endlessly fooling myself that this time a country would be for keeps. Maybe the NATO guy was right: Maybe I was just naïve.

Despite all the noise, U.S. diplomats were predictably quiet. In any other country such an obvious slap in the face of democracy like suspending the chief justice would lead to some level of censure, some comment by the U.S. administration. In any other country, such a spontaneous movement for an independent judiciary would draw praise. But in Pakistan, the United States still banked on Musharraf, one-stop shopping for support in their war on terror. Complaints about Musharraf's behavior were muted, halfhearted, vague. One top U.S. diplomat said he brought a message to Pakistan of "strong friendship" and "excellent partnership." All our eggs remained in the same basket, with Musharraf, who had just shot himself in the foot and was bleeding all over the place.

CHAPTER 14
HIGHWAY TO HELL

As the lawyers danced, the Red Mosque boiled. The mosque-and-madrassa compound increasingly resembled an Islamic militant training camp in the heart of Islamabad, a city known more for its ability to incite sleep than jihad. Young men patrolled the high walls carrying long sticks. They burned piles of threatening videos like *Free Willy* because they were supposedly against Islam. Young female students, referred to as "ninjas" because of their all-encompassing black garb, kidnapped alleged prostitutes and dragged them to the compound for deprogramming. The Red Mosque's leaders talked of Islamic law, of all-out war.

The government threatened to shut down the Red Mosque; the Red Mosque clerics threatened holy war.

But this was no simple story. Some of the savviest Pakistanis I knew believed that the establishment had engineered this militant uprising in the capital to divert everyone's attention from the chief justice's movement—especially in the West, easily distracted by militants waving shiny things. The brothers who ran the Red Mosque were certainly old friends of the ISI, since the time of the jihad against the Soviets in Afghanistan.

So two groups vied for the nation's attention—the lawyers and the zealots. The lawyers said the spy agencies created the zealots. The zealots said they were defending Islam.

In the middle of that tug-of-war of July 2007, as the lawyers and the zealots threatened to pull Pakistan apart, I decided to go on vacation. I figured I could get away with a short trip to Greece. I was so very wrong. Within those two weeks, everything would be over. Kind of.

First, Pakistani security forces stormed the Red Mosque compound. More than a hundred and fifty people, including women and children, were killed. One head cleric, who had always been a charming host to foreign journalists, died violently. His more elusive brother was arrested when he tried to sneak out the back in a clever disguise: a burqa. If this raid were an attempt to distract the country from the chief justice controversy, it would have devastating consequences. Islamic militants and many ordinary Pakistanis didn't just see some kind of elaborate, duplicitous plot gone wrong. They saw Pakistani security forces purposefully killing Muslims inside a religious compound—an act that some felt demanded vengeance.

Sitting on the Greek island of Santorini, I didn't know about any of the fallout yet. I just knew I was missing the action. I also knew I'd never make it back to Pakistan in time, not with a ferry ride, a long drive, and fires nipping at the edge of Athens. As I fretted, more news landed. The country's supreme court reinstated Chaudhry as chief justice—a slap in Musharraf's face and an indication that the pushback to his regime was not going away.

As soon as I could make it back to Islamabad, I tried to play catch-up. I talked to a top medical official, who spun a story about all the children killed at the Red Mosque and buried in a nearby field. He told me that hundreds of deaths had been hidden, and spoke cryptically about how they had died. I sipped my sweet milky tea and decided to cut through the conspiracy drama. I asked my test question, the one that I had started using in Pakistan regularly.

"So . . . do you think any Jews were killed in the World Trade Center?"

He looked at me. The switch in topic was dramatic.

"Well, I don't know," he said. "I don't think so."

I stood up. "I'm out of here. You've lost all credibility."

Shocked, he tried to explain himself.

"If Jews died, why don't they put it on the Internet? Why don't they name all the Jews who died on a website? Then I'd believe it."

"You want the Jews to make a list of the dead. Seriously, that's what you want?"

"Yes."

"Right after 9/11, I talked to the families of dozens of Jews who died. You're educated. You're a doctor." I turned to leave.

"Maybe you should put up a website," he said. "Maybe you should make a list."

I reached back and grabbed a cookie, eating it on the way out the door. The entire interview lasted ten minutes.

My patience had frayed. I was slightly sad to be back here, lonely in Islamabad, a city that didn't have nearly as crazy a social scene as Kabul. But despite living in the region for more than three years, longer than most correspondents lasted in this South Asian sweatshop, I wanted to stay. Just a little longer, I kept telling myself. I wanted to see how the story ended, even if I had to live in Islamabad, a manufactured capital built in the 1960s with wide boulevards, lots of grassy medians, and the vibe of Sacramento on tranquilizers. People joked that Islamabad was a thirty-minute drive from Pakistan. A former U.S. ambassador once quipped that Islamabad was half the size of Arlington National Cemetery and twice as dead. A group of us invented our own fun. We dressed up for parties at embassies. On Fridays, we dropped by the UN club or restaurants at the two top hotels in town, the Serena and the Marriott. But meeting anyone new or seeing anything surprising was about as likely as Shakira touring the tribal areas. One night our table of eight was the only one at a restaurant called Riffi's, which blasted "The Girl from Ipanema" repeatedly. That was entertainment.

Regardless, while in Greece, I had decided to move to Islamabad. Maybe then I could unravel Pakistan. With another correspondent recently moving to India, I was also superfluous. And I was tired of being a woman without a home, who theoretically lived in New Delhi but was never there. An Afghan refugee had spent more time in my apartment this year than I had. In Pakistan, at least, I knew I would be home more. I envisioned nesting.

And I had Samad in Islamabad—a driver I had found in the spring of 2006, a young man of about twenty who was as skinny as a coat hanger and as efficient as a Japanese train. He wore sweater vests and hipster rectangular glasses and had no beard, even when he was living in his car-rental agency because his brother had kicked him out of the house for not paying enough rent. I trusted him so much that I gave him my bank card and the code to my account— or maybe I was just that lazy. Samad called me "boss." Often he wouldn't look me in the eye—he looked down at the ground, his hands clasped behind his back. This was part of the country's class system, most likely a hangover from the caste system of India or the deference paid to the British. Like other foreigners, I tried to establish a more egalitarian workforce. I sat in the front seat next to Samad instead of in the back. We played a game whenever he parked. I would grab my bag and try to open the car door. He would run around the car and try to open my door first. Samad would also follow me, picking up the crumpled money that fell out of my purse, occasionally the forgotten passport. Samad was as prepared as a new father. He had stocked his trunk with lemon juice, vinegar, bandannas, and cheap Speedo swimming goggles, defensive weapons against tear gas. Without Samad, I was a mess. With him, I almost functioned. He was the closest person I had to a Farouq here.

I figured I would lead a cloistered life in Islamabad, given the lack of options. But at a press conference with one of many visiting U.S. officials in the basement of the Serena, I noticed a reporter I hadn't seen before. Blue eyes, graying hair, a beard. I wondered who he was, and in Islamabad, it didn't take long to find out. The following weekend, at a party at the Australian embassy, I spotted him talking to mutual friends. Fueled by the courage of whiskey and sodas and a short black skirt, I introduced myself to him, shortly after realizing that I was dancing sexy in a circle of women, which was fine but not the message I was trying to send.

"So I just realized I was dancing in a circle of women," I said, master of the pickup line. "I figured I'd rather introduce myself to you."

Sitting in the grass and watching everyone else dance, Dave and I talked for more than an hour about the horrors of Islamabad, the pressures of work. He rode a motorcycle, spoke three languages, and planned to quit his journalism job soon to write a book in Afghanistan. I could have interpreted that as an adrenaline addiction. I chose to see it as passion. From the beginning I thought Dave could be the answer to the question of work-life balance. A reporter like me, who liked to live overseas like me, who liked adventure like me. All this ran through my head in thirty seconds. Within days, we settled into an easy romance—curry egg sandwiches in the morning, occasional episodes of *Fawlty Towers* in the afternoon, motorcycle rides in the evening to the only Italian joint in town that served wine. Then, of course, we had our date at a riot, where we dodged tear gas, rocks, and lawyers, me limping because I had dislocated a pinky toe on a piece of furniture while railing about Musharraf. As usual, work overshadowed everything. Soon the political landscape would make it even worse.

Rumors swirled about a potential power-sharing deal between Musharraf and Benazir Bhutto, the former Pakistani prime minister who had been in exile for eight years. Since her early popularity, her reputation had been stained, particularly because of credible claims of corruption against her and her husband. But even in exile, Bhutto was the most popular civilian leader in the country, maybe because of the lack of options. The Americans and the British had pushed a Bhutto-Musharraf deal, seeing it as a way to bring stability to Pakistani politics. That way, the government would have a civilian face and the West would still have its favorite military strongman. Pakistan could then focus on what the West saw as crucially important—the war on terror.

The pieces of the deal fell into place. Bhutto announced her return. Musharraf signed a controversial ordinance granting amnesty to Bhutto, her husband, and the hundreds of other politicians facing pending criminal charges. The next day, the parliament overwhelmingly elected Musharraf president, more democracy in action.

On October 18, we waited with the sweaty masses near the airport in Karachi. Bhutto, the woman of the people, had tried to balance her need for security with her need to shake hands. A large armored truck had been fitted with a platform, railing, and bulletproof screen on the top so Bhutto could stand outside but still be protected. Dozens of unarmed Bhutto supporters wearing T-shirts that said they would die for her planned to surround her bus. Their actual role was left unsaid—these volunteers were human shields, expendable. The government had provided little security, indicating that any deal between Bhutto and Musharraf was shaky. Barricades had been set up, but they were as substantial as Tinkertoys. Rabid fans pushed back a police line near the airport, flooding inside. No one was searched.

To get out of the crush of people, Dave, another friend, and I climbed onto the roof of a colorful Pakistani jingle truck, painted with fluorescent scenes of Pakistan—pink trees, purple skies. On a wooden platform just above the driver, we watched the crowd of tens of thousands swell.

Eventually Bhutto was whisked out of the airport and into her truck. She soon swept onto the platform in a green salwar kameez and a white gauzy headscarf, waving gracefully. Chaos, clapping, cheering, screaming. I was happy I wasn't in the crowd. A kind of fervor, a lunging, hungry fever spread down below, with people lurching toward the T-shirts near the bus, trying to get close to their queen. But the scene was also joyful, seen from above, and as usual, the Pakistanis started dancing to their own inner music. Bhutto treated the bulletproof screen like a nuisance and leaned over the railing instead. We rode along with the convoy for about five hours, or less than a mile, before climbing down, near our hotel, and going inside to write. Like everyone else, I wanted to file a story, sleep for a few hours, and join the convoy in the early morning.

After writing, Dave and I checked the news, set the alarm, and fell into bed before midnight, still wearing our clothes. Then my cell phone rang. A close friend.

"What?" I said.

"A bomb, turn on your TV," she said, sounding panicked.

I turned on CNN. Nothing.

"Are you sure it was a bomb? It's not on CNN."

"That's what they're saying."

She told me to check a Pakistani station. I did, and saw the first images of an explosion, of flames and carnage. I groaned.

"Gotta go."

Dave and I looked at each other, sighed, ran to the lobby, and begged and bribed our way into a taxi. No driver wanted to go near Bhutto's convoy or any explosion—rumors were already spreading. The cab dropped us blocks away, and we ran toward the sirens. Bhutto's truck sat there, surrounded by mangled car parts, people with bloody salwar kameezes, police. I saw friends and body parts, and pulled out my notebook and started taking notes. Dave and I split up. The scene was a free-for-all, no police tape, no sense of preserving evidence. A police officer called me over. He lifted up a white sheet, to show me a head.

"Bomber," he said.

Over the years my notebook had become my insulation. Around such destruction, such death, I simply took notes. I could deal with it emotionally later, but right now, I had to work.

"Head," I wrote. "Possibly bomber."

I wandered around, talking to people, eventually deciding to climb the ladder on the back of Bhutto's truck to see what was there. The police escorted me as if I were an investigator. On the deck of the truck, I saw blood, shrapnel, pieces of twisted metal. A Bhutto supporter showed me bullet dings in the bulletproof screen, insisting that someone was shooting at the truck when the bomb—or bombs, no one was certain—exploded.

Tired, I grabbed the railing of the truck, and felt something wet. I froze for a few seconds, not wanting to look down. Finally I glanced, realizing what I had done. I swallowed and looked at my left hand, wondering what I should do now. I wiped my hand on my jeans, then wrote in my notebook: "Pieces of people on the railing of truck." More than a hundred and forty people had died, including many who had sworn to give their lives for Bhutto, who was unharmed. I had seen more death—the tsunami, two different earthquakes. But I could somehow understand natural disasters. This was a human disaster, and I couldn't make sense of the hate. We flagged a ride back to the hotel from a man named Mujahid. I walked quickly to the lobby bathroom, pulled off my tennis shoes, and yanked hand towels off the roller as fast as I could, pumping soap onto them and drenching them in hot water. Then I scrubbed my shoes, trying to get the paper towels into the grooves of the soles, trying to clean them. I cried as the water ran pink, then clear. I shut off the water, looked in the mirror, dabbed my eyes, and walked back to the hotel room in my socks. I dropped my shoes outside the door, next to my boyfriend's. I went inside to write.

Looking back, if my adrenaline addiction had a rock bottom, this was it—wiping my bloody hand on my pants, scrubbing the blood of strangers off my shoes, pushing away the tears so I could write a story. Years later, I realized that never again would I get this close to a bomb scene, never again would I report inside the perimeter, because never again would I want to. But at the time, a mark of how far down the rabbit hole I had fallen, I saw it as just another tragedy I needed to stuff in the growing box in the back of my head. Shut the top and move on.

The next days were a blur. Of going to the morgue and seeing people try to identify family members from limbs, and smelling that peculiar, unmistakable stench of death—sweet but overripe, overwhelming but still unable to cover the something rotten beneath. Of sobbing family members, hair-pulling grief. Of squeezing past angry crowds to slide into Bhutto's compound.

Bhutto decided to meet with a few foreign reporters, but after years in exile, she miscalculated the new vibrant national press, who saw it as a major insult that Bhutto was favoring foreign journalists. As we waited for Bhutto, Pakistani reporters pushed inside and started arguing. Bhutto tried to calm everyone down. An old woman shoved her way into the room, grasping at Bhutto. There seemed to be no security, no real attempt to protect her. The old lady was hustled out, the bickering continued.

At one point, bored, I rolled my eyes and made faces at friends standing on the other side of the room. Unfortunately, I was standing next to Bhutto, and the Associated Press chose that moment to take a picture. My eyes bugged out of my head, as did my hair. I looked like a cartoon character. It was, most definitely, the worst photograph ever taken of me in my life. It would run in newspapers around the world, and I would hear from people I hadn't talked to in years, asking what had happened to me overseas.

But now, oblivious, I sat down to the right of Bhutto and introduced myself.

"I interviewed you on the phone once."

She nodded. "Of course, I remember you, Kim."

She introduced herself to everyone, and we were all instantly smitten. Up close, Bhutto didn't show all of her fifty-four years. She still had ink-black hair, a regal narrow nose, a crooked smile, and only a few wrinkles around her eyes. She wore a gauzy white headscarf that she used like a prop—it would slip back on her head or her shoulders, and she would gracefully put it back in place. We all knew about her cynicism, about the deal she had made with a dictator. But Bhutto had that power that only the rare leader does—to make every person feel like the most important one in the room.

After a few days, I flew back to Islamabad and waited for the next bomb, the next fracture in this fractured country. Dave flew to England, where I planned to meet him soon for a well-earned vacation. I chose to ignore rumors that Musharraf was contemplating declaring an emergency. If I paid attention to every rumor in Pakistan, I'd never sleep.

One morning I popped awake at 6:30 with a stabbing sensation in the middle of my upper back. I couldn't turn my head. I felt as if there had been a crank in the middle of my back, and it had been turned and turned, until at one point, something snapped. In tears, I called Samad, who picked me up and rushed me to the hospital. I called a friend to meet me there, just before being dumped in a bed and injected with drugs. Woozy, drowsy, I vaguely noticed a team of men and women in white coats surrounding me. One, with a long, fundamentalist beard and no mustache, asked if he could take my pulse. An Islamic fundie. I could recognize one anywhere, even when I was high.

"Yes, fine," I whispered.

Before I knew it, he had unzipped my jeans and started feeling for the pulse in my groin. This man would probably never even shake my hand, but here he was, grabbing around inside my pants. The crowd leaned forward to look. I was in so much pain and on so many painkillers, I barely registered the many easier places to check a pulse. My friend showed up, just in time to add some modicum of decency to the nurses' decision to check my breasts.

"What is going on here?" she announced, pulling the drapes closed. "Who's in charge?"

"I have no idea," I replied.

I never saw the fundie again, and the doctors shot me up with enough drugs so I no longer cared. But I clearly needed a break. I needed to be left alone, to sleep for a month. Once my pinched nerve subsided, I hopped on a plane for London. Unfortunately, it was November 3, 2007. It would be the shortest vacation of my life.

CHAPTER 15
GOD SAVE THE QUEEN

I walked off the plane exhausted but excited. Finally, I would be able to relax with Dave. Finally, we could do couples' things we had never experienced in Pakistan, radical activities like holding hands in public. Finally, we could see what was between us.

But as soon as I spotted Dave in Heathrow, I knew something was wrong. He wore a sad smile and patted me like he was putting out a fire.

"What? What happened?"

"I'm sorry, babe. Musharraf just declared an emergency."

I felt as if someone had kicked me in the head.

"No. No. I can't."

"You can. You have to," he said.

I felt sorry for us, sorrier for Pakistan. Every month seemed to bring a fresh crisis, a new attempt to drive the country into a brick wall at a hundred miles an hour. Musharraf had suspended the constitution, actually fired Chief Justice Chaudhry instead of just suspending him, suspended the country's other independent top judges unless they signed a new oath, and placed them all under house arrest, blocking off the entire judges' enclave with riot police, barricades, and barbed wire. In a hilarious justification, Musharraf said he declared the emergency because of the increased threat of Islamic militants and interference by the judiciary. It seemed much more likely that Musharraf wanted to preempt an expected ruling by the supreme court that would have tossed out his recent reelection.

The country's security services started rounding up the bad guys. No, not the nefarious Islamic miscreants Musharraf usually complained about. Instead, the tin men hauled away thousands of lawyers, opposition politicians, and human-rights activists. From London, I frantically called people in Pakistan—some talked in hushed tones because they had already been detained. Others talked, but by the end of the day, their phones just rang incessantly or not at all. Tammy went into hiding.

By the next day, I was back on a plane, bound for Islamabad.

Musharraf's extreme action provoked some allies to finally turn against him—at least somewhat. The Dutch government suspended aid. Britain announced it would review its aid package. The European Union said its members were considering the dreaded "possible further steps." President George W. Bush told reporters in the Oval Office that the United States wanted elections as soon as possible, wanted Musharraf to strip off his uniform, and wanted to work with Musharraf "to make it abundantly clear the position of the United States."

"We made it clear to the president that we would hope he wouldn't have declared the emergency powers he's declared," Bush said. "And at the same time, we want to continue working with him to fight these terrorists and extremists."

As always, America's relationship with Pakistan was all about the terrorists. Meanwhile, Musharraf met with foreign ambassadors in Islamabad and tried to justify himself. He said he was committed to completing the transition from military rule to democracy, a three-phase process he had yammered on about for years, and said the top judges in Pakistan had "paralyzed various organs of the state and created impediments in the fight against terrorism." Musharraf figured that he just had to wave a terrorist bogeyman at the Western countries to get their support. Usually it worked.

His actions raised a major question: What would Bhutto do? She remained fairly quiet at first, obviously hoping to preserve her power-sharing deal. But it soon became clear that Bhutto had to do something—she had to distance herself from the military ruler or risk her entire political base. So she announced a rally for that Friday in neighboring Rawalpindi—symbolically important for her, the army-garrison town where her father had been hanged by General Zia twenty-eight years before.

Early on the morning of the scheduled rally, the show unfolded. Bhutto was placed under house arrest in Islamabad. Dozens of journalists waited near the concrete barriers, barbed wire, and hundreds of government security forces outside her house. The scene would have been funny to watch from above—one journalist heard a rumor that Bhutto was supposed to speak at one spot, and sprinted down the block. The rest of the herd followed, running, holding cameras and notepads, and dropping samosas and pakoras and other fried food. Then another journalist talked quietly on a cell phone and started running, and we all followed in another direction. At one point, two friends and I just started running, to see if everyone followed. They did.

Twice, Bhutto tried to leave her house unsuccessfully. She then gave an impromptu press conference from her bulletproof white SUV, ringed by cops, just on the other side of the barrier. She stood up inside the vehicle, speaking against Musharraf from the open sunroof, an image that would later haunt me.

Musharraf soon ended his temper tantrum. After years of promises, he finally stepped down as army chief. Weeks later, he ended emergency rule, restored the constitution, and announced that he believed emergency rule had saved his country. Case closed.

But damage had been done, and not just to the country's institutions. While the government was distracted, the militants had gained strength. Largely reacting to the siege on the Red Mosque months earlier, more had vowed revenge against the Pakistani government, instead of just attacking foreign troops and Afghan security forces across the border in Afghanistan. A neo-Taliban group in the South Waziristan tribal agency had been blamed for the attack on Bhutto's homecoming parade. (Soon the group would be dubbed the Pakistani Taliban.) Two suicide bombers blew themselves up at almost the same time, near ISI targets in Rawalpindi, the seat of the military's power—an indication of how strong the militants were growing. In Peshawar, the capital of the beleaguered North-West Frontier Province, which bordered Afghanistan and the lawless tribal areas, bombs had started exploding, small ones, outside video shops, seen as un-Islamic and full of Western propaganda. The senior superintendent of police in Peshawar told me that he was exasperated with what had happened in the previous year.

Then his phone rang. Another bomb, carried by a woman, had just blown up near the local ISI office.

"Please excuse me," he said, standing up. "I have to go."

The militants, largely a creation of the omnipotent ISI and the Pakistani military, were now blowing back on their creators like a version of Frankenstein. But still, knowing the truth was practically impossible; Bhutto blamed the establishment for her homecoming attack, not militants. And many Pakistanis blamed India for all the bombs—with, of course, no proof. The double game was practically a quadruple game.

I took breaks when I could, sometimes staring at a wall. I celebrated the Islamic holiday of Eid al-Adha with Samad's mother, father, sister, and various cousins, eating a goat sacrificed for the occasion. Every time I visited his tiny apartment, his mother treated me like royalty, kissing me on my cheeks, pinching me, laughing at me. Her gray hair was always colored with bright orange henna; she continually tried to talk to me in Urdu, finally falling back on the few Urdu words I seemed to remember.

"Samad *ganda*," she said, laughing. That meant "Samad dirty," completely untrue, but always funny. While we ate, a bomb exploded at a mosque near the tribal areas, killing more than fifty worshippers.

Too much death. I was homesick and lonely. After our abrupt vacation, Dave had returned to Islamabad, wrapped up his job, and departed for Afghanistan to launch his new project. I hunted for some Christmas spirit, helping a friend buy sugar, flour, and tea for care packages for Afghan refugees. But when Samad drove us to the refugee camp in Islamabad, everyone started fighting as soon as they spotted our bounty. Desperate for help, the women and children surrounded us, grabbing bags of goodies out of our hands, grabbing our hands. We shimmied our way back into the car. They pounded on the windows. We barely made an escape without running over a child.

"That did not make me feel good at all," I said.

My friend, the same one who had rescued me from the hospital breast grab, who spent weeks planning this act of charity, just looked out the window.

I tried to convince my bosses to let me go to the States for the holidays.

"What could happen between Christmas and New Year's?" I asked.

My boss sat silently on the other end of the phone, letting me fill in the blanks. The earthquake in Iran, the tsunami in Asia?

"OK, fine," I said. "Something could happen. But given all that's happened this year, what are the chances?"

"You can't leave Pakistan," he said. "I'm sorry. I know you're tired. But we can't take the chance."

"Can I go to Karachi?"

He finally agreed. Tammy lived in Karachi, the port metropolis that actually had culture, restaurants, and grit, as opposed to the sterile capital. She had invited me to spend the holidays with her family. Over the past seven months, Tammy had become one of my closest friends, even though she was superficially my opposite. She had thick long black hair—the kind people pay to turn into wigs—and pale skin, and wore designer jewelry that often matched her delicate shoes. Her hair was always perfect; her outfits were always perfect; her nails and makeup were always perfect. Tammy was a member of the elite in Pakistan, the daughter of a former cricket hero, the sister of a man who ran one of the country's largest stock exchanges, the sister-in-law of a media mogul. She attended one of the same elite Pakistani private schools as Benazir Bhutto. Tammy, however, was far more than she appeared. A former New York corporate lawyer, she now hosted a talk show on her brother-in-law's TV station and wrote columns for the English newspaper *The News*. She used her celebrity and intellect to whip up support for the lawyers' movement against Musharraf, even though both her brother and brother-in-law liked Musharraf. Conversations at the family's dinner table were often bitter disagreements about the country's future. Watching them was the Pakistani version of *Crossfire*.

Regardless of any political disputes, Tammy's family was warm and welcoming to anyone who entered her realm. Her mother and father immediately embraced me like a daughter, inviting me to stay whenever I wanted. Their art collection rivaled that of museums; their generosity rivaled that of anyone I ever met. Through Tammy's family, I had a window into the upper class of Pakistan, the movers and shakers who ate elaborate dinners at midnight and would never think of receiving guests without offering delicate crustless sandwiches, various deep-fried packets, and sweet milky tea. Yet unlike many of the movers, who believed that the country's economic future rested with Musharraf, Tammy was passionate about the need for a functioning legal system. Tammy counseled me repeatedly to hold my temper with the ass grabbers; she navigated countless reporting trips for another close friend and me; she dodged tear gas and rocks at lawyers' protests in Islamabad, running from danger in high heels.

Tammy's family, although Muslim, saw nothing wrong with

observing Christmas, as did other moderates, since Jesus Christ is considered to be a major figure in Islam. As soon as my boss gave me the go-ahead I immediately flew to Karachi. I ate a lot of food, walked down a beach, and touched my first actual Christmas tree in four years. I relaxed.

Two days after Christmas, Tammy and I prepared for the shooting of the TV reality show *Enter the Prime Minister*, where Pakistanis could vote on their favorite candidate for prime minister. It was like *American Idol* meets C-SPAN, reality TV for political junkies, only possible in a politically obsessed country like Pakistan. Tammy was a judge. I planned to write a story. So I packed a backpack—my computer, a notebook, two cell phones. I didn't bother to bring my power cords, as I planned to be back at Tammy's house in a few hours. Unfortunately the show was as scintillating as static. At one point, bored and concerned about how I would ever make a reality show about politics interesting, I checked the news wires. Somebody had fired shots at a rally of Nawaz Sharif, who like Bhutto had just returned from exile. I worried that I was in the wrong place, out of position again.

During a break in filming, I told Tammy and the show's other participants about the attack. A few crowded around my computer. Then I checked the Pakistan news again. This time a breaking-news bulletin flashed an attack on Bhutto's rally in Rawalpindi, although the former prime minister was safe. Most of the high-powered people on the TV show were friends of Bhutto, and they started making calls. The head of Pakistan's human-rights commission soon received a text message saying that Bhutto had been wounded. Minutes ticked by, all confusion. Then Bhutto's longtime friend from the human-rights commission answered a phone call. She cried out and hung up.

"She's gone."

Benazir Bhutto, the daughter of the East, had been killed at a rally a few miles from where her father had been hanged, as she stood and waved out the sunroof of her white SUV. Maybe a bomb, maybe a gunshot, the conspiracy machines were already spinning. Like the country, I found this impossible to process. But I had no time. Events soon overtook even her death. Tammy and I looked at each other; she had been frustrated with Bhutto's willingness to make a deal with Musharraf, but she still saw Bhutto as a preferable alternative to the military. Almost immediately, Tammy started to cry.

"This is very bad," she said. "It will rip this country apart."

She needed to visit Bhutto's relatives and friends, so I rode with her to the home of one, a cousin. The receiving room was elegant, chandeliers and wooden furniture. Everyone hugged and sobbed. I was the stranger, the lone non-Pakistani, the lone journalist, the other. At one point, I slid out my notebook, figuring I should write something down. Tammy glanced at me and shook her head. Her message was clear: This was not the place, and I should have known better. She soon sent me off in a carload of people from the TV show toward the Pearl-Continental Hotel, where they were staying.

"You can grab a cab home from there," she said. "I need to stay."

But the turbulent city of Karachi was Bhutto's home, and it was catching fire. As darkness fell, young men threw rocks at the Saudi embassy; others set fire to tires in the middle of intersections. Already Pakistanis marched with flags of Bhutto's Pakistan Peoples Party and yelled "Bhutto lives!" Some fired guns in the air. In my car, crammed with seven people, one woman threw a scarf around my head.

"Cover yourself," she said. "You're an American. You never know what will make these guys angry. It's very volatile."

Eventually we made it to the Pearl-Continental. I called Tammy.

"You'll never make it back tonight," she said. "They're already rioting. Cars are on fire. The neighborhood has been sealed off."

I was in poor shape. The hotel was sold out. I had no computer plug and only about thirty minutes of battery power remaining. I had two cell phones—but each was close to running out of batteries. I camped out in the business center, writing a story on a hotel computer. Eventually the hotel manager found a last-minute vacancy, a suite that cost slightly less than $400. I jumped at it.

By 3 AM I was asleep. I woke up early the next day, trying to figure out a plan. Bhutto would be buried that day, near Larkana, her ancestral home, a short flight from Karachi. Tammy called and told me a special plane was taking journalists and relatives to the funeral. She gave me the name of a party official; he told me the plane was leaving in fifteen minutes.

"I don't think you'll make it," he said.

But nothing ever left on time in Pakistan, and on this morning, fearful of what could happen, no one was yet on the road. The highway, normally a parking lot that constantly vexed me, was empty, and the taxi sped to the airport at fifty miles an hour. On the sides of the road, cars were piled together, all burned-out husks, still smoking. I tried to count them, but lost count around a hundred. After the taxi pulled up in front of the airport terminal, I sprinted for the door. I bought one of the last two tickets for the plane, rushed through security, and then ran to the gate. Somehow I made it.

Then I contemplated my decision. I had no fixer. I had no phone chargers, no computer charger. I had only the clothes on my back— a black-and-white slightly ripped long-sleeved shirt that barely covered my rear, and baggy black pants. I had not showered. I was not fit for a funeral. I called Tammy.

"There's no way we can get out to send your stuff," she said. "You'll figure it out. Just find something to cover your hair."

"OK," I said.

"Oh and one last thing," she said. "If anyone pinches or grabs you, don't yell or punch them. It's a funeral. You have to stay calm."

"Yeah. Calm. Right."

Luckily a friend from the *Guardian* was on the same plane. Unfortunately, he had a different computer and a different phone.

He and I were the only foreign journalists on this trip because we were the only two who happened to be in Karachi when Bhutto was killed. We flew to a town called Sukkur and were picked up by trucks and vans to drive to the funeral, about an hour away. With a police escort, we moved quickly, past smoldering gas stations and cars and banners that said WELCOME, BENAZIR. The air smelled like burning tires.

We stopped at Bhutto's family home. Her wooden coffin, draped in the green, red, and black flag of her party, was slid into the back of an ambulance. People clutched at the coffin and ran after the ambulance, crying. Our convoy then pushed on toward the mausoleum Bhutto had built for her father and two brothers, who also died violent deaths. We stopped when we hit the crowds, climbing out of our van to walk across the desert toward the white tomb, which resembled a cut-rate version of the Taj Mahal. Thousands of Pakistanis also trudged toward the tomb, waving the flag of Bhutto's party, beating their chests. They came by tractor, by hanging off the back of buses or trucks, by foot. Men held up posters of Bhutto and notes she had written them. Women sobbed, clutching at me. Angry young men held guns and long bamboo sticks and vowed revenge.

Pakistanis practicing English tried to talk to me. I asked one to help get something to cover my hair—he quickly procured a large piece of dark red, blue, and white material, which I wrapped over my head and chest. I walked around, talking to people who spoke English. The funeral started. The prayer of the dead was read outside, and men held their palms to the sky. At least, most of them did. Sure enough, in the middle of the prayer, someone pinched me. I spun around, mindful of what Tammy had warned, quietly outraged.

"Here?" I whispered. "At a funeral?"

But one of my broken-English pals had seen what had happened. "Don't worry, sister," he whispered.

He linked arms with some friends, who formed a human protection chain. Together we walked around, and no other hands got through. I wondered where the reporters who had chartered a plane from Islamabad were, but I couldn't call them—the Pakistani government's one nod to security was blocking all calls in the area. Nobody checked for weapons or bombs. No government official trekked here, and the funeral hardly befitted a former head of state. Instead the funeral was probably how Bhutto would have wanted it—a public, messy, spontaneous outpouring of grief, not necessarily for the leader she was but for the leader she aspired to be.

A hole had been cut in the white marble floor next to Bhutto's father's grave. The ambulance backed inside the shrine, and supporters threw rose petals as her coffin, simple and wooden, was pulled out. Bhutto's husband and son, who had flown to Pakistan after she was killed, helped lower her into the ground. They threw handfuls of sandy soil on top, helped by supporters. Slowly the coffin and Benazir Bhutto disappeared from view. She was gone. The country burned.

We eventually hitched a ride to the hotel where the other foreign journalists were staying—the chartered plane had made it to the nearest airport in time for the funeral, but the journalists had not been able to find a ride. The sold-out hotel was the only one not set on fire the previous night. It was decrepit. The pool was filled with trash and dead leaves—a BBC correspondent, talking on her phone while walking with her computer, accidentally fell in. A friend from the *Washington Post* loaned me his computer cord and a phone charger, and said we could stay in his room. His kindness was rewarded. When he went to the bathroom, someone flushed the toilet in the room above, which leaked on him below.

About 4 AM, after finishing my third story of the night, I shoved the *Guardian* reporter to one side of a mattress on the floor and laid down on the other side, wearing the same clothes I had been wearing for more than two days. I passed out for four hours. That morning, the *Post* reporter and I decided to flee.

"This is the worst place on earth," he said.

"I'm never coming back here again," I agreed.

We hitched a ride to Karachi, avoiding roadblocks of burning tires and cars and slogan-shouting men. Broken glass carpeted parts of the road. Trucks at gas stations were set on fire; so were some gas stations. Black plumes of smoke and the wreckage of grief could be seen everywhere—a torched building at a district court complex, a dozen blackened trucks near a gas station, a gas tanker, and a truck once filled with sand, still flickering with flames.

We waved a flag from Bhutto's party out the car window, our visa on this dangerous stretch. "Bhutto lives!" we shouted as our password whenever men stopped us. "Bhutto lives!" the men shouted back. In one town, we saw hundreds of men carrying sticks and marching down the road ahead of us. We veered off, down a side street to the right. Nationwide the scene was little better. Life was at a standstill. Trains were halted; stores were closed. Some towns reported fuel and food shortages, or that only rickshaws and donkey-pulled carts could move.

We made it back to Karachi in seven hours—relatively quickly, with no traffic and no police preoccupied with pulling over speeders. In the rubble of the riots, boys already played cricket, normalcy already reasserting itself, the typical cycle of tragedy and mourning and recovery compressed because tragedy was such a usual event.

No one ever claimed responsibility for killing Bhutto, although the newly anointed Pakistani Taliban leader was again blamed, the newest bogeyman for the country. At a press conference three days after his mother died, Bhutto's nineteen-year-old son, who had spent almost half his short life outside Pakistan, was named the future leader of the party. Until then the party would be run by her widower, Asif Ali Zardari, otherwise known as Mr. Ten Percent for past corruption allegations. The choice would be controversial.

I found a pharmacy in Karachi that was somehow open, and plunked down $10 for a potpourri of sleeping pills, available over the counter. I needed instant sleep, the kind that chased away any nightmares.

CHAPTER 16

STRAY CAT STRUT

With Bhutto gone, I needed to meet the lion of Punjab, or maybe the tiger. No one seemed to know which feline Nawaz Sharif was nicknamed after. Some fans rode around with stuffed toy lions strapped to their cars. Others talked about the tiger of Punjab. By default, Sharif, a former prime minister like Bhutto, had become the most popular opposition leader in the country. He was already the most powerful politician in Punjab, which was the most powerful of Pakistan's four provinces, home to most of the army leaders and past rulers. Some people described Sharif as the Homer Simpson of Pakistan. Others considered him a right-wing wing nut. Still others figured he could save the country.

Sharif was once considered an invention of the establishment, a protégé of the former military dictator in Pakistan, General Zia, but like all politicians here, he had become a creature of himself. During his second term, Sharif built my favorite road in Pakistan, a hundred and seventy miles of paved, multilaned bliss connecting Lahore to Islamabad; named Musharraf as chief of the army; and successfully tested the country's first nuclear weapon. He also cozied up to the Taliban in Afghanistan and briefly considered declaring himself the "commander of the faithful," an often-claimed Islamic title waved around by such luminaries as Taliban founder Mullah Omar. In other words, his record was mixed. Sharif's fundamentalist phase occurred just before he bloomed into full megalomania, believing that a civilian leader of Pakistan could actually sack his army chief. He fired Musharraf in 1999 while the general was in Sri Lanka; Musharraf immediately hopped on a plane home, and Sharif followed up his original folly by refusing to allow Musharraf's plane to land in Pakistan. Meanwhile, top generals in Pakistan, used to such shenanigans, seized power and allowed the plane to land ten minutes before it ran out of fuel. In gratitude, Musharraf jailed Sharif, accused him of attempted murder, and eventually banished him to Saudi Arabia. That would teach a civilian leader to take on the army.

While in exile, Sharif joined forces with his former nemesis, Bhutto, and reformed his fundamentalist image, going so far as to get hair plugs. Many people counted Sharif out—even Western diplomats, who typically laughed when asked if his party had a chance to regain power in the upcoming parliamentary elections. But Sharif's party—not Bhutto's—had become the major backer of the lawyer protests, and Sharif had gone on at length, even eloquently, about the need for justice in Pakistan. (The irony of this was lost on no one. While Sharif was in office, in 1997, his backers had actually stormed the supreme court and forced it to suspend contempt proceedings against him.)

So Sharif was now the darling of the more moderate forces in Pakistan, even if they remained slightly suspicious. One of Sharif's friends tried to explain him to me: "He might be tilting a little to the right, but he's not an extremist. Extremists don't go do hair implants. He also loves singing."

I had attempted to see Sharif when he first tried to return to Pakistan a few months earlier, in September. But commandos had stormed his plane shortly after it landed. Within five hours, he had been shipped back to Saudi Arabia, looking bewildered.

Sharif had finally flown home in late November, weeks after Musharraf declared an emergency. Samad had driven me to the airport in the eastern city of Lahore, Sharif's home territory and the capital of Punjab Province. Tens of thousands of supporters waited behind fences across from the airport entrance. Some shouted for the lion of Punjab—others waved stuffed toy tigers or tiny cardboard Sharif cutouts. It was a classic botched media event. Reporters were herded into a tiny area in front of the airport, surrounded by barriers covered in barbed wire. Thousands of supporters eventually broke through the fences, screaming and running toward us. More and more people pushed into the journalists' pen, squeezing everyone and driving us toward certain impalement on the barbed wire. Samad guarded a shorter friend of mine. My translator tried to protect my back. I stood in a basketball stance, an immovable force. But not for long. A Pakistani journalist from Aaj TV pushed past me, elbowed me in the ribs, and shoved me to the side. I pushed back.

"You don't see me standing here?" I said.

He shrugged. "Women should not be here anyway. This is a man's job."

The crowd swayed back and forth, and I tried to keep my balance. A man grabbed my butt, a message to my fist, and before my brain knew it, I managed to punch him in the face. Not professional, not at all, but still somewhat gratifying.

That was the chaos just before Nawaz Sharif and his brother walked out of the airport, with me worried about my rear, my position, the barbed wire, a mob, and a potential bomb. Supporters lifted the Sharifs onto their shoulders and spun them around in circles because they had no room to walk. Nawaz Sharif looked shell-shocked. He somehow clambered onto a rickety wooden table next to a taxi stand. The contrast with Bhutto was obvious—she was smooth, a master performer, charisma personified, always in control. Sharif seemed more like a baffled everyman, nondescript and beige.

The crush of men waved their arms in the air and shouted that they loved Sharif. He spoke into a microphone, but it was broken and no one could hear anything he said. Speech over, Sharif climbed down from the counter and slipped into a bulletproof black Mercedes, courtesy of his good friend, King Abdullah, who had also shipped Sharif back to Pakistan in a Saudi royal plane.

Now, six weeks later, it was January 2008. Bhutto was dead and Sharif was the only living senior politician in Pakistan. He had been banned from running in the upcoming parliamentary elections—likely because Musharraf still hated him so much—but he would be a major factor in those elections. Sharif was trying to appear like a figure of reconciliation, above all the politics. He publicly cried after Bhutto's death, and talked about how she had called him for his fifty-eighth birthday, two days before she was killed. I called everyone I knew to try to get an interview.

"You only get fifteen minutes with Mian Sahib," Sharif's press aide finally told me, referring to Sharif by his honorary title. "Maybe twenty at the most."

I flew into Lahore on a Friday morning, and we drove for an hour toward the town of Raiwind and Sharif's palatial home and palatial grounds. The closer we got, the more Sharif. The place may as well have been called Nawaz Land, given the amusement-park feel and the fact that his name and picture were on everything, from the hospital to giant billboards. Everywhere I looked, Sharif—amiable, slightly pudgy, topped with hair plugs—stared at me like the Cheshire cat. Guards checked me at the gate, searching my bag meticulously. The grounds of Raiwind resembled a cross between a golf course and a zoo, with several football fields of manicured grass and wild animals in cages, leading up to a miniature palace that looked slightly like a wedding cake, with different layers and trim that resembled frosting. The driveway was big enough for a limousine to execute a U-turn. I walked inside and was told to wait. The inside of the house appeared to have been designed by Saudi Arabia—a hodge-podge of crystal chandeliers, silk curtains, gold accents, marble. A verse of the Holy Quran and a carpet with the ninety-nine names of God hung on the walls of Sharif's receiving room, along with photographs of Sharif with King Abdullah and slain former Lebanese prime minister Rafik Hariri. Finally I was summoned.

"Kim," Sharif's media handler said, gesturing toward the ground. "Come."

I hopped up and walked toward the living room, past two raggedy stuffed lions with rose petals near their feet. So maybe Sharif was the lion of Punjab. Inside the room, Sharif stood up, wearing a finely pressed salwar kameez, a navy vest, and a natty scarf. He shook my hand and offered me a seat in an ornate chair. The sitting room was a study in pink, rose, and gold, with golden curlicues on various lighting fixtures and couches, and crystal vases everywhere. Many of the knickknacks were gifts from world leaders. His press aide tapped his watch, looked at me, and raised his eyebrows. I got the message and proceeded with my questions, as fast as I could. But it soon became clear that this would be unlike any interview I had ever done.

"You're the only senior opposition leader left in Pakistan. How are you going to stay safe while campaigning?"

In Pakistan, campaigns were not run through TV, and pressing the flesh was a job requirement. Candidates won over voters by holding rallies of tens and hundreds of thousands of people. Even though Sharif was not personally running, his appearance would help win votes for anyone in his party.

Sharif looked at me, sighed, and shook his head.

"I don't know. It's a good question. What do you think, Kim?"

"I don't know. I'm not the former prime minister of Pakistan. So what will you do?"

"Really, I don't know. What do you think?"

This put me in an awkward position—giving security advice to Nawaz Sharif.

"Well, it's got to be really difficult. You have these elections coming up. You can't just sit here at home."

"What should I do?" he asked. "I can't run a campaign sitting in my house, on the television."

I had to find a way to turn this back on him.

"It's interesting," I said. "You keep asking me questions about what I think. And it seems like you do that a lot—ask other people questions. It seems like you're also willing to change your mind, if circumstances change."

"I do take people's advice," he said. "I believe in consultation."

After twenty minutes, Sharif's aide started twitching. I fired off my questions about Musharraf, the man Sharif had named army chief, only to be overthrown by him.

"I do not actually want to say much about Musharraf. He must step down and allow democracy. He is so impulsive, so erratic."

"Come on. You named this man army chief, then tried to fire him, then he overthrew you and sent you into exile, and now you're back. What do you think about him?"

Sharif nodded, then tried to duck the question.

"Appointing Mr. Musharraf as chief of army staff—that's my biggest mistake."

I stood up. Sharif's aide was already standing.

"I should probably be going," I said. "Thanks very much for your time."

"Yes, Mian Sahib's schedule is very busy," Sharif's handler agreed.

"It's all right," Sharif said. "She can ask a few more questions."

I sat down. I had whipped through most of my important questions, so I recycled them. I asked him whether he was a fundamentalist. Sharif dismissed the idea, largely by pointing to his friendship with the Clintons. I tried to leave again, fearing I was overstaying my welcome. But Sharif said I could ask more questions.

"One more," I said, wary of Sharif's aide. Then I asked the question that was really on my mind.

"Which are you—the lion or the tiger?"

Sharif didn't even blink.

"I am the tiger," he said.

"But why do some people call you the lion?"

"I do not know. I am the tiger."

"But why do you have two stuffed lions?"

"They were a gift. I like them."

Curiosity satisfied, I decided to get out of Pakistan and the madness there while possible. A colleague flew in from India so I could take a week's vacation. Dave, just back from Afghanistan, and I left for a much-deserved holiday, a beach in Thailand. Before moving to Asia, I had never liked beach vacations. I had wanted to visit historic sites, move hotels every day, run all the time. But after the past six months, all I wanted to do was sit catatonic in front of an ocean and read bad thrillers. I didn't want to move from my reclining chair. Even ordering a drink with an umbrella or dipping my toes in the ocean seemed too demanding. I also really didn't want to argue with Dave, even though he was upset that I only had a few days off. We had fought after the emergency was declared—I wasn't being supportive enough. We had fought after he returned from his first trip to Afghanistan, and again after I went to visit Sharif in Lahore, both times because I was not paying enough attention to our relationship. He was probably right.

I hoped that this vacation could fix us—because all we had been doing since meeting was working harder than I could ever remember and fighting more than I ever had. Maybe having time off would stop the arguments, which I still believed were a sign of intensity, of passion. By the time we flew back to Pakistan—after hardly a week of vacation—I was still burned out, unable to think rationally, unable to comprehend that for the first time since moving overseas, I was no longer happy. My joy was gone, my soul was sapped, but I would only realize this much later. At least I had weaned myself off the sleeping pills and my nightmares had stopped. At least the fighting had calmed down. I dug into my reserves. Looked forward to when I could go back to Afghanistan, where things may have been bad but never this bad.

Once home from Thailand, I picked up my Pakistan cell phone from my colleague, who had borrowed it.

"So, you got a few phone calls," she said. "One interesting one."

"Who?"

"Nawaz Sharif," she said.

I had almost forgotten about the story—I had mentioned his hair plugs, twice, and said Sharif's genial personality made him seem more like a house cat than a tiger or lion. Ouch.

"Oh. Him. What did he say?" I asked.

"He wanted to talk to you. I said you were on vacation, and he told me to tell you that you wrote a very nice story, and he liked it."

"Really?"

Well, that was good news, and meant Sharif was remarkably down to earth. Clearly he had a sense of humor. Bhutto had certainly never called after any story I wrote. I soon called Sharif, to see if I could campaign with him.

"You're the most dangerous man in Pakistan, the top living opposition leader," I told him. "I want to see what it's like to be around you."

"Welcome anytime, Kim," he said.

In mid-February, I met Sharif at the government's Frontier House, just outside the judges' enclave, where the country's former top justices were still under house arrest. Eventually, after slipping through the mob, I climbed into Sharif's bulletproof black SUV, surrounded by similar SUVs, and we took off, heading for two speeches outside the capital. We left Islamabad. One of Sharif's security officers somehow sent us down narrow, bumpy dirt roads, where we ended up in traffic jams. Not encouraging.

"That was bad planning," Sharif muttered. He sat in the front passenger seat. I sat behind the driver, next to Sharif's aide.

After various detours, we ended up at the dirt field where Sharif would speak. Thousands of people waited. He was mobbed when he tried to step out of his vehicle, and his bodyguards bounced around like pinballs, trying to get in between well-wishers and their charge. I stood near the dusty stage, but I didn't want to walk out. Despite Bhutto's killing, the security at this event resembled that of a high-school pep rally. The podium didn't even have a bulletproof glass screen, which was supposed to be there. "I don't know where it is," Sharif told me, shrugging. "Sometimes the police give it to me, sometimes they give it to someone else."

Onstage he didn't seem to care about potential attacks, thundering against dictatorship to the crowd. But I did. This country made me feel insecure, much more than Afghanistan.

We drove to the next rally. I looked at my BlackBerry and spotted one very interesting e-mail—a Human Rights Watch report, quoting a taped conversation from November between the country's pro-Musharraf attorney general and an unnamed man. The attorney general had apparently been talking to a reporter, and while on that call, took another call, where he talked about vote rigging. The reporter had recorded the entire conversation. I scanned through the e-mail.

"Nawaz," I said. I had somehow slipped into calling the former prime minister by his first name. "You have to hear this."

I then performed a dramatic reading of the message in full, culminating in the explosive direct quote from the attorney general, recorded the month before Bhutto was killed and just before Sharif flew home:

"Leave Nawaz Sharif . . . I think Nawaz Sharif will not take part in the election . . . If he does take part, he will be in trouble. If Benazir takes part she too will be in trouble . . . They will massively rig to get their own people to win. If you can get a ticket from these guys, take it . . . If Nawaz Sharif does not return himself, then Nawaz Sharif has some advantage. If he comes himself, even if after the elections rather than before . . . Yes . . ."

It was unclear what the other man was saying, but Human Rights

Watch said the attorney general appeared to be advising him to leave Sharif's party and get a ticket from "these guys," the pro-Musharraf party, the massive vote riggers.

Sharif's aide stared at me openmouthed. "Is that true? I can't believe that."

"It's from Human Rights Watch," I said. "There's apparently a tape recording. Pretty amazing."

Sharif just looked at me. "How can you get a text message that long on your telephone?"

"It's an e-mail," I said, slightly shocked that Sharif was unconcerned about what I had just said. "This is a BlackBerry phone. You can get e-mail on it."

"Ah, e-mail," he said. "I must look into this BlackBerry."

Sharif soon whipped out a comb, pulled the rearview mirror toward him, and combed his hair. I watched, fascinated. His hair plugs were in some ways genius—not enough to actually cover his bald spot but enough to make him seem less bald. He had the perfect hair transplant for a Pakistani politician who wanted to look younger while still appearing like a man of the people. But with every pull of the comb, I counted the potential cost—$1,000, $2,000. At the next speech, Sharif spoke in front of a metal podium with a bulletproof glass screen that ended three inches below the top of his head. I wondered if Musharraf was trying to kill him.

The election was three days away. And as much as Sharif seemed to be slightly simple, he was also increasingly popular, largely because of his support of the deposed judges. While Bhutto's widower campaigned on the memory of his dead wife, Sharif campaigned against Musharraf and for justice. Bhutto's party would win the most votes. But I thought Sharif would perform better than anyone suspected.

The day of the election, two journalist friends and I drove to polling stations in Islamabad and neighboring Rawalpindi. Everywhere we heard the same name: Nawaz Sharif. It was rather spooky. At one point, we found a man who had spent the entire night cutting up white blankets, gluing them to his new car, and then painting them with tiger stripes. He finished the project off with black-feather trim.

"What are you going to do if it rains?" I asked the man.

"God willing, it won't," he said.

I snapped a photograph with my BlackBerry. By the end of the day, the results were clear—Musharraf's party had received barely any votes. Secular parties had triumphed over religious ones. Bhutto's party had won the most seats, as predicted. But Sharif's party had won the second-highest amount of votes, a surprise to many Western observers. Through the election, Sharif had exacted revenge on Musharraf. And Bhutto's party needed Sharif to have enough seats to run the country.

After more than eight years of political irrelevance, Sharif was back. I sent him a text message and asked him to call. A few hours later, he did, thrilled with his victory.

"I saw a car today, where a man had glued blankets to it and painted it like a tiger," I told him at one point.

"Really?" he asked.

"Yeah. It was a tiger car."

He paused. "What did you think of the tiger car, Kim? Did you like the tiger car?"

Weird question. I gave an appropriate answer.

"Who doesn't like a tiger car?"

CHAPTER 17
LUCKY STAR

Buried by the bombs and political wrangling of Pakistan, I had not been to Afghanistan for months. Stepping on the plane in Islamabad felt like freedom. Walking off the plane in Kabul felt like going home, even if I was allergic to that home. Outside the airport, Farouq smiled widely when he saw me. I sneezed. If we were alone, we would have hugged—it was March, and we hadn't seen each other in six months. But in public, where all the taxi drivers and assorted men crowded around like paper clips near a magnet, we could only muster a vigorous shaking of hands. Farouq threw my bags into the back of his car. He was doing predictably well. Ever the businessman, Farouq had opened an Internet café and was clearing $1,500 a month, despite the fact that he had banned anyone from looking at pornography. As one of the country's senior fixers, Farouq commanded up to $300 a day, primarily from visiting TV journalists, who blindly paid whatever was asked. But Farouq only earned money when journalists were in town, and he needed everything he could get. His wife was pregnant again.

"Oh man," I said. "She's going to kill you."

Farouq laughed. His wife had wanted to have a small family, and she had wanted to work. But less than four years into their marriage, she was pregnant with her third child.

Regardless, whenever I was in the country, Farouq still charged me only $125 a day to drive and translate, even though it was difficult to drive and organize stories at the same time. He sometimes complained, but halfheartedly, almost like he felt he should complain. Many friends who had watched Farouq and me described us like an old married couple. We had worked together for almost five years. We knew each other's quirks and bickered in shorthand. Farouq raised his voice whenever we disagreed. We always had the same exchange.

"Farouq, why are you upset?" I would ask. "Why are you raising your voice?"

"Kim. I've told you a million times," he would reply, loudly. "I'm not upset. It's just the way I talk."

But now, after I had been gone for so long, we were excited to catch up and report good stories. I had only a week here—I wanted to make it count, even while juggling work and Dave, who had flown into Kabul after a grueling six-week embed that involved hiking all night through the snow.

So Farouq and I drove around the city, something we always did when I had been gone for a while. Kabul was slightly tense. Armed men patrolled the neighborhood of Shir Pur, that den of corruption and various crimes against architecture. Predictably, this was all because of Sabit, my estranged Afghan grandpa and the country's wayward attorney general. Abdul Rashid Dostum, the Uzbek warlord famous for his love of booze and horses, had sent men to beat up a rival and his family members. In a bold attempt at law enforcement, Sabit had ordered police to surround Dostum's mirrored and pillared monstrosity in Shir Pur. Dostum, in turn, ran up to the roof of his house and beat his chest, an Afghan King Kong. The standoff lasted for hours, until finally Sabit was called off. Dostum's armed henchman now lurked on street corners. Sabit hid in his office. This passed for rule of law in Afghanistan—warlords trumped all. Sabit, the great white-bearded hope for the Afghan judicial system, had become the symbol of its failure.

I didn't write about it, didn't feel like kicking Sabit when he was down. No, I wanted something joyful, a happy story, a small good thing in all the gloom.

So Farouq and I made plans to see *Afghan Star*, a reality show modeled on *American Idol* and the most popular show in Afghanistan. This show, like other programming on the country's most popular station, Tolo TV, started by savvy Afghan-Australian siblings, had angered conservative mullahs and established some kind of pop culture for Afghanistan's young people. For the first time, a girl had made it to the final four. And she was a Pashtun from Kandahar, shocking because Kandahar was a conservative stronghold. Many Pashtun women from the south weren't allowed to work, and they definitely weren't allowed to sing, a profession akin to prostitution. I called a friend at the TV station to get two tickets. Then I told Dave.

"I want to go," he said. "Can you get me a ticket?"

"I don't know," I replied.

And I didn't. In truth, I was reluctant to bring him, to report alongside him. I hadn't dated a journalist in years, and I was still leery. When we had reported together on breaking stories in Pakistan, it wasn't necessarily fun. We were interested in different parts of a story. We had sniped at each other while on deadline in a shared hotel room. He had a temper. I was stubborn. While working, we didn't necessarily play well. I was also reluctant to introduce him to Farouq and my life in Afghanistan, which had always been my separate world. Out of everyone, Farouq and his opinion mattered. He had seen me through every relationship overseas. Despite our ups and downs, Farouq was the constant. And although he never passed judgment, any silence spoke volumes. My boyfriends usually ended up with nicknames, none flattering.

So I said I would try to get Dave a ticket, and then I changed the subject. But I didn't try. Even though we had talked about sharing a house in Islamabad, even though I wanted to make us work, I didn't necessarily want to work with him. And I was selfish. This was my story. No one had yet written about the Pashtun female finalist, even though a woman had never performed this well.

The day of the show, I called Dave as Farouq and I drove to the taping. I thought he had forgotten about it. But he fumed.

"You didn't even try to get me a ticket, did you?" he said. "You knew I wanted to go."

"It's difficult," I replied.

"Is it? You don't want me to go."

Farouq could overhear the argument.

"Kim," he whispered. "Tell him to come. We'll get him in."

Realizing my worlds were colliding, I invited Dave. Farouq and I parked outside the Afghan Markopolo Wedding Hall, a phantasm of mirrors and columns, and walked past the crowds of young men waiting outside. We showed our passes to the burly security guards and climbed the stairs. Being here was like attending any celebrity event anywhere, only tinged with the possibility of an insurgent attack. Farouq looked for someone in charge.

"I'm going to schmooze some people," he said, using a word I had taught him.

"Schmooze away."

Farouq easily found the media guy and convinced him to let Dave into the show. That handled, we found seats, saving a seat next to Farouq, so he could translate for both of us. Dave soon showed up, wild-eyed and out of breath.

"I was just assaulted," he said. "A bodyguard just slammed me in the chest. He took the wind out of me. He thought I was a Pashtun."

I considered that objectively. With his coloring and beard, Dave did resemble a Pashtun. A beefy Afghan who had clearly been pumping iron in one of the many bodybuilding gyms of Kabul then walked up to him.

"I'm sorry again, sir."

Dave started yelling at him. "You can't treat people like that. I'm a journalist."

Farouq looked at me, his eyebrows raised. Dave had a point. But the security guard had apologized, several times. Now Dave was shaming him in public, which contradicted any Afghan code imaginable. His anger was spilling over from me to the world. What had he seen on his embeds? I didn't know, because he didn't want to worry me, but I imagined bombs, gunfights, the kind of violence that I had somehow avoided. Dave had started to change. Always passionate and intense, he now seemed just angry.

Finally he sat down, still upset, barely speaking to me because of the ticket fiasco. This was not a fun date. Poor Farouq was stuck in the middle.

But we were all soon distracted. White lights flashed, and the loudspeakers pumped music. The host ran onstage, announced "In the name of God—hello," and called out the four singers. They walked out and stood nervously, waiting to hear who lost in the previous week's voting. Lima Sahar was the only woman and the only Pashtun.

"Who is the person who should stay with us?" the host asked the audience, who booed Lima. Some of the three hundred or so audience members felt that Lima had made it this far in the competition not because of her talent but because of a massive Pashtun voting bloc. And they were upset for another reason.

"Why are they booing her?" I asked Farouq.

"She's a woman," he whispered. "They aren't used to it."

I felt bad for her. Lima was kept home during the Taliban years, and although she was eighteen, she was only in the eighth grade. She could speak little Dari, the main language in Afghanistan. When Lima was in Kandahar, she wore a blue burqa whenever she left the house. But onstage she wore blue glitter in her hair, a matching headscarf, a long electric-blue tunic with gold-sequin flowers, matching pants, fake eyelashes, and the makeup of a televangelist's wife. She gripped her elbows in front of her chest like a life preserver and stared straight ahead, looking past the boos of the audience.

The host paused, dramatically delaying the judges' decision. "I can tell you this time, something strange has happened."

Something strange had indeed happened—the most popular singer had been knocked off. And Lima had made it to the final round of three.

When Lima sang, I could see why some people questioned her ability. She seemed more like a karaoke performer, perhaps even a not-so-good karaoke performer. She danced almost as an after-thought, with the rhythm of Whitney Houston and the enthusiasm of lumber. Her voice was sometimes off-key. Yet she was also slightly flirty, a bit subversive. She sang one song with almost a sneer, changing the words of a traditional Pashto song from a male perspective to a female one. In Afghanistan, that passed for rebellion.

"If I blacken my eyes with eyeliner, it will kill you," she sang, with a slight hip sway. "Especially if I wear these bangles from Kandahar."

My story was scheduled for the front page the next Thursday, the same day that Lima happened to be voted off the show. But Dave's ran first, days earlier, meaning that I had helped him scoop me. That was hardly the only problem. Unknown to anyone at the *Tribune*, a reporter at our sister newspaper, the *Los Angeles Times*, also owned by the Tribune Company, had written a story weeks earlier about *Afghan Star* that had not yet run in the newspaper. It was a very different story, and didn't even mention Sahar, but it was about the same TV show. Then, in a decision that would haunt me for months, the *Los Angeles Times* decided to run its story about *Afghan Star* on the same day as mine.

Our newspaper company had just been bought by the eccentric billionaire Sam Zell, an alleged maverick who liked wearing jeans and swearing. The deal was complicated and somehow involved cashing in all the stock owned by employees, but since it had gone through in the weeks between the emergency and Bhutto's death, I paid little attention. Zell, who resembled a cross between a Keebler elf and a garden gnome, was not a newspaperman. He was a compul-sive bargain hunter, the self-proclaimed "grave dancer," making billions largely by buying troubled companies, somehow fixing them, and then selling them. So far he had tried to ingratiate himself with employees by removing the barriers to porn on the Internet, under the theory, I guess, that newspapers shouldn't have any censorship and because everyone loves porn, even at work. After appearing at a *Los Angeles Times* plant in Orange County in February, he was quoted on his philosophy: "Everyone likes pussy. It's un-American not to like pussy."

In theory, he should have loved my story about *Afghan Star*. But soon after the competing stories appeared on March 13, they came to Zell's attention. He allegedly got angry and used some four-letter words. I could understand his point—two of his newspapers had expended resources on the same feature story in Afghanistan, hardly a smart investment. So as Zell toured around his newspapers in the coming weeks, he would complain about *Afghan Star*. And by inference, me.

But I wouldn't know about the fallout for months. Oblivious and trapped in a hotel room with a man who felt neglected, I wrote other stories. I tried to spend time with Dave, but I also ate dinners with various sources, a time commitment that annoyed Dave more than my ticket stunt. Then my friend Sean, the British adrenaline junkie, called. I hadn't seen him since the barbecue the previous summer at the Fun House, where the Afghan Elvis had peddled cocaine smuggled in toothpaste tubes.

"Meet me for dinner," he said. "I need to talk to you about something. It's very sensitive."

I wanted to say yes. I knew I couldn't.

"I can't," I said. "Lunch?"

I didn't tell Sean I had a man in my hotel room because I didn't want to mix the two men. Sean would be fine, but Dave would be jealous. Sean invited me to the Gandamack. As soon as the waiter took our order of chicken salads, Sean looked from side to side and leaned in closer.

"So, I have to ask you about something," he started, vaguely.

"Yes?"

"I have an opportunity. An invitation to go meet someone. Someone important. But it could be difficult. I'm wondering if you think I should go."

"Tango?" I said. By now, I slipped easily into his conspiracy lingo.

"Not Tango. Someone senior. I can't tell you."

"Hekmatyar?" I said, naming the renegade leader of Hezb-i-Islami, the militant group in the east.

"No. Let me finish. I have been invited to meet a senior commander who's very important. But the meeting would be over the border, in the tribal areas of Pakistan. What do you think?"

I didn't have to think long. "I think you're a fucking idiot and you're going to get kidnapped."

"They promised me security," Sean said.

"I think you're a fucking idiot and you're going to get kidnapped," I repeated.

"Keep your voice down," he said. "You know, I'm a little worried. I was supposed to meet the contact a few days ago, but Sami didn't have everything together and it felt weird, so we canceled. And our contact said, 'No problem, we can reschedule.' That seemed strange. Normally you have to push and push to get these guys to talk to you."

I sighed. Sean knew everything I was telling him. His translator, Sami, knew everything. They knew this was a bad idea, but Sean still wanted his fix.

"Tango in Pakistan is not like Tango in Afghanistan," I said, knowing that Sean knew this. "The ISI's involved. You can't just walk into the tribal areas without them knowing. You're probably in more danger from the ISI than from the militants."

The Inter-Services Intelligence Directorate, Pakistan's conflicted top spy agency, was known for some members supporting insurgents.

"Who are you seeing?" I asked again.

"Someone important."

"Haqqani?" I asked.

Militant commander Jalaluddin Haqqani, an old Pakistani pal of the CIA and ISI, had helped fight the Soviets in Afghanistan in the 1980s and supported the Taliban while they were in power. Three main groups based in Pakistan now fought against foreign troops and the Afghan government, even though the groups were usually just lumped together and called the Taliban. One group was Mullah Omar's Taliban, suspected to be based in the Pakistan city of Quetta, in western Baluchistan Province. Another was Hezb-i-Islami. The third group was the one formed by Haqqani in the North Waziristan tribal agency and now run mostly by his son Sirajuddin. Haqqani's group was generally regarded as the most ruthless, sophisticated, and evil of all the militant factions, responsible for a spectacular attack two months earlier at the Serena Hotel in Kabul.

Sean smiled slightly. "I can't say. Maybe."

"You're a fucking idiot and you're going to get kidnapped. Why would you go meet him? Nobody in the West even knows who he is. He's not worth it."

"I can't say exactly what I'm doing."

I shook my head and looked at him. I knew what he would decide.

"When would you be back?"

"Easter. I told my boys I would be back home in time for Easter."

"I still think it's a bad idea," I said. "But knowing you, everything will work out great."

Sean laughed. "I'll let you know. But keep it quiet. I don't want anyone else to know about it."

So I left Sean and the Gandamack, and a few days later, I left Afghanistan. Sean also asked several mutual friends their opinions of his planned trip—as with everything else, Sean couldn't keep his mouth shut. But I would only find this out later because Sean had told them, like me, to stay quiet. We all stayed·quiet, until we couldn't anymore. Only then would I learn that everyone told Sean the same thing: that the trip was too risky, and that he was acting like an idiot.

CHAPTER 18

SUSPICIOUS MINDS

My new house in Pakistan was the nicest I had seen in Islamabad, nicer than anywhere I had ever lived during my resolutely middle-class life. Brick with white trim, it was an over-the-top knockoff of a colonial mansion, with a ridiculous five bedrooms, an even more ridiculous five bathrooms, a giant two-story living room with floor-to-ceiling windows, a view of the Margalla Hills, a roof deck, bunny planters, and a landlord who was a colonel. I figured I deserved it. To save the company money, for almost a year I had either slept at friends' houses in Islamabad or rented a cheap room, while the company continued to pay for the bulk of my apartment in India. But after giving up my Delhi apartment the previous summer, my expenses had dropped to a dangerously low level. I didn't want my increasingly cheap company to get used to it. I also wanted my own space again, and since Dave had no place to live in Islamabad anymore, as he was spending most of his time in Afghanistan, getting a house together made sense.

At least, that's what I told myself. Moving in after only a few months of dating seemed crazy, especially considering his anger issues and my lack-of-support problems, but, hey, this was a crazy lifestyle. We were both mature. Somehow we could make it work. And we needed it, needed the anchor. The Italian restaurant where we had always gone for dates had just been blown up, the night after Tammy, Dave, several other friends, and I ate dinner there. Dave bought us a pool table. I bought us a wooden bar and stools. All the foreigners were creating their own havens, to stay out of the Pakistani madness. Our mantra had become like my misanthropic father's: Outside bad, inside good.

My trusty driver Samad cleaned up the house, picked out new lighting fixtures, and supervised the painting of the walls, which the previous German tenants had desecrated with pink-and-rust triangles. He told me he wanted to be the gardener.

"I love this work, Kim."

So I made him the gardener. I even let Samad move into the tiny maid's room, with its own entrance, so he had a place to stay during the day and sleep if I made him work late. I gave him a piece of carpet, a DVD player, a spare TV. He brought in a mattress. I watched how Samad worked, how he was so meticulous, so trustworthy for a kid of twenty-two. I wanted to find a way to help him.

Samad did not own his own car. He took whatever car his company handed him—which meant that en route to Peshawar one morning, after making various clanking sounds, our car broke down. The engine appeared to be held together by duct tape and staples. I spent the next ninety minutes berating Samad for not checking the car, an experience that made me feel slightly dirty, like kicking a puppy. Samad needed a new car, one of his own. He needed it for our safety. So we cobbled together loans, from me and others and Samad's helpful boss, to get him a sleek black 2008 Toyota Corolla. He started crying when he showed up at my house with it. He washed it about thirty times a day and cringed whenever I climbed inside holding a large cup of coffee.

So my new life was set: new house, new car, new live-in if long-distance boyfriend, and inevitably, new intrigue.

Samad soon drove me to a lunch date with a political officer at the Afghan embassy. I had known him for years, ever since he had run for parliamentary elections in Afghanistan in 2005 under the randomly drawn symbol of One Camel. (Unfortunately, his position on the ballot was right next to a man running as Three Camels, which led to much confusion and One Camel's general depression.) One Camel had actually run a campaign in Afghanistan, and he had not been connected to any warlord, which meant his candidacy was doomed. So he landed here, at the Afghan embassy in Islamabad, where he had helped me get visas on short notice. Now One Camel wanted to go to lunch. In repayment for all his help, I said I'd take him and his female translator to the buffet at the Serena Hotel, the fanciest hotel in Islamabad. We ordered fresh orange juice, which tasted slightly rancid, and then picked up plates filled with various lukewarm curries. One Camel told me vague generalities about drugs and corruption across the border. He leaned forward and whispered, as did his translator. At the end of our lunch, we stood up to leave. He muttered something; I asked the translator what he said.

"ISI," she said with a shrug.

"My spies," One Camel said, smirking and nodding at three men sporting mustaches and wearing crisp cream-colored salwar kameezes at a table near the entrance to the restaurant.

"What do you mean?" I said.

"My spies. They follow me."

I started laughing. "Seriously?"

"I go, they go."

Sure enough, as soon as we walked out of the grand lobby of the Serena, the men stood up and walked out. Of course the ISI, Pakistan's premier intelligence agency, would want to pay attention to an Afghan political officer, just like it paid attention to Indian diplomats and various journalists. The ISI was not like the CIA—not exactly. It expended most of its resources inside Pakistan, and its operatives were really, really obvious and occasionally too close with Islamic militants like the Taliban.

"Bye," I told One Camel. "Good luck with your spies."

Ever watchful for me, Samad pulled up in his fancy new car. I told him to stop at the Marriott Hotel so I could pick up my dry cleaning. I ran inside, handed over a fistful of rupees, grabbed my freshly cleaned Islamic gear, and walked outside. A man in a cream-colored salwar kameez stood outside Samad's door, showing him something, bending over to talk to him. I hustled across the street. Samad said something. The man looked up, saw me, and walked away quickly.

"Who was that?" I asked.

"ISI."

"Seriously?"

"Problem, Kim. Man come up, say ISI, hand me ISI card. He say, 'Who is boss?' "

"What did you say?"

"You know. I say, 'I'm a small boy, no read, no understand, I don't know she. My boss send to Serena to pick she up, I pick up. I don't know she.' "

"Good work."

That was always Samad's act, whenever the ISI asked about me. At least, that's what Samad said he told the ISI. How could I know for sure? My gut trusted Samad, but I didn't really understand the ins and outs, all the levels to this Pakistan fun house. Tammy said Samad seemed trustworthy, but given all the double games being played here, given how many times my gut had been wrong, how many times I had been played, how many times other friends had been played, I had no idea if Samad was telling the truth. Part of the reason I had hired Samad in the first place was that he didn't work at the Serena or the Marriott—both of which were known for hiring staff members who made extra money by informing to the ISI. He also came recommended by a Pakistani journalist friend—but again, some Pakistani journalists played for the ISI team. The ISI was everywhere, in newspapers, TV, shopping malls, hotels, and most definitely lurking inside our cell phones.

A few months earlier I had tried to report on a suicide attack at an ISI office in Rawalpindi. But whenever we tried to talk to anyone, someone else showed up, telling us to leave, shoving us back, refusing to show any identification. The busybodies pulled people away mid-interview and threatened to arrest them—and us. When we left Rawalpindi, a car of spooks tailed us to Islamabad, until we made a few quick turns.

So on this afternoon, I looked at Samad.

"Let's see if they follow us."

We pulled out of the parking lot and drove in the direction of my house. A white car followed. Samad turned right. The car followed. Samad turned left. The car followed. These guys were hardly sophisticated. Being followed by the ISI in Pakistan felt like being chased by the Keystone Cops, like the *Mad* magazine cartoon *Spy vs. Spy*. I would like to say the song from *Mission Impossible* played in my head, but it was more like "Mahna Mahna" from *The Muppet Show*. It certainly didn't feel serious. After one too many turns, I decided I had enough.

"Pull over," I told Samad.

We stopped on the side of the road. The white car had no choice but to drive slowly past, the two men inside looking out the window at us. Clever. Samad waited and then dropped me at home.

The next morning he showed up, looking mopey. When I opened the door, he stood in his button-up shirt tucked into his hiked-up jeans, staring at the ground like he wished it would open up and swallow him.

"Problem, Kim."

"What happened?"

"Last night, the ISI come to my home. Because of car, they know my home. They show up, ask about boss. They say they arrest me if I don't tell them."

"So you did, right?"

"So sorry, my sister, I did."

"It's OK, it's fine. Don't worry about it."

It's not like it mattered that much—I wasn't doing anything wrong. Samad seemed like he felt bad. He seemed like he really considered me his sister. But how could I know for sure? The next Sunday, I needed him to drive me to a meeting. I called, once, twice, three times. But Samad didn't pick up the phone. I started to panic. Could he have run away with the car, after I loaned him money? Could he betray me? I worried that I was being played. That night, Samad called.

"So sorry, Kim, I go to cousin brother's home," he said. "I forget phone."

I soon flew to Afghanistan for some stories, putting the Pakistan spy intrigue and Samad aside for a while.

But after a few days, another intrigue knocked at the back of my mind. I wondered where Sean was. He was supposed to be back in London by Easter—it was May, long past Easter. I hadn't heard from Sean in weeks. Farouq hadn't heard from Sami. And no one had seen Sean since the week after I spoke to him—since he told me about his wacky plan to meet a top insurgent in the tribal areas of Pakistan.

"Oh, you know how Sean is. Disappears for weeks at a time," a friend said. "Don't worry."

"Yeah. I don't know, I'm worried."

I called Tom, the British journalist and my former housemate at the Fun House.

"He's probably fine," Tom said. "But I haven't heard from him. He was supposed to check in ten days ago."

"Ten days ago?"

"I know. I'm going to Jalalabad tomorrow to try to talk to him and track down Sami's family. I'm also in touch with his driver in Pakistan. But you know how he is, Kim. He's probably fine."

We hung up. The next night, I had a nightmare that Sean was kidnapped. I woke up convinced that he would be killed. I called Tom.

"It doesn't look good," said Tom, who had driven to the eastern city of Jalalabad near the Pakistan border with his fixer, Tahir, who besides Sami was the only Afghan fixer we knew with serious Taliban contacts. "The driver said he'd meet us. But then he turned off his old phone numbers. Tahir had to make a lot of phone calls but finally got a new number for the driver. He said he'd come up to Jalalabad from Peshawar to meet us. But then he switched off his phone."

"That doesn't sound good," I said.

"No. Tahir is still trying. I'll let you know."

Days passed. I worked on a story about pornography and soap operas invading Kabul—something easy and light that I could focus on, although Farouq and I shared the uncomfortable task of looking at various DVDs we had bought, making sure they were porn and trying to see if Afghans were involved. Still, almost seven years since this notion of democracy was thrust into Afghanistan, many Afghans, especially the young ones, saw it as a veneer for "anything goes," for sex, drugs, and booze, and music about sex, drugs, and booze. Freedom was just another word for losing yourself in excess. I tried to do stories on this culture clash whenever I could, seeing it as a way to write about how Afghans lived, not just how they died.

"This is really, really embarrassing," Farouq said, popping a porn DVD out of my computer. "People are really sick."

"I am aware," I said, popping one that involved a watermelon into my DVD player.

Tom became more and more cryptic. Then, finally, he called.

"I wanted you to hear this from me," he said. "But Sean has been kidnapped."

I felt ill. As far as Tom had been able to figure out, Sean and Sami had been taken hostage in late March, immediately after crossing into Pakistan to meet their contact. Brilliant, as Sean would say.

Dave flew to Kabul on his way to another embed with NATO troops. He was unsympathetic to my fears about Sean, blaming him for being an idiot. As usual, Dave and I fought late at night, him yelling at me for some perceived slight. I curled up, facing the wall. He apologized, saying that he was under stress. But I stared at the paint. It was nothing I wanted to deal with at that moment, but I knew I would eventually have to face the truth. This would never be that fairy tale I thought I wanted, the dream of the overseas life, the family, the full-meal deal. I just couldn't face it now. I didn't want to be alone in Pakistan. With everything happening, I didn't want to be alone at all.

I flew back to Islamabad for a few days before leaving on a trip to the States, where I planned to have minor surgery that would hopefully fix all my sinus and allergy problems. Sean was kidnapped, Dave was a war junkie, and, on nowhere the same level, I was facing a deviated-septum repair and the removal of a blueberry-sized polyp from my right nostril. I was in no mood for any more stress. I walked upstairs to the freezer, where I kept the booze. Procuring alcohol in Islamabad involved a bootlegger, a friend, or cumbersome red tape that meant you basically had to declare yourself a Christian alcoholic. I chose the friend option—one had earlier sold me about a dozen bottles, including syrupy concoctions like banana liqueur and Midori, a sweet, green, disgusting melon-flavored drink made from Japanese honeydews. Only fifteen-year-old girls would drink it. But in an Islamic country, I took whatever was offered, under the theory that at some point, at some time, life might become as desperate as me sitting beneath the pool table, swigging banana liqueur, bombs falling outside.

When I looked in my freezer, I noticed the gooey liquor bottles were missing. Dave would never drink those. The next morning, I asked the housekeeper. He immediately blamed Samad—almost predictable, as the two hated each other. Samad was a Punjabi, and as the driver, should have been relegated to the outside. The housekeeper was an Afghan-born Pashtun.

"Samad's been sleeping in the main house," the housekeeper volunteered.

"What?"

"Yes," he said. His eyes grew large. "Inside, on the floor, I found him one day."

I grabbed my office manager, hired three months before.

"Has Samad been sleeping here?"

"Well . . . I don't know about every night, but I know one morning when you were gone, I came inside and he was sleeping on the floor of the office," she said.

"He brings girls here," the housekeeper said. "He has parties. He plays with the balls upstairs."

He must have meant the pool table.

"Is that true?" I asked the office manager. "He's playing with the balls upstairs?"

I envisioned Samad having sex on the pool table. The office manager shrugged. "I don't know," she said. "I've seen him with a girl out near his room in the back."

"What? Who? Why didn't anyone tell me? Girls?"

The housekeeper shrugged. He appeared to be settling into his story. "You don't want to hear anything bad about Samad. He was also having girls in your house. Maybe in your bed."

I called Samad. "Where are you?"

"Five minutes, boss."

He showed up in twenty. I practically dragged him inside. He denied everything—the booze, the girls. He said he had slept once on the floor of my office because he was worried about security.

I didn't believe Samad, but I kind of shared the blame. He was only twenty-two, a poor kid who lived in a one-bedroom apartment with his mother, sister, and various other relatives. I had handed him the keys to a five-bedroom house that he knew would be empty. I had helped him buy a car. I had given him my bank card and my bank code—although I would later figure out that he had never taken any money. I had handed him temptation. What did I think was going to happen?

"Give me the house keys," I said.

Samad looked at me, eyes brimming with tears, chin quivering. He handed me the keys.

"We're hiring guards, so you don't have to worry about the house. We need to get locks for the alcohol. You're not allowed to bring women here. You're not allowed to bring friends here. You're not allowed to come inside anymore. You're going to have to earn back my trust."

Samad sulked as he drove me to an interview. I snapped at him, suspicious that he had been stealing money from me.

"You probably work for the ISI," I said.

"No, Kim," he said. "You are my sister. No ISI. I don't do anything."

"I don't believe you."

That silenced him. He stared straight ahead and drove. For days, we barely talked. Eventually Samad drove me to the airport, and I flew back to the States, where things would be even worse.

CHAPTER 19
REBEL, REBEL

Something needed to give—my nose or my lifestyle. For my entire life, I had suffered from allergies, asthma, sinus infections, bronchitis. But in Asia, those illnesses had become my usual state. I was allergic to mold, pollen, grass, anything green, anything with four legs, but primarily I was allergic to dust, and in every country I visited, the dust was an unwelcome companion. I was always sick. Even though Farouq was a doctor, there wasn't much he could do. Whenever I arrived at the airport in Kabul, the air immediately assaulted me. It supposedly had a very high percentage of fecal matter; the dust was called "fecal dust," the air, "fecal air." About eight times a year, a sinus infection knocked me out, and Farouq brought me antibiotics, a large IV bag of sterile saline water to shoot up my nose, nasal sprays with foreign lettering, and decongestant pills. Nothing really helped.

I opted for surgery in Portland, Oregon, so my father could take care of me. The surgery was actually very simple, and I had soon healed enough to travel. I couldn't fly, so I rented a car to drive to Chicago. This would give me a chance to visit my relatives and evaluate my relationship with both Dave and the United States. I planned to think about this, and not at all about Sean and what might be happening to him.

Along the road, I saw my brother in Seattle, who was soon moving to London, making my parents wonder just what they had done wrong; my grandmother in Montana, who took me to a funeral and introduced me as a Pakistani; and a police officer in South Dakota, who made me sit in his police car with his police dog while he wrote me a warning ticket for speeding. Finally I pulled into Chicago. This was my so-called "home leave." Every two years, the *Tribune* paid for its foreign correspondents to come back for a week, to make sure we didn't go native while abroad. I was so far gone, even walking into the newspaper building seemed like entering another time zone.

But my newspaper was now a foreign country. I had always loved the Tribune Tower, a megalomaniacal Gothic temple to the industry. Pieces of landmarks from around the world had been embedded in its outside walls, from the pyramids of Egypt to a remnant from the World Trade Center. A piece of the moon even sat in a special window. For a journalist, entering this building had always meant something. Famous quotes about freedom of speech were carved into the walls of the lobby. From the time I first walked in here as a college student, I had felt awed by these constant reminders that journalism mattered. Now I had a hard time convincing the guards that I actually worked here.

"Kim Barker," I said, repeatedly.

"You're not in the system," the guard said, staring at a computer screen of employees.

I leaned over the counter and looked at the screen. "Not Baker. Barker."

He still looked at me suspiciously.

"You need to call someone."

No one answered on the foreign desk, but luckily a secretary remembered me so I was allowed to walk inside, past the display cases that in the past blandly advertised the Tribune Company's various services. Now the four cases blasted a different message— change. One window even featured a picture of Bob Dylan, and the lyrics from "The Times They Are a-Changin.'"

They were. Advertising and circulation were down, panic was up. I walked a few feet forward and glanced in front of me, toward the elevators that led to the newsroom. And there I saw something horrific, something that would give me nightmares, something that told me life would never, ever be the same again. The quotes on the walls were the same, from writers such as Flannery O'Connor and Albert Camus. But right in front of the elevators sat a statue. A giant hideous multicolored statue of a fat businessman in a red-and-black-striped tie with six legs entitled *Bureaucratic Shuffle*. I gave it a wide berth, but I couldn't help but stare.

"What the hell?" I asked myself, out loud.

I pushed the button for the fourth floor. Walking into the newsroom now felt like walking into the newsroom during Christmas—it was depressing, and most of the desks were empty. Only it was June, and many desks were empty because of layoffs and buyouts. Friends told me to keep my head down. For years, like everyone else, I had suffered through cost-cutting measures, grounded for a month or two at a time, forced to stay put in New Delhi or Islamabad and keep my spending small. I would stay with friends or in the cheapest hotels I could find. I had refused to give Farouq a raise—something that had started to grate on him. Even moving to Pakistan had saved the company money compared to the cost of India. My expenses the month before in Afghanistan had run about $125 a day, as I charged the newspaper only for Farouq and paid for everything else myself. During the Afghan presidential election in 2004, I had spent an average of $285 a day.

My scrimping was nothing compared with the devastation here. A photographer told me she wasn't allowed to travel to Cairo for a great story. She meant the Cairo in Illinois. A top editor—the first man who sent me overseas, who had written my name on the back of the used envelope—asked me to lunch.

"Do I need a backup plan?" I asked him.

"It never hurts to have a plan B," he said, carefully.

The editor of the paper had time to meet with me, and not the usual fifteen minutes. Instead, she had an hour, and seemed unusually calm for a woman who had spent the past months fending off requests that she cut more money. I was suspicious about why. The rumors stacked up—that the foreign desks of the *Los Angeles Times* and the *Chicago Tribune* would be combined, or that we would all be fired and the *Tribune* would buy foreign coverage elsewhere. I begged another top editor to let me meet Sam Zell. But I was told no—no one could meet with Sam, even though his e-mail address started out "talktosam."

The foreign desk tried to prove its relevance. Because our new owner and top management did not fully understand that a dateline of "Kabul, Afghanistan" meant the reporter actually was in Kabul, company newspapers had started being much more explicit about their datelines and correspondents. As part of our new self-promoting mission, all *Tribune* foreign correspondents were asked to give travel tips to readers—our best of the world, the hidden delights that tourists should enjoy. Other correspondents wrote about cities and regions people might actually visit. I sat in Chicago and wrote about Islamabad, a town with practically no social life except for what we invented. This was the newspaper equivalent of a burlesque performance. "Plus, most of the other places I once took guests have closed because of security fears or nearby suicide blasts," I wrote, explaining why I took visitors to the Serena Hotel. Guests? I had never had guests in Pakistan. Friends and family members were more likely to vacation in prison.

My immediate boss and I decided to go to a Chicago Cubs baseball game, another exercise in futility. Before we left, I heard him pick up the phone.

"Yes. Yes, well, she's actually right here."

He talked some more before punching the hold button.

"Kim. The caller says he's from the Chicago Police Department, and that you've been a victim of identity theft."

"What?"

"That's what he says. Don't tell him anything. You need to figure out if he's really a cop."

I picked up the phone.

"Is this Kimberly Barker?" the alleged police officer asked.

"Yes."

He identified himself as a cop.

"Kimberly Barker, you have been a victim of identity theft," he then said, in a game-show voice that just as easily could have told me I won a million dollars.

"What?" I said.

He explained to me that a woman had been arrested with a fake Indiana driver's license with my name, and with real credit cards and a bank card with my name.

I opened my purse. My wallet was gone. And I didn't know where I had lost it because I had been carrying my driver's license, my current bank card, and the only credit card I used separately. Whoever stole my wallet pocketed no money. The credit cards were all useless, either expired or never activated, and the bank card was old. Yes, I had done a very poor job keeping current plastic.

"Yeah, that's me." I sighed. "But what makes this identity theft? It sounds like regular theft."

"The fake license."

My identity on the run, I agreed to drive to the police station on Chicago's South Side and file a report. It was kind of embarrassing. I had covered wars and tragedies overseas, but I had never been robbed. With the ever-ballooning recession, the United States had turned into its own kind of war zone, an economic one.

At the station the detectives took me upstairs and sat me at a long table spread with papers. They specialized in identity theft. I asked them what had happened. The day before, police had responded to a report of an illegal weapon in a nearby park and questioned people there. This woman had handed over a fake Illinois driver's license with a fake name but her correct address. The cops then searched the master criminal, pulling up more fake ID cards, and then a fake ID with my name and an assortment of my plastic. She was clearly an idiotic identity thief, arrested for fraud or theft at least eighteen times. After catching her, the police struggled to find me. That was considerably tougher. Some of the credit-card companies had no way to track me. The police called my working credit-card company and my bank, but the number listed for me was an old one.

"We were starting to think you didn't exist," the lead detective said.

"I can understand that," I replied.

But my bank and the police kept trying, eventually waking up my father at 5:30 AM, who instead of telling the police that I was in Chicago and giving them my cell-phone number, said he didn't know what country I was in but I was definitely a foreign correspondent for the *Chicago Tribune*. And that's how they found me, my bank and the Chicago police working together.

"That's kind of impressive," I said. "Fast."

The police asked me questions. From what I could tell, my wallet was missing for at most twenty hours before the cops recovered my identification.

"So . . . can I talk to her?" I asked.

"No you can't talk to her," the lead detective said.

We talked more. They asked about my job. I pumped up the macho.

"Yeah, I talk to the Taliban," I said. "I've hung out with them before."

After spending almost an hour at the station, I asked my question again.

"So can I talk to her? Come on."

The detectives looked at each other, shrugged.

"Bring her out of lockup," the lead detective said. "Get the room ready."

I had watched a lot of TV cop shows overseas while on embeds, while flying from one country to another. I figured I could interrogate a perp. The police escorted me into a tiny white room, where my identity thief sat, handcuffed to the wall. She was a squat African American woman squeezed into a white tank top and black shorts. In a way, we looked similar—I wore a long-sleeved white blouse and black pants. She was visibly confused, with a wrinkled forehead and question-mark eyes. This was not protocol. I thought about how I would proceed. Macho. Over the top. Bad cop. Out of control.

"So I spend years overseas, dealing with assholes like the Taliban, risking my life, then I come home and an asshole like you steals my identity. How did you get my credit cards?"

She looked at me, mumbled that she didn't know anything.

"Oh, you know. You know, bitch."

Here, I was channeling a multitude of TV cop shows.

"Tell me. I can go easy on you, or I can go hard. It's up to me how this case is prosecuted. If you cooperate, I'll go easy. If you don't, you'll wish you never were born."

"Yeah," interjected one of the officers, who had adopted the role of good cop. "Help yourself."

Eventually, I was able to get the name of the man who had allegedly given her my stolen cards, and the time of day she had allegedly got them. Not much, and no idea if it was true, but the experience was good training for a new career.

I walked out of the room with the two cops. We all started laughing. The lead detective was congratulatory.

"Man, you're good," he said. "You got more out of her in fifteen minutes than we did in six hours."

I had still not dropped my fake-cop persona.

"Well, you know—I kind of do this for a living. We're all on the same side."

Where was I getting this? I left the cop station in time to see the Cubs lose. My thief would eventually be sentenced in a plea bargain, to about thirty minutes in jail.

But no matter. I soon heard my best news in months, the news I had been waiting for. Sean and Sami had been released after three months in captivity. Sean was spirited out of Pakistan to London, and Sami had crossed back to Afghanistan. After a flurry of e-mails with friends, I managed to get Sean's new phone number in London—he was trying to lay low. While driving to Springfield to meet people from the Illinois National Guard, about to deploy to Afghanistan, I called Sean and left a message. He called back almost immediately. He sounded manic, jumping from subject to subject like a fly in a roomful of candy, tasting each one briefly before moving to the next.

"Hey, do you remember the last conversation we had?" he asked.

"You mean the one when I told you that you were a fucking idiot and were gonna get kidnapped?" I asked. "Yeah, I remember."

"I kept thinking about that."

But most of our conversation was one-sided, just a monologue from Sean, a run-on sentence.

"I lost some teeth," he said.

"Uh-huh," I said.

"At one point, I was inside one safe house. I heard BBC on a radio outside, and they were doing a story on Taliban training camps in Pakistan, and Pakistani officials were denying any training camps, but I couldn't hear the story that well because of all the gunfire from the Taliban training camp outside my door."

"Uh-huh," I said.

"Sami almost lost it, at one point he was convinced we were going to be killed, and he just didn't want to translate anymore, and without him, I had no way to communicate, so I had to tell him to pull it together."

"Uh-huh," I said.

Altogether, between driving to Springfield and back to Chicago, through various phone calls, I talked to Sean for almost four hours. Or I listened to Sean. Sami and Sean had been kidnapped almost as soon as they met their crucial contact, although they didn't realize it at first. They had been moved several times—their captors would torture them, by doing things like brandishing guns, even pretending to shoot them in the head with an unloaded weapon. Sean didn't know if he would ever be released. What got him through, he said, was thinking about his two sons, about what that would do to them, and about getting home. He felt guilt so heavy it threatened to smother him. He rarely felt hope.

It was unclear who originally took Sean—possibly criminals—but he was eventually traded up to members of the Haqqani network, the worst bad guys in Pakistan. Press accounts said his TV station had paid a total of $300,000 to free Sean and Sami. Sean didn't want to talk about money. That also made him feel guilty—any money would go to nothing good and would make all of us targets. I said I'd see him soon in London.

My nose felt brand new, and it was time to leave. After the long break, I knew that I wanted to keep my job, wanted to stay overseas. Four years into this gig, my whole identity was wrapped up in it. If I wasn't a foreign correspondent, then who was I? But after almost two weeks in Chicago, hearing the various plans to save the newspaper, I had become a pessimist. Something had to give. With few ads, dropping subscriptions, and no other business model, the newspaper seemed like it was imploding. I worried that I would have to move back to Chicago, find a new job, or make Dave get an actual job, if we could even make us work. Nothing else seemed likely. I calculated the odds. Chicago or Dave getting a job seemed like the most realistic bets. I talked to Dave. He really didn't want to get an actual job yet.

"But I'm pretty sure they're going to get rid of the foreign staff," I said. "We can't both freelance. So I may have to move back to Chicago. We may have to move."

"I really hope that doesn't happen," he said. "I'd miss you."

"Wouldn't you come with me? You can work there."

"I don't want to live in Chicago. I don't want to run into all your ex-boyfriends all the time."

"All my ex-boyfriends? There's maybe one."

"I don't want to just be a trophy on your arm there, Kim."

"A trophy? You're hardly a trophy."

I thought about what he was saying.

"What about a compromise, D.C. or New York?"

"I don't want to live in the U.S. I have no interest."

All my doubts clicked into place. Freedom Fries and all, this was still my country. I didn't want to move back to the States yet, but I didn't want to rule out the possibility of ever living here again. I had reverted to my fantasy of normalcy, children, the things I was supposed to want, rather than facing the fact that this relationship was doomed. The fights had just gotten worse; objects had been thrown. I would much rather be alone than ever yell again, even if it meant being alone in Pakistan.

I walked into the Tribune Tower to say goodbye to my bosses and churn through some paperwork before flying home to Islamabad. Within three months, most of the glass offices would be filled with different people. Most of the top editors would quit, including the man who had written my name on an envelope, the editor in chief, and the editor who wouldn't let me talk to Sam. The motto of the *Tribune* would change from the hopeful "World's Greatest Newspaper" to the realistic "The Midwest's largest reporting team." That evening, I stepped off the elevator and walked past the inexplicable six-legged statue on my way out the door. I glanced at the nearby quote from Flannery O'Connor. It seemed apt: "The truth does not change according to our ability to stomach it." My limbo was becoming my life.

CHAPTER 20
WHY CAN'T WE BE FRIENDS?

I flew back to Pakistan to pick up the pieces. As I trudged out of the Islamabad airport into the summer swelter, Samad spotted me and grabbed my purple suitcase, big enough for him to fit inside. "Hello, boss," he said, looking down at the pavement. This was a test run, to see if he could handle working for me again. He had disappeared for more than a month after I left for the States, unavailable whenever my office manager called. But he had finally surfaced to explain why he had been acting so strange. He was not an ISI spy. He had been seeing a girl—his fiancée.

Although he was engaged, Samad was not supposed to talk to his fiancée. This was an arranged marriage. Samad and his fiancée would not be allowed to marry for years, not until his older brother had married, and not until Samad and the girl were considered old enough. This decision had the force of law because the father of the bride, who didn't trust Samad, was also Samad's oldest brother. Samad and his future bride were related in a second way—her mother was his cousin. So Samad was his fiancée's uncle and second cousin. This was hardly unusual in certain circles in Pakistan, Afghanistan, or even India. Such marriages consolidated family ties and family belongings. Only the middle class and the elite picked their own spouses, and not always.

After Samad got his car, he figured he had the status to merit a wife. But his older brother said no. So Samad and his cousin/niece had eloped. Samad's older brother had reacted predictably, vowing to kill Samad for insulting his honor and marrying his eighteen-year-old daughter.

This, also, was typical. Because Samad and his bride had disobeyed their family, both could be killed. So for weeks, Samad and his new bride were on the run, sheltered by friends in Lahore and sympathetic family members. Finally his mother helped broker a truce. Samad and his wife moved back home. And Samad started calling my office manager, begging for his job back.

I felt I didn't have a choice. I didn't want to train a new driver. And I blamed myself for tempting Samad, giving him too much trust and responsibility. He had reacted like any young man to an empty house, a pool table, and free booze—actually, he had reacted better than most. And I had bigger issues to worry about than a missing bottle of Midori liqueur. Dave was moving out. We had broken up, and the split was hardly amicable. Just before flying in from Kabul, he sent me an e-mail, apologizing for the hurt he had caused but saying he had wanted to be honest about his feelings. "I have no doubt you'll be run off your feet when I come through, as it always was," he wrote. "Maybe I do need someone who has time to tend for me when I come in."

Maybe so. Samad helped him move out, even though it was confusing for him, a bit like subjecting a three-year-old to a divorce. Samad had bought all three of us key chains, each with our first initial. He had been thrilled when I started dating Dave, talking about my wedding and naming our firstborn before our one-month anniversary. Although divorce and single adults over thirty were quite common in my Pakistani circle of friends, in Samad's family such things were scandalous.

While packing up, Dave was kind and polite. I wondered if we were making a mistake. But then friends forced me to go out for dinner instead of moping at home, and to go to the UN club for a drink.

"I don't know," I said. "That's where he always goes."

"That's where everyone in Islamabad goes," a friend said, reminding me how miserable our options were. "You can't let him run your life."

So we went, hiding in the back garden because Dave had been spotted inside. After a while, my curiosity won out.

"What was he doing?" I asked.

"Singing karaoke," a friend said.

"What song?"

" 'My Way.' "

Meanwhile, Pakistan started to simmer again. It was August 2008. President Pervez Musharraf, who had managed to hold on to his presidency even as his popularity, power, and army post had been stripped away, finally stepped down. He didn't really have a choice—his enemies had recruited enough votes in parliament to impeach him. He gave a speech, punctuated with tears. "God protect Pakistan," he ended it. "God protect you, Pakistan, forever. Long live Pakistan." And then Musharraf collected his note cards and tried to stand up, with some difficulty. With that, all vestiges of the country's military rule were finished, at least for now.

Instead of resolving the political quagmire, his move only sharpened it. Pakistan's fragile new ruling coalition was falling apart. The coalition had agreed to restore the judges fired by Musharraf within twenty-four hours of him leaving the presidency, but that deadline quickly passed. The tiger of Punjab, Nawaz Sharif, still defending the judiciary, threatened to pull out of the coalition. But Bhutto's widower, Asif Ali Zardari, did not want to restore the judges. He probably suspected that they would throw out Musharraf's controversial ordinance granting amnesty to hundreds of politicians for past crimes; Zardari had faced accusations of corruption for misappropriating as much as $1.5 billion. Mr. Ten Percent also had his eye on a new prize he had once claimed that he never wanted—the presidency.

The militants exploited the government's many distractions. Two suicide bombers killed at least sixty-seven people during a shift change at the Pakistani army's main weapons factory outside Islamabad. The insurgents also spread their control in the tribal areas, where the government had never held any sway. This time the Pakistani army tried to push back, moving into the Bajaur tribal agency and even bombing homes. As many as 260,000 civilians, or almost half the residents, fled Bajaur. Shoddy relief camps were set up, where children died of diarrhea and families slept on the ground. In some areas the militants did a better job of providing relief than the government. At a meeting with top UN refugee agency officials, Zardari offered his own creative solution to the insurgency in the tribal areas: Build a cement factory, where people could work, and build bulletproof homes, where they could live. He had even drawn up the plans for such houses himself, demanding that his minions hand them over to the UN.

Capping the chaos, Nawaz Sharif then dropped out of the government. This shocked me—he had repeatedly threatened to end his party's support for the coalition, but I didn't think he would, as this chess move would in effect checkmate himself, eliminating any power he had. I called Sharif for the first time in months, and he invited me over to the Punjab House in Islamabad. He had always been unfailingly polite and soft-spoken with me. He seemed old-fashioned, speaking my name as a full sentence and rarely using contractions.

This time, in a large banquet hall filled with folding chairs and a long table, Sharif told his aides that he would talk to me alone. At the time, I barely noticed. We talked about Zardari, but he spoke carefully and said little of interest, constantly glancing at my tape recorder like it was radioactive. Eventually, he nodded toward it.

"Can you turn that off?" he asked.

"Sure," I said, figuring he wanted to tell me something off the record.

"So. Do you have a friend, Kim?" Sharif asked.

I was unsure what he meant.

"I have a lot of friends," I replied.

"No. Do you have a friend?"

I figured it out.

"You mean a boyfriend?"

"Yes."

I looked at Sharif. I had two options—lie, or tell the truth. And because I wanted to see where this line of questioning was going, I told the truth.

"I had a boyfriend. We recently broke up." I nodded my head stupidly, as if to punctuate this thought.

"Why?" Sharif asked. "Was he too boring for you? Not fun enough?"

"Um. No. It just didn't work out."

"Oh. I cannot believe you do not have a friend," Sharif countered.

"No. Nope. I don't. I did."

"Do you want me to find one for you?" Sharif asked.

To recap: The militants were gaining strength along the border with Afghanistan and staging increasingly bold attacks in the country's cities. The famed Khyber Pass, linking Pakistan and Afghanistan, was now too dangerous to drive. The country appeared as unmoored and directionless as a headless chicken. And here was Sharif, offering to find me a friend. Thank God the leaders of Pakistan had their priorities straight.

"Sure. Why not?" I said.

The thought of being fixed up on a date by the former prime minister of Pakistan, one of the most powerful men in the country and, at certain points, the world, proved irresistible. It had true train-wreck potential.

"What qualities are you looking for in a friend?" he asked.

"Tall. Funny. Smart."

I envisioned a blind date at a restaurant in Lahore over kebabs and watermelon juice with one of Sharif's sidekicks, some man with a mustache, Sharif lurking in the background as chaperone.

"Hmmm. Tall may be tough. You are very tall, and most Pakistanis are not." Sharif stood, walked past the banquet table toward the windows, and looked out over the capital. He pondered, before turning back toward me.

"What do you mean by smart?" he asked.

"You know. Smart. Quick. Clever."

"Oh, clever." He nodded, thought for a second. "But you do not want cunning. You definitely do not want a cunning friend."

He looked out the window. It seemed to me that he was thinking of Bhutto's widower, Zardari, his onetime ally and now rival, a man universally considered cunning at business who many felt had outsmarted Sharif in their recent political tango.

"No. Who wants cunning?"

"Anything else?" he asked. "What about his appearance?"

"I don't really care. Not fat. Athletic."

We shook hands, and I left. In all my strange interviews with Sharif, that definitely was the strangest.

Pakistan's spies soon seemed to kick up their interest in me, maybe because I had written a few controversial stories, maybe because of Sharif. Sitting in my living room, I complained to several friends about a man named Qazi, a former army colonel who worked as part of intelligence over foreigners.

"Qazi," I said. "That guy. He always calls me and asks me what I'm doing."

My friend's phone started ringing. He looked at the screen, then at us.

"It's Qazi," he said. "I'm not answering it."

Then my phone started ringing. Qazi. I felt I had no choice.

"Hey, Qazi."

"Hello, Kim, how are you, how is everything, your house?"

"Fine. I'm kind of busy." I rolled my eyes, looked at my friends.

"So did you like Taxila?"

"What?" A friend had recently driven me through Taxila, a town near Islamabad where I had bought a plaster-of-paris disco ball and a five-foot-tall mirrored plaster-of-paris flower vase. But how could Qazi know this?

"Did you like the shopping there?"

My tone grew sharp. "How do you know I was there?"

He started laughing. "Oh, you'd be surprised what I know. I have eyes everywhere."

"OK, then. I gotta go." I hung up.

That was creepy, but I didn't have time to think about it. Zardari was soon elected president, ending his quest for the power that he had repeatedly claimed not to want. As one of his first official moves as president, Zardari would travel to New York and call vice-presidential candidate Sarah Palin "gorgeous" and threaten to hug her. Pakistan: Spreading love and good feelings, around the world.

It would soon be Ramadan, the fasting month that made working in an Islamic country almost unbearable, so I decided to leave for a short reporting trip to India. But I still didn't have my annual Pakistani visa, despite applying more than a month earlier. My current visa was about to expire. I was stuck. Two days after Zardari's election, a man rang my doorbell in the late afternoon. He said he was from the Interior Ministry and was following up on my visa application, but he was probably a spook. He had a slight brown beard and light gray eyes, and was wearing a button-up plaid shirt and gray pants. He looked gray—how appropriate. He called me "lady," and not in a nice way.

"Lady, give me your CV," he insisted.

I didn't have a curriculum vitae or a résumé.

"What's your name?" I countered.

"Lady, give me your CV. CV," he repeated.

"What's your name—are you ISI?" I asked.

"Interior Ministry. Lady, CV," he demanded.

"Give me your card."

He ignored me.

"I don't have a CV."

"Lady, you have to have a CV."

It was like a Jerry Lewis skit.

"Calling me lady like that—it's rude," I said.

But he was right—I should have a CV. I should have been looking for a job, now that he mentioned it, but instead I was stuck, hoping desperately to hold on to this one. He was growing upset, standing on my front porch. I knew I needed to handle this, or he'd just keep coming back, so I invited him inside my house, and then inside my office. That's what he wanted—to check out me and my surroundings. Many Pakistanis believed American journalists were actually American spies—a suspicion only bolstered by past claims of American spies to be working as journalists. My spook stared at the difficult-to-obtain maps of the tribal areas pinned to the walls, the map of Afghanistan, and then walked over to my computer.

"Lady, what is *Chicago Tribunal*?" he asked.

"It's the *Tribune*. It's a newspaper. Didn't they tell you anything?"

"I've never heard of it. Lady, I've never heard of you."

He told me he started his job the previous March, but he would not give me his name or his card or his title.

"Why you not have a CV? Why not?" he asked, growing angry.

I needed to somehow turn this around, and now, this guy was very suspicious.

"I can write a CV and deliver it to you tomorrow morning."

"No," he said. "I will interview you, and do it that way."

He sat down and pulled out a notebook. He asked where I worked, my dates of employment, where I graduated college, where I was born.

"Montana," I said.

He squinted. "Lady, I've never heard of it." Then he thought for a second. "Montana bikes. I've heard of them."

"I don't know what you're talking about."

"What's your ancestry?"

This time I squinted. "Why?"

"Not for work," he said. "Because I'm curious."

But it was for work. He wanted to know if I was Jewish. They always wanted to know if we were Jewish.

"I bet you're German," he said.

"German Irish," I said.

"Religion?" he asked.

"Catholic," I claimed.

We were getting along now. I apologized for my rudeness. He apologized for calling me lady. Then he demanded to see my most recent story and my website. He immediately became suspicious again.

"That picture doesn't look like you," he said, looking at my mug shot online. "She looks a lot younger. She looks a lot nicer."

"Well, it's from a few years ago."

The man finally stood up.

"Don't go anywhere for ten days," he said, as he walked out my front door.

I worried I would never get my visa.

But I stayed busy. Zardari was sworn in as president the day after my spook visit. At a press conference with Afghan president Hamid Karzai at the president's house in Islamabad, both men pledged to cooperate against militants but didn't say how. I sat in the back row, near the exit, as the event featured absolutely no security, no metal detectors, no bag searches, even though the list of people who wanted to kill either man was surely the size of a New York phonebook. I sent a text message to a colleague outside, letting her know the reason if anything should explode. Afterward, we were escorted out through the kitchen. I stole a Diet Coke.

The next night, Samad drove some friends and me to a dinner

inside the diplomatic enclave. My phone beeped with a text message from a number with a British international code.

"Hello, Kim, I arrived London yesterday. Congratulations on AZ becoming the new president, how is he doing and how have the people taken it? I am working on the project we discussed and will have the result soon. Best wishes and warm regards."

I had no idea who sent the message. My brother? Sean? No, this sender clearly knew me from Pakistan. And what was the project? What had I discussed? I read the text message to my friends, and we pondered the sender. Then, finally, I remembered reading that Nawaz Sharif had flown to London so that his sick wife could have some tests.

"Is this Nawaz?" I replied.

"You are correct," he responded.

The project. That was funny. Everyone in the car, even the man from the U.S. embassy, agreed that I needed to see this through. And I thought—well, we all did—how hilarious it would be if Sharif actually found an option that worked.

CHAPTER 21
LONDON CALLING

After finally being promised a visa that would allow me to return to Pakistan, I flew to India to write some stories. Nawaz Sharif asked for my number there. He needed to talk about something important, outside Pakistan. One early evening, he called from London. Sharif wondered whether I would be back in Pakistan before Eid al-Fitr, the Islamic holiday at the end of Ramadan. Maybe, I told him. He planned to go to Pakistan for a day, and then to Saudi Arabia for four days.

"I am working on the project," he said.

"Day and night, I'm sure," I replied.

Sharif said the real reason he was calling was to warn me that the phones were tapped in Pakistan.

"Be very careful," he said. "Your phones are tapped. My phones are tapped. Do you know a man named Rehman Malik? He is giving the orders to do this, maybe at the behest of Mr. Zardari."

Everyone knew Rehman Malik, a slightly menacing figure who was the acting interior minister of Pakistan. He was known for making random word associations in press conferences and being unable to utter a coherent sentence. He also had slightly purple hair.

"Is this new?" I asked. "Hasn't it always been this way?"

"Well, yes. But it has gotten worse in the past two or three months."

So true. He had a solution—he would buy me a new phone. And give me a new number, but a number so precious that I could only give it to my very close friends, who had to get new phones and numbers as well.

Very tempting, but I told him no. He was, after all, the former prime minister of Pakistan. I couldn't accept any gifts from him.

"Sounds complicated. It's not necessary. And you can't buy me a phone."

He said I needed to be careful. We ended our conversation, and he promised to work on the project.

"Don't be—what is it you say? Don't be naughty," he said before hanging up.

Naughty? Who said that? The conversation was slightly worrying. I thought of Sharif as a Punjabi matchmaker determined to find me a man, not as anyone who talked naughty to me.

While watching TV in the Indian coastal town of Mangalore—a misnomer if there ever was one—I found out the Marriott Hotel in Islamabad had been blown up and fifty-four people had been killed. I saw the flames and the destruction and a friend from CNN climbing over the rubble and explaining how bad this was. Normally I would have been upset that I was out of position for such an attack. But this time I was just numb and, in fact, happy I wasn't there. I had lived at the Marriott for weeks at a time, and even when I lived elsewhere, I had visited several times a week. Like the Serena, the Marriott was an oasis for expatriates and Pakistanis. I had joined the gym there, ate at the Thai and Japanese restaurants, and drank high tea with sources. The bombers exploded their truck at the worst time possible—in the evening, just as the guards sat down to break their daily Ramadan fast with an evening meal. The attack was one of the worst ever in Islamabad and marked a whole new level of sophistication for militants attacking inside Pakistan, a whole new level of cruelty. I had known some of the dead—the front-desk greeters, the people who worked at the metal detector.

I stayed in India longer than I should have. Samad picked me up at the airport.

"Do you want to drive by Marriott?" he asked.

"No," I said. "I really don't."

Pakistan increasingly depressed me. I had once hoped that the lawyers could actually change the country and that Pakistanis would finally get the government they deserved. Instead, they got a second-hand trashy veneer of democracy. The political machinations were yet another example of how the country's priorities were completely upside down. Finally Pakistan had a civilian government, a rarity. But instead of focusing on the real problems in the country—the bad economy, the war, the Pakistani Taliban—the civilian leaders bickered with one another. The military and spy agencies seemed unwilling to abandon the reins of Pakistan and fixated on India rather than homegrown militants. And the rare offensives the military ever announced here showed that the country was only willing to take on a certain kind of militant—the ones attacking inside Pakistan, and never the ones training and planning strikes against international troops and civilian targets in neighboring Afghanistan.

The United States was also to blame, losing massive popularity in Pakistan by supporting Musharraf until almost the end and failing to adequately push nonmilitary aid. America was seen as hypocritical, championing democracy in countries like Iraq or Afghanistan, but not in Pakistan. And the U.S. drone attacks in the tribal areas had provoked a backlash in much of the country. Many Pakistanis blamed the militants' growing power on the country's promise to help America, not on the establishment's decision to play a double game with the militants. Of course, some Pakistanis blamed the militants on rival India, talking of eight—or was it eighty?—Indian consulates in Afghanistan along the border with Pakistan, all fomenting rebellion.

In short: None of this was Pakistan's fault. The country had a reluctance to look inside, much like a chain-smoker refusing to accept responsibility for lung cancer while blaming it on a nearby factory. That view was dangerous. If Pakistanis didn't see this war as their war, as a fight for the nation's survival, then more and more bombs would explode, and the country would continue its downward spiral. If Pakistan didn't own this war, the militants would keep spreading, recruiting through money, refugee camps, intimidation, religion, tradition, and help from invisible friends. The militants had already set up shop throughout much of the tribal areas, where the government had no influence, and the army had only small sticks and little staying power.

I planned a trip to Afghanistan, where the politics were much less murky, where the suicide bombers were much less effective, to write about alleged negotiations with the Taliban.

That's why I had to see Nawaz Sharif again. Emissaries from the Afghan government and former Taliban bigwigs had flown to Saudi Arabia for the feasts that marked the end of Ramadan. But they had another goal. Afghan officials had been hoping that the influential Saudi royal family would moderate negotiations between their battered government and the resurgent militants. Sharif, in Saudi Arabia at the time, was rumored to have been at those meetings. That made sense. He was close to the Saudi king. He had supported the Afghan Taliban, when the regime was in power.

I called Sharif and told him why I wanted to see him.

"Most welcome, Kim," he said. "Anytime."

We arranged for a lunch on a Saturday in October—I was due to fly to Kabul two days later. Samad and I decided to drive the five hours from Islamabad to Raiwind instead of flying. Samad showed up on time, but I overslept, having been up late the night before. I hopped out of bed and rifled through my Islamic clothes for something suitable because I liked to dress conservatively when interviewing Pakistani politicians. I yanked out a red knee-length top from India that had dancing couples embroidered on it. Potentially ridiculous, but the nicest clean one I had. We left Islamabad.

"You're gonna have to hurry, Samad," I said. "Possible?"

"Kim, possible," he said. It always cracked me up when I got him to say that.

We made good time south, but got lost at some point on the narrow roads to Raiwind. Sharif sent out an escort vehicle with flashing lights to meet us. We breezed through security—we actually didn't even slow down—and I forced Samad to stop in the middle of the long driveway leading up to Sharif's palace. I had forgotten to comb my hair or put on any makeup. I turned the rearview mirror toward me, smoothed down my messy hair with my hands, and put on some lipstick. Twenty seconds. "Good enough," I pronounced my effort, and flipped the mirror back to Samad.

We reached the imposing driveway. Sharif actually waited in front of his massive front doors for me, wearing a blue suit, slightly snug around his waist. He clasped his hands in front of his belt. It was clear that our meeting was important. Sharif was surrounded by several lackeys, who all smiled tight-lipped before looking down at the ground. I jumped out of the car, sweaty after the ride, panicked because I was late. I shook Nawaz's hand—he had soft fingers, manicured nails, baby-like skin that had probably never seen a callous.

"Hello, Kim," he said.

"Hey, Nawaz. Sorry I'm late."

In the sitting room, I immediately turned on my tape recorder and rattled off questions. Was Sharif at the negotiations? What was happening? He denied being at any meetings, despite press reports to the contrary. I pushed him. He denied everything. I wondered why he let me drive all this way, if he planned to tell me nothing. At least I'd get free food.

He looked at my tape recorder and asked me to turn it off. Eventually I obliged. Then Sharif brought up his real reason for inviting me to lunch.

"Kim. I have come up with two possible friends for you."

At last.

"Who?"

He waited a second, looked toward the ceiling, then seemingly picked the top name from his subconscious. "The first is Mr. Z."

That was disappointing. Sharif definitely was not taking this project seriously.

"Zardari? No way. That will never happen," I said.

"What's wrong with Mr. Zardari?" Sharif asked. "Do you not find him attractive?"

Bhutto's widower, Asif Ali Zardari, was slightly shorter than me and sported slicked-back hair and a mustache, which he was accused of dying black right after his wife was killed, right before his first press conference. On many levels, I did not find Zardari attractive. I would have preferred celibacy. But that wasn't the point. Perhaps I could use this as a teaching moment.

"He is the president of Pakistan. I am a journalist. That would never happen."

"He is single."

Very true—but I didn't think that was a good enough reason.

"I can call him for you," Sharif insisted. I'm fairly certain he was joking.

"I'm sure he has more important things to deal with," I replied.

"OK. No Mr. Z. The second option, I will discuss with you later," he said.

That did not sound promising. We adjourned our meeting for lunch in the dining room, where two places were set at a long wooden table that appeared to seat seventy. We sat in the middle of the table, facing each other over a large display of fake orange flowers. The food was brought out in a dozen courses of silver dishes—deep-fried prawns, mutton stew, deep-fried fish, bread, a mayonnaise salad with a few vegetables for color, chicken curry, lamb. Dish after dish, each carried by waiters in traditional white outfits with long dark gray vests. Like the good Punjabi that Sharif was, he kept pushing food on me.

"Have more prawns. You like prawns, right?"

He insisted on seconds and thirds. It felt like a make-believe meal. I didn't know which fork to use, not that it mattered in a culture where it was fine to eat with your hands, but the combination of the wealth, the empty seats, and the unspoken tiger in the room made me want to run screaming from the table. I needed to get out of there.

"I have to go."

"First, come for a walk with me outside, around the grounds. I want to show you Raiwind."

"No. I have to go. I have to go to Afghanistan tomorrow."

Sharif ignored that white lie and started to talk about where he wanted to take me.

"I would like to take you for a ride in the country, and take you for lunch at a restaurant in Lahore, but because of my position, I cannot."

"That's OK. I have to go."

"I am still planning to buy you a phone. Which do you like— BlackBerry, Nokia, iPhone?"

So now he knew what a BlackBerry was. But I would not bend.

"You can't buy me a phone," I said.

"Why not?"

"You're the former prime minister of Pakistan. No."

"Which do you like?" He kept pressing, wouldn't let it go. Black-Berry, Nokia, iPhone, over and over. That scene from *The Wizard of Oz* started running through my head: Lions and tigers and bears, oh my!

"BlackBerry, Nokia, or iPhone, Kim?"

"The iPhone," I said, because I already had a Nokia and a Black-Berry. "But I still can't take one from you."

As we left, Samad insisted on getting our picture taken with Sharif. Samad was a Bhutto man, which meant he should have been a Zardari man, but increasingly, like many of Bhutto's followers in

Pakistan, Samad had grown disenchanted with Zardari. And increasingly, Samad liked Sharif. Everyone liked Sharif. Behind the scenes, the tiger of Punjab was growing very powerful. His decision to break with Zardari over the issue of restoring the judges had proved to be smart. As Zardari's government floundered and flip-flopped, Sharif looked more and more like an elder statesman.

Regardless, I told my boss it was no longer a good idea for me to see Sharif. He was married, older, rich, and powerful. As a pleasant-looking, pedigree-lacking American with hair issues, I was an extremely unlikely paramour. But Sharif had ended our visit with a dangling proposition—the mysterious identity of a second potential friend. I decided to stick to a tapped-phone relationship.

CHAPTER 22

DEADBEAT CLUB

As soon as I landed in Kabul, Farouq and I drove to the Defense Ministry to ask about negotiations with the Taliban. Farouq parked the car. We started walking. I had always regarded this long path, leading past halfheartedly practicing Afghan soldiers, as my own personal march toward sexual harassment. I thought happy thoughts. Farouq talked our way past the first checkpoint. But then we reached the second checkpoint.

"Keep going," Farouq muttered.

I kept walking, staring straight ahead. But it was no use. The women had spotted me. One lifted up the lacy curtain over the door in the concrete guardhouse. She started yelling. I kept walking. Finally I was stopped by a man with a gun and sent back to the women, inside the dreaded room where the bad things happened. One took my purse and opened up every single zipper, pulling out every lipstick and crumpled bill. Another took me. I held my arms out to the sides and grimaced. She ran her hands under my armpits, grabbed my breasts, squeezed.

"Nice," she said.

"Just give me one example of an American woman who would blow herself up," I said to her. "Just one. Doesn't happen. We could never commit that much to anything."

In response, she smiled, grabbed my butt, and ran her hands up my inner thighs, all the way to my crotch. She was barely as tall as my rib cage. Then, assault finished, she smiled, pinched my cheek, announced "Very pretty," and patted me on the back. I walked out, feeling dirty.

For years, whenever people asked how foreign women were treated in Afghanistan, I always said better than in Pakistan. We were rarely felt up in public, and we had an easier time than the male reporters. We could interview women who would never reveal their secrets to a man. And we got bizarre access to the men, even the conservative mullahs, who seemed secretly charmed by the idea of Western women running around. We were the third sex, immune to the local rules for women and entitled to a more exclusive status than Western men. But the checkpoints were bad. We were felt up roughly and searched far more than our male counterparts—by women, no less, who had tried to take my lipstick and held up tampons in a threatening manner, asking what they were for. It was a problem in Pakistan and India as well—it was as if the women hired for these jobs were told that they were being hired because women had different parts than men, so they figured their primary duty was to search only the female parts. At every checkpoint, for every foreign woman, it was the same. Walk inside some dark room with several women drinking tea. Assume the position—arms out to the sides, legs spread. Grit your teeth through the groping. Often a security check consisted of a breast squeeze, a crotch grab, and a slap on the back. Sometimes male guards would come watch the show. Meanwhile Afghan men like Farouq were barely touched.

In Kabul, two places were known as the ninth level of female guard-box hell. The presidential palace, where the women had shoved me up against the wall, once becoming alarmed because I had neglected to wear a bra. And the Defense Ministry, which featured five checkpoints, two with very assertive women.

So on this day, Farouq and I pushed on to the third and fourth checkpoints. Both men, both easy. Then I faced the last and worst checkpoint, inside the ministry headquarters. A shriveled woman with bright-orange-hennaed hair and white roots waved me inside. She grabbed, pulled, yanked, squeezed, searched. I felt like a vegetable. I turned to go, but not fast enough. She pointed at her cheek and puckered her lips. She wasn't letting me leave until I kissed her. So I kissed her on both cheeks. "Good," she said. She patted my cheek.

Then, finally, we made it to the office of a Defense Ministry official, who was nicknamed the Silver Fox for his hair and manners. He stood up, laughing and raising his hands when he saw us. He pointed to one cheek. I kissed it. This was not Afghan protocol—in most places, an unrelated woman kissing a man on the cheek was akin to having sex—but it had always been Silver Fox protocol. He pointed to the other cheek, then the first one. "Three," he announced.

I couldn't seem to go anywhere today without kissing half a dozen Afghans. And no one would tell us anything about Taliban negotiations. After struggling for a few days to set up interviews, Farouq sat me down. Although we were still close friends, we had been growing somewhat distant from each other professionally, largely over money and job strains. I had been honest with Farouq about the situation at the *Tribune*, telling him that he had maybe a year at best and that we had no money. I was under so much stress, so worried about my job, my entire identity, that I couldn't help but pass on my fears to Farouq, which caused him to worry about his job. A certain bitterness had crept into my dealings with work, and since I spent more time with Farouq than anyone else, a certain amount of my bitterness rubbed off on him. Now he was honest with me.

"We need a driver," he said. "I know money is tight, but I can't drive for you at the same time I'm a fixer. It's too complicated. I can't talk on the phone while I'm driving. And someone needs to stay with the car while we're doing interviews. Because of the situation."

"The situation"—the nondescript description of how bad things were getting in Afghanistan. Farouq was probably right. I had recently done an unscientific tally of how many people I knew in Afghanistan who had later been killed. I lost count. The latest example: A top anti-drugs judge had just been shot on his way to work in Kabul, months after telling me that the government refused to give him an armored car despite repeated threats.

The situation was also getting worse for foreigners. Sean's kidnapping was only one example. A female Canadian journalist was kidnapped at a refugee camp near Kabul—she would eventually be freed, after protracted negotiations. Men on motorcycles shot and killed a Western woman walking to work in Kabul. The Taliban claimed responsibility—allegedly because she was a Christian trying to convert Muslims. Five days later, a disgruntled employee gunned down the two foreigners who ran DHL. More journalists were kidnapped. A Dutch woman, who wrote for a soft-porn laddie magazine, decided to perform a sympathetic interview with the Taliban; her magazine paid $137,000 for her release. A *New York Times* reporter on book leave went to meet the Taliban with the fixer Tahir—along with their driver, they were kidnapped and eventually traded to the Haqqani network, where Sean had earlier landed. After years of gambling with the Taliban, Tahir, the third Afghan fixer who had been willing to work dangerously, was betrayed. Tahir and the reporter would be held for more than seven months before escaping; their driver would manage to leave soon after.

So the situation was bad and getting worse. I told Farouq that we could hire a driver. I hoped that my bosses wouldn't notice that I was now paying an extra $25 a day—$150 total, or $100 for Farouq, and $50 for the driver—but the security worries merited it. Farouq recruited a young man from his Internet café, who spoke little English and seemed unclear where anything was. Sometimes Farouq opted to drive himself, whenever the young man frustrated him or the drive was tricky.

"He's learning," Farouq said. "And his most important job is to watch the car."

We drove out to Pul-i-Charkhi prison, the former home of

superpatriot Jack Idema—or Farouq drove, as the area near the prison was a frequent Taliban hangout. I figured if I could meet the Taliban in prison, then I could find out what they thought about negotiations or anything else, while remaining safe. About 3,500 inmates now crammed into Afghanistan's largest prison, a grim concrete catacomb that looked exactly like you'd expect an Afghan prison to look. Always affable, the guards agreed to bring a few Taliban members to talk to me, easy because about 1,500 of the inmates were allegedly insurgents. Farouq and I sat in the jail commander's office, decorated with a dozen startlingly fluorescent pink-and-green-flower bouquets celebrating his recent promotion. Eventually three alleged Taliban militants were paraded inside. They sat down on the overstuffed couch across from me. Farouq then left the room to help a photographer friend get inside the prison. Suddenly I realized we were alone. No cops, no fixers, just me and the Taliban, who were not handcuffed or restrained in any way. I smiled at the Taliban. The Taliban smiled at me. I nodded. They nodded. Most likely, this was not safe. Some of these men were probably killers.

"Farouq?" I said loudly, still smiling. "Is this safe?"

"You're fine," he answered from the hallway.

We smiled and nodded some more. Farouq and the commander walked back into the office. A prison guard then poured green tea—first for the commander, then the Taliban, then Farouq, then me. I knew my place so I didn't complain. The guard slapped down trays of chewy candies and bitter almonds for us to eat, before slumping in a chair in the corner. A fourth alleged Taliban member walked into the room.

"If somebody gives me a suicide vest, I will be the first one to blow up these guards," proclaimed the man, sentenced to eighteen years for allegedly killing four Chinese construction workers. He gestured toward the guard in the corner, who appeared to be falling asleep. "If I get out, I will fight them. If some Islamic country could pay me, I am ready."

The commander laughed.

The men I talked to that day were not much help with the overall goals of the Taliban or negotiations. Some said they were never Taliban. Others said they joined the Taliban after being unjustly imprisoned. But I learned how pervasive corruption was alleged to be in the justice system. All said they had been asked for bribes of tens of thousands of dollars to get their sentences reduced. All said they could not afford that much, but that other accused Taliban members had paid the bribes and were now free. One Taliban inmate insisted that Afghanistan didn't have actual defense lawyers. Instead, inmates had brokers, middlemen between them and the judge or prosecutor.

Two senior police officials had earlier told me that many prisoners had paid off police officers to escape. The year before, fifteen prisoners had been taken to be executed, the first mass execution since Karzai's election. Although this was supposed to send a message to Afghans that the country's justice system was now functioning, it sent quite a different message. The executions were sloppy, mass shootings against a wall. And three guards had allowed the escape of Afghanistan's most famous criminal, who had been sentenced to die for kidnapping, rape, and murder. In this environment, with such a topsy-turvy and often corrupt justice system, it was difficult to dismiss the claims of these alleged Taliban members.

One man sounded particularly credible. He said he was a low-level Taliban member when the regime was in power, but after Karzai came, he reconciled with the government. When three Afghan army soldiers were kidnapped by the Taliban in his district, near Kabul, he helped mediate their release. He said he was arrested because of false information given by a man who owed him money. The former Taliban member was then sentenced to seven years in prison. He told me he would rejoin the Taliban when he got out.

"I am from a tribe of three hundred and fifty young men," he said. "They are all against what's been done to me. Of course, they are also now against the government."

His story—of leaving the Taliban, only to be arrested later because of a personal rivalry—was familiar. So was his story of entire clans turning against the government for a perceived slight against one member. The Afghan government seemed to be losing the Afghans. In the south, clerics who had backed Karzai or stood against the Taliban had been killed, one by one. Many Afghans drifted toward the Taliban-led militants because they seemed more powerful and more committed. Others leaned toward the Taliban because of disillusionment with corruption and civilian casualties.

My onetime shooting buddy, Sabit, had failed so miserably as attorney general that his name was now a joke. I felt bad for him, even if I was still wary of seeing him. His moral high ground had been gradually eroded, his credibility erased. Warlords had continued to humiliate him publicly. His temper had alienated everyone. Western diplomats had started treating him a bit like a drunk uncle at a holiday party. But even as I pitied him, Sabit also shared the blame for the broken justice system and what it had become—one of the biggest failures of the international community and the government.

Finally Sabit had gone too far, even for Karzai. The previous summer, in a fit of pique, Sabit announced he was running for president. Karzai immediately fired him. The jokes started—a video appeared on TV and on YouTube, allegedly showing Sabit dancing at a party. The video was fuzzy, and Sabit's face couldn't be seen, but it was entitled "Afghanistan Attorney General, Dancing Drunk." The *New York Times* later sealed the deal, reporting that the video showed Sabit dancing giddily, slurring his words, apparently drunk. I didn't think that the dancing man was Sabit—but as usual in Afghanistan, the truth didn't matter. His fall was complete. Afghanistan's Don Quixote, who rode to power tilting at brothels and booze, was finished.

Things deteriorated further. I was going slightly stir-crazy after imposing my own security lockdown due to all the attacks and kidnappings. So right before leaving Afghanistan, I decided to see old friends, making use of my new driver. On a Friday afternoon, I dropped by a going-away party for a stranger at a security-guy hangout with its own bar. Within half an hour, I wanted out. After extensive instructions, my driver picked up three of us to go to L'Atmosphère. He couldn't find it. Our conflicting directions probably didn't help.

"Doesn't he know where anything is?" a friend asked.

"Apparently not," I answered.

"How did you find this guy?"

"Farouq."

"This isn't safe," she said. "The situation's too bad to be just driving around with no idea where we are. I want to talk to Farouq."

I called Farouq. This was probably not a good idea. This was Friday, Farouq's day off. In an attempt to show how productive I was, how useful I was, I had been pushing Farouq harder than in years, harder than he was used to working. I listened to my friend tell Farouq how the young man didn't know enough to be a driver. She was right—but this conversation would have fallout. She was challenging Farouq's Pashtun-ness and questioning him in a way that was not good. Farouq wanted to talk to the driver, then me. He was icy.

"He is just a boy. He is just learning. And you're making him work too late at night."

"If I'm paying $50 a day for a driver, he has to work," I said. "And it's only eight o'clock."

The next week, Farouq told me the driver could not work in the evenings.

"Because of the situation," Farouq said. "He's just a boy."

The attacks in Afghanistan were almost always between seven and ten in the morning, and we had adjusted our schedule accordingly. Only one major attack had been at night.

"I don't get it," I said. "Nothing ever happens at night."

"Something might," Farouq said.

Right before I left Kabul, the driver again couldn't remember where a restaurant was. Farouq wasn't in the car.

"I can't believe this," I complained. "My company is paying a lot of money for a driver, and you can't remember where anything is."

I had assumed I was paying $50 for a driver, and $100 for Farouq. But apparently Farouq and his employee had a different deal. The poor guy, struggling with his English, tried to understand me. He looked at me, and tried to explain himself in a combination of Dari and English.

"No. Not a lot."

"How much do you make?"

"Five." He held up his hand and waved his fingers and thumb.

I should have seen it coming. That Farouq, the master operator, would figure out a typical Afghan workaround, a way to get more money out of the *Tribune* in the last days of a regular paycheck. By my calculations, hiring a driver was now netting Farouq $145 a day, as opposed to the $125 he made when we didn't have a driver. I tried to look at this from Farouq's point of view. The driver was driving Farouq's car, and $5 a day was a lot for most Afghans, most of whom made $1 or $2 a day. And it's not like he drove much. Essentially, he was being paid to car-sit.

I filed the information away, but considering what was happening with our company, considering how Farouq's job was under threat, I didn't confront my old friend about something so comparatively small. I figured everything would work out soon. I just didn't know how.

CHAPTER 23
EYE OF THE TIGER

I flew to London to meet my brother for Thanksgiving. But just as we stepped out of a cab to meet Sean for dinner, my phone rang. A boss.

"Where are you?" he said.

"London."

"Damn. That's right. I'm assuming you know about the Mumbai situation. Any thoughts?"

"What Mumbai situation?"

A situation, as I had learned, was never good.

He sighed. This was the same editor who had years earlier informed me about the tsunami—eleven hours after it hit—because I had taken the day off. He explained something about gunmen storming hotels in Mumbai in a coordinated attack.

"What?"

He told me to check the news and think about getting on a plane. My brother and I walked into a seafood restaurant to meet Sean, the first time I had seen him since our fateful lunch. We hugged, sat down, and ordered a bucket of seafood. I was distracted by Mumbai, and I kept searching the news on my BlackBerry. I knew I should head for the airport. India looked very, very bad. And I could tell who was responsible for it. Someone in Pakistan. Had to be.

But I decided I could wait until after dinner. My brother, a law-yer, asked Sean questions about every second of his kidnapping.

"Is this OK?" I asked Sean.

"It's fine," Sean said, and he regaled us with a story told so often it no longer seemed real.

But Sean seemed twitchy and different. He had a ten-o'clock shadow, and he kept leaving the table to smoke outside. He talked about his sons, and how guilty he felt seeing how old his parents looked when he returned from Pakistan. He hadn't worked much since the kidnapping. He wasn't sure what he would do in the future. He wanted to be in Mumbai. We finished dinner. My brother and I left.

"Really interesting guy," my brother said. "I liked him. Pretty damaged, though."

Indeed, Sean was damaged. I thought about him, and my own life. Since moving overseas, I had seen my brother for only three meals—two dinners and a breakfast. I had missed a family wed-ding, countless holidays. I had skipped out on helping my mother recover from the death of her husband. I had not been around for my father's various health problems. Back home, I was the relative no one recognized. And here I was, on my first night of a short visit to my brother, thinking about flying back to Asia. What was I sacri-ficing everything for? I loved my job, but my job clearly did not love me. The messages from the new overall bosses featured ominous phrases such as "your partner in change" and did not mention for-eign coverage. I had never even met the new editor of our newspa-per. As the cherry on my sundae of doom, owner Sam Zell had just been interviewed by the editor of *Portfolio* magazine, in which he again complained about my story on the TV show *Afghan Star*. He was like my grandmother with my marital status—he wouldn't let it go. It's possible he thought I lived in Chicago.

"The entire focus is on becoming an international correspon-dent," he complained. "I mean, I know that because our newspaper sent somebody to Kabul to cover the 'Afghan Idol Show.' Now, I know *Idol* is the No. 1 TV program in the world, but do my readers really want a firsthand report on what this broad looked like who won the 'Afghan Idol Show'? Is that news?"

So I added up everything—my brother, Sean, Sam Zell, all that death in Mumbai. If I had learned one thing in Afghanistan and Pakistan, it was that there would always be another major tragedy. If I had learned another, it was that family was important. I had rarely put any family first, or put anything or anyone first except my job. I had lost relationships over work, friendships over work. It was time to let go.

"So you have to leave, right?" my brother asked. He knew the drill.

"I'm not going anywhere," I said.

I called my boss.

"So is there anyone else who can go?" I asked. "I'm a little sick."

He may have known I was exaggerating my slight sinus infection, but he definitely knew how many vacations I had cut short, how tired I was. So he said I could stay in London for a few days.

I still flew back a day early, to Islamabad. Once the horrific siege of Mumbai was finished, killing 171 people over three days, the focus of the story switched to Pakistan, hardly a shock to the world. The one surviving militant had allegedly told Indian authorities that he was from a town called Faridkot. But at least three towns were named Faridkot in the province of Punjab alone. I had no interest in running after a ghost, in driving to town after town. I wanted the right Faridkot. I also needed to go to Lahore, the capital of Punjab, to look into the charity that American and Indian authorities claimed was a front for the militant group Lashkar-e-Taiba, blamed for the Mumbai attack. This group—"Lash" for short—had been formed with the help of the Inter-Services Intelligence Directorate (ISI), the Pakistani spy agency, in the late 1980s, just after the Soviets were driven out of Afghanistan. It had originally served as an unofficial arm of the Pakistan military, doing its dirty work in the Indian-controlled part of Kashmir.

After Lash was blamed for attacking India's parliament in late 2001, Pakistan banned the group and distanced itself—in theory, at least. Like other banned militant groups, leaders were placed under house arrest, but only for a few months. Like other groups, Lash simply changed its name. Most militancy experts and Western diplomats believed that Lash was now publicly operating as the charity Jamaat-ud-Dawa. The same man had started both groups, the groups had shared the same leaders. Even before the siege of Mumbai, the United States had imposed financial sanctions on the founder and listed both groups as terrorist organizations.

Still, despite a public crackdown on Lash, the charity had run relief camps during a major earthquake and during the internal refugee crisis. A few weeks before Mumbai, the charity held two large meetings in Punjab Province, the first since Lash was banned. Almost a million people attended each meeting. The founder talked in vague terms about jihad, a phrase that in Islam usually meant "a personal struggle against temptation" but with these groups was often code for fighting in defense of the religion, which in recent years had included striking first. Some women in attendance were so impressed with the founder's speeches, they handed over their gold jewelry for the cause.

Now India and the West accused Lash of planning the Mumbai attack. Given the group's historic ties to the ISI, the group had either gone rogue or someone linked to the agency had known what was happening. I needed to go to Lahore, where the main mosque for Jamaat-ud-Dawa was. And I knew, with plenty of reservations, that I needed to go to Lahore because of Nawaz Sharif. If anyone knew the right Faridkot, he would.

That Friday, Pakistan seemed to have launched its typical crackdown on the charity—in other words, lots of noise, little action. A charity billboard in the heart of Lahore proclaimed: "We can sacrifice our lives to preserve the holiness of the Prophet." I sent my translator into the group's mosque because I wasn't allowed. There, flanked by three armed guards, the founder of Jamaat-ud-Dawa and Lash preached to about ten thousand men. His bluster was typical Islamic militant stuff—about sacrifice, about Eid al-Adha, the upcoming religious festival where devout Muslims would sacrifice an animal and give part of it to the poor. The holiday honored Ibrahim, or as Jews and Christians knew him, Abraham.

"Sacrifice is not just to slaughter animals in the name of God," the founder said. "Sacrifice also means leaving your country in the name of God. It means sacrificing your life in the name of God."

His meaning seemed fairly clear.

Meanwhile, the spokesman for the charity tried to rewrite history. He said the founder was barely involved with Lash—despite founding it—and insisted Lash was now based in India. The spokesman also drew a vague line in the sand, more like a smudge—he said the charity talked about jihad, but did not set up any training camps for jihad. The man who ran the ISI when Lash was founded denied having anything to do with the group. "Such blatant lies," he told me, adding later that Jamaat-ud-Dawa was "a good lot of people."

These men seemed convinced of their magical powers, of their ability to wave a wand and erase a reporter's memory. This obfuscation was not even up to Pakistan's usual level.

With a heavy heart, I knew I needed to see Nawaz Sharif. I figured I might be able to get something out of him that he didn't know he wasn't supposed to tell me—as former prime minister, he'd certainly be told what was happening, but because he wasn't a government official, he wouldn't necessarily know that he was supposed to keep the information quiet. But this time, I planned to bring my translator along, a male chaperone. Samad drove our team out to Raiwind. I sat in the back of the car, writing up my story about the charity on my computer, trying not to think about what Sharif might try to pull this visit.

Eventually, we walked inside Sharif's palace. Sharif looked at my translator, then me, clearly confused. He invited us both into his computer room, where we sat on a couch. Sharif sat on a chair, near a desk. When he answered my questions, he stared at my translator. My translator, embarrassed to be there, stared at the ground.

Sharif told me the right Faridkot—the one in Okara district, just a couple of hours from Lahore. He gave me the phone number for the provincial police chief. He told me what Indian and Pakistani authorities had told him about the lone surviving militant. For us, this was big news—a senior Pakistani confirming what the government had publicly denied: The attackers were from Pakistan.

"This boy says, 'I belong to Okara, and I left my home some years ago,'" Sharif said, adding that he had been told that the young man would come home for a few days every six months or a year.

"He cut off his links with his parents," Sharif also told me. "The relationship between him and his parents was not good. Then he disappeared."

Once the interview was finished, Sharif looked at me.

"Can you ask your translator to leave?" he asked. "I need to talk to you."

My translator looked at me with a worried forehead wrinkle.

"It's OK," I said.

He left. Sharif then looked at my tape recorder.

"Can you turn that off?"

I obliged.

"I have to go," I said. "I have to write a story."

He ignored me. "I have bought you an iPhone," he said.

"I can't take it."

"Why not? It is a gift."

"No. It's completely unethical, you're a source."

"But we are friends, right?"

I had forgotten how Sharif twisted the word "friend."

"Sure, we're friendly, but you're still the former prime minister of Pakistan and I can't take an iPhone from you," I said.

"But we are friends," he countered. "I don't accept that. I told you I was buying you an iPhone."

"I told you I couldn't take it. And we're not those kind of friends."

He tried a new tactic. "Oh, I see. Your translator is here, and you do not want him to see me give you an iPhone. That could be embarrassing for you."

Exasperated, I agreed. "Sure. That's it."

He then offered to meet me the next day, at a friend's apartment in Lahore, to give me the iPhone and have tea. No, I said. I was going to Faridkot. Sharif finally came to the point.

"Kim. I am sorry I was not able to find you a friend. I tried, but I failed."

He shook his head, looked genuinely sad about the failure of the project.

"That's OK," I said. "Really. I don't really want a friend right now. I am perfectly happy without a friend. I want to be friendless."

He paused. And then, finally, the tiger of Punjab pounced. "I would like to be your friend."

I didn't even let him get the words out. "No. Absolutely not. Not going to happen."

"Hear me out." He held his hand toward me to silence my negations as he made his pitch. He could have said anything—that he was a purported billionaire who had built my favorite road in Pakistan, that he could buy me a power plant or build me a nuclear weapon. But he opted for honesty.

"I know, I'm not as tall as you'd like," Sharif explained. "I'm not as fit as you'd like. I'm fat, and I'm old. But I would still like to be your friend."

"No," I said. "No way."

He then offered me a job running his hospital, a job I was eminently unqualified to perform. "It's a huge hospital," he said. "You'd be very good at it." He said he would only become prime minister again if I were his secretary.

I thought about it for a few seconds—after all, I would probably soon be out of a job. But no. The new position's various positions would not be worth it. Eventually, I got out of the tiger's grip,
but only by promising that I would consider his offer. Otherwise,
he wouldn't let me leave. I jumped into the car, pulled out my tape
recorder, and recited our conversation. Samad shook his head. My
translator put his head in his hands.

"I'm embarrassed for my country," he said.

After that, I knew I could never see Sharif again. I was not
happy about this—I liked Sharif. In the back of my mind, maybe
I had hoped he would come through with a possible friend, or that
we could have kept up our banter, without an iPhone lurking in
the closet. But now I saw him as just another sad case, a recycled
has-been who squandered his country's adulation and hope, who
thought hitting on a foreign journalist was a smart move. Which it
clearly wasn't.

The next morning, Samad drove us to Faridkot. As soon as we
pulled into town, dozens of men in cream-colored salwar kameezes
flanked our car. One identified himself as the mayor—he denied all
knowledge of the surviving militant and his parents. Other Pakistani journalists showed up—we had all found out about the same
time that this was the Mumbai assailant's hometown, a dusty village
of ten thousand people in small brick houses along brick and dirt
paths. My translator said many of the cream-attired men here were
ISI. Another journalist recognized an ISI commander. Their job: to
deny everything and get rid of us.

They tried flattery. I was their first foreigner ever. Would I like
some tea? Sure, I said.

Then they tried intimidation. Two journalists who worked
for an international news agency started filming. Alleged villagers
screamed about the privacy of their women, rushed the journalists,
and punched and kicked them. Someone took their cell phones and
digital-video cassettes (DVs). The mayor called us inside a building

to talk. I figured we were getting somewhere. But in a dark room, the mayor's lackeys put my translator and me in rickety chairs. "Just wait," the mayor said.

Outside, Samad stood near his precious car, worried that we had been kidnapped. A few men talked about smashing its windows and stealing my purse, locked inside. "Just burn their car," one said.

Samad started yelling. He called my translator on his phone and shouted what was happening outside. We pushed past the men watching us and ran down the stairs. A boy ran up to us.

"I know everything," he said.

"Just keep quiet," a man told him.

"Are you mad?" another asked.

Finally we were allowed to walk around, but only down one street, and only flanked by an escort of about twenty so-called villagers.

"This is entirely pointless," I said, as one man after another told us that no, this was not the Faridkot we were looking for.

"We should go," my translator said.

Upon hearing our plans to leave, the mayor asked me to wait. He then ran inside a house and ran out, holding a large white scarf embroidered with pink-and-green flowers. He presented it to me in front of the alleged villagers.

"Because you are our first foreigner," he said.

I took it. The crowd of alleged villagers clapped. I made a grand speech.

"Thanks so much for this. Your hospitality—threatening to beat us up and set our car on fire, refusing to let us walk around, lying to us consistently, and now this, handing me this scarf so I can cover myself up—it's truly been amazing. I'm speechless."

My translator looked at me.

"I really hope none of them speak English," he said, before sanitizing my speech for the masses. They clapped again. I waved, tossed the scarf in the backseat, and hurtled into the car.

We stopped first at the press club in the neighboring town. A club officer confirmed that the surviving militant was from this Faridkot. A TV journalist who had visited Faridkot earlier said all the villagers said the man was from this Faridkot—off the record.

"But on the record, they refused," he told us.

While in the press club, my translator's brother called in hysterics. A police official had just called to tell him that we had been kidnapped. Classic ISI intimidation, designed to scare us into leaving. A friend, another journalist, later called me, saying that he had been told that my translator and I had been beaten up—his glasses and my computer had been broken.

We left. But we also visited the police commander for Okara district and told him about our reception. "I can't say anything," he said. A bit later, when the news-agency journalists came to complain about their stolen phones and DVs, the commander made a call.

"Sir," he said, "your men have snatched the journalists' DVs and telephones. You can erase the images, but please give them back to the journalists."

Nothing odd going on, nothing at all.

Wary of the reach of both the ISI and Nawaz Sharif, Samad and I decided to drive all the way to Islamabad that night, dropping off our translator on the side of the road near Lahore.

"I'm leaving town for a while," he said. "I'll probably go underground. You won't be able to reach me."

This cloak-and-dagger show could strangle the country. One journalist we met was arrested after my story. I later tried to help another journalist, threatened by the ISI after his TV report aired, get out of Pakistan, without success. Even a year later, any journalist who went to this Faridkot would risk arrest or harassment by the agencies, who stalked this corner of nothing like a traffic cop looking for his quota.

My story ran on the front page. The next day was Eid. I opened my front door and saw rivulets of blood running down the street from all the animals gutted to mark the holiday. A man in a tan salwar kameez stained with blood walked down the middle of the street, holding a dripping knife, his eyes glazed. Anywhere else in the world, I would have run away screaming. Here, this was normal. Considering everything happening in the country, all the blood and gore, I barely noticed that the Tribune Company had just filed for bankruptcy. Sacrifice? I was a newspaper reporter working for a bankrupt company in the middle of the war on terror. I was standing in line like a dumb steer in a chute in Montana, and I didn't even know it.

CHAPTER 24

BAD LIVER AND A BROKEN HEART

The threat of war loomed between Pakistan and India. I had been through this before—back in 2002 and 2003, when the two countries bumped chests the last time around, after the attack on India's parliament was blamed on Lash militants. Because of our history, I treated this display of force between the two neighbors as what it was—a chest-thumping drama worthy of an Indian movie. Now that both countries had nukes, and now that both countries salivated for U.S. approval, war was unlikely. Still, we all wrote stories about the two nations being on the verge of hitting the button. Everyone pumped it up like a championship football match.

Unfortunately, I had planned a real vacation between Christmas and New Year's Eve for the first time in years. I was supposed to go to California for a friend's wedding. I had even bought a ticket.

"Nothing's gonna happen after Christmas," I told my boss.

"I'm not even going to respond to that," he said.

"But I'm supposed to be on vacation."

"We'll see."

Until his verdict, I worked. While Samad and I were about ninety minutes outside Lahore one afternoon, reporting on how the main Jamaat-ud-Dawa campus was up and running despite Pakistani claims to have shuttered the charity, I glanced at my BlackBerry. Farouq had written an e-mail. He was slightly hurt because I hadn't told him I was coming to Afghanistan the next day to interview President Karzai. I called him.

"What interview with Karzai?"

"I heard you had an interview with Karzai."

"No. I've repeatedly asked for one. But they haven't told me anything."

Farouq, helping the *New York Times* with the kidnapping of its reporter, said a photographer told him I had an interview with Karzai.

"What? No. I think they would have told me."

We hung up. I thought for a minute. I had been pushing for an interview for months, relying primarily on my good friend Barack Obama. My argument went like this: Obama was probably going to be president. Obama thought Afghanistan was really, really important. Obama was a U.S. senator from Illinois. I worked for his hometown newspaper. Therefore, the president of Afghanistan should talk to me. Now that Obama had actually been elected, this ridiculously thin argument may have actually worked. It would be a coup—Karzai had granted very few interviews in recent months. I called Karzai's spokesman, aware of the government's incompetence.

"Do I have an interview with Karzai tomorrow?" I asked.

"Yes," he said.

"Maybe someone should have told me."

"I thought I did," he said. "I sent you a note on Facebook."

"I didn't get it."

"Sorry about that," he said, although he clearly wasn't. "Can you be here at noon?"

"No. I'm in Pakistan, and I'm in the middle of nowhere, Pakistan. I think it's highly unlikely I could get there by noon."

"How's four?"

I said I'd check. The morning flight to Kabul was sold out, but my travel agent, a friend, promised to get me on the plane if I could make it back to Islamabad. Samad drove us back the six hours, pulling into the capital before midnight. The next morning, he rushed me to the Afghan embassy where I picked up a visa in a record fifteen minutes.

After a quick flight and a harried attempt at scribbling questions, I was ushered in to see Karzai, who looked tired and gray, a dehydrated version of his earlier self.

"It's nice to meet you, ma'am," he said, standing to shake my hand.

I didn't tell him that we'd met before. Our interview was strange and rambling, and Karzai jumped from subject to subject, failing to take any responsibility for all that had gone wrong in his country. He blamed the U.S.-led coalition for hiring "thugs or warlords or whatever," and then going with "those thugs to the homes of hundreds of elders and community people," which "frightened them into running away from Afghanistan." I had a hard time understanding exactly what Karzai meant. At some points, he seemed distracted. His voice occasionally went up several pitches—when he said "high time," the "high" sounded a good sixteen notes higher than "time." His face twitched continually, evidence of an attack on him years earlier. Karzai made sense when he talked about the failures of the international community—they didn't understand the damage from civilian casualties, didn't train the police, didn't focus enough on militant sanctuaries in Pakistan. But he seemed completely oblivious to his own failures, except that he had been too soft with his initial complaints to the international community. His points on the Taliban were just bizarre. He wanted to negotiate with the Taliban but didn't know where to find them.

"I try to find them, I keep sending them messages, I don't know their address," he told me. "That is another big problem. The Afghan Taliban not having an address."

I nodded. A big problem, yes.

At the end of the interview, Karzai returned to the subject of whether he was too isolated, always surrounded by bodyguards.

"There's that man, the governor of Punjab in India, whenever he goes anywhere he has hundreds of bodyguards around him," Karzai said. "Isn't that right?"

"Right, sir," his spokesman said.

"I'm much less isolated," Karzai said.

"Right, sir," the spokesman said.

They both looked at me.

"I have no idea," I said.

I left. The interview was so sprawling, I knew I'd need to put a direct transcript online to do it any justice. After the transcript appeared, the president's spokesman thanked me, saying the transcript had been translated into different languages and delivered to various embassies. I did not think that was a smart move. Afghan friends asked whether Karzai had lost the plot.

Within days I was back in Pakistan, since my bosses and most of the world believed the country was about to explode.

"I'm supposed to be going on vacation," I said.

"Yeah, I know," my boss said. "I'm really sorry. You can take your vacation in Pakistan. Unless something happens, and then you'll have to write."

Or I would be blown up in a nuclear conflagration. Either option sounded like a bad holiday. But I agreed to the new vacation plan, wary of recent rumors that the *Tribune* and the *Los Angeles Times* were launching Ultimate Fight Challenge and would require all the correspondents to punch it out for the few jobs left. I drank my way through Christmas Eve, and then I drank my way through Christmas Day. Depressed, lonely, worried about the lack of balance in my life, I was hardly alone. The small international community in Islamabad made the best of the season, of celebrating a Christian holiday in the middle of a potential nuclear war between an Islamic country and a largely Hindu one.

The day after Christmas, I wrote a story about Pakistan moving troops from the tribal areas to the border with India. Then I went back on vacation, which meant hiking in the Margalla Hills above Islamabad and watching true-crime shows on TV. After three days of this, I wasted a day on the Internet. I checked Facebook, looking to see if pictures had yet been posted of my friend's wedding. Then I noticed that my ex-boyfriend Chris, the man who had moved to India before descending into paranoia, had changed his relationship status. Twice. In fourteen minutes, he had gone from single to being in a relationship to being engaged. This was a surprise. We had stayed friendly—we were friends on Facebook—and I knew that we never would have stayed together, even in the States. He had managed to heal himself after his journey into darkness in Delhi, but had stopped communicating with me over the previous summer. I wrote on his Facebook wall "wow, congratulations"—because that seemed the proper response to a Facebook engagement announcement.

That night I sat at home, vaguely sad. I didn't want to be married to Chris. I didn't necessarily want to be married. But I didn't want to be where I was, with the threat of war and an employment ax hanging over me every day. With a new year fast approaching, I felt sorry for myself, a mood that grew quickly boring. Maudlin and self-obsessed, I dressed up for New Year's Eve, always an exercise in unmet expectations and amateur drinking. I slipped on a short black dress that probably qualified more as a shirt, tights, and high-heeled black boots with silver buckles up the side. Over the years, I had amassed my own ridiculous wardrobe for an Islamic country.

The party was at the Canadian embassy, featuring a bad buffet and the same lame Pakistani DJ who played the same songs in the same order at every single Islamabad party, almost daring people to dance. I pledged myself to a good time, and immediately grabbed a glass of red wine. I tried dancing, but teetered on my heels and towered over most of the crowd. At one point, I sidled up to a male friend, a journalist I had developed a slight crush on. But he was busy working the diplomats. He dared me to ask a short Middle Eastern diplomat to dance. I did, fairly certain that my slight crush was trying to get rid of me. At midnight, my friends and I all kissed each other on our respective cheeks. I tossed back red wine like water.

Later, in the bathroom, I looked at myself under harsh fluorescent lights. My black eyeliner was now smudged. One eye looked like I had been slugged. I had bits of red wine in the corners of my mouth. My tongue was stained purple, the color of cheap boxed wine, as were my teeth. I looked puffy, trashy, and drunk, the opposite of sexy. But I stayed late. My slight crush drove me home, after almost backing into the British embassy. I poured myself out of his car, into my front door, and fell asleep in my dress and boots. I popped awake the next morning at nine.

I needed a new start. It was a new year, after all, and Obama was going to be president. Afghanistan and Pakistan were finally on America's radar, the biggest story in the world. I focused on work, on cultivating new sources, on winning Ultimate Fight Challenge. I vowed to do embeds, blogs, video, interviews, cartwheels, breaking news, long features, recipes, algebra. If there was going to be some kind of contest over my job, I was going to fight as hard as possible to win. I channeled the theme from *Rocky*. I would cancel all holidays, write at all hours, say yes to every editor. I wasn't going to just roll over and play dead. But I was hungover, still lying in bed, and I narrowly avoided strangling myself in competing clichés and resolutions.

Why did I want to stay so much, in a region that was falling apart, as my newspaper was dying? Because despite the missed vacations, despite everything, this still felt more like home than anywhere else. Only in this madness was it possible to feel such purpose. I was paid to watch history. In a small way, I felt that I was part of something much bigger, like I mattered in a way I never did back home. Every dinner conversation felt important; every turn of the screw felt momentous. This was my life. I wanted to know how the story ended. And if I left here, I wanted to leave on my terms because I had decided it was time to leave, not because someone back in Chicago decided to pull the plug.

So I came up with targets, on both sides of the border, stories that would appeal back home, sources who could deliver scoops. I had recently met a man in the Pakistani military. He was on the inside. He knew what was happening with the troop movements against India. He called me in code, as he knew our phones were tapped. It was all very conspiratorial and promising. He called me from an unknown number.

"This is that one person you met," he said. "Do you know who I am?"

"Oh yes, you. Of course."

Through cryptic text messages and calls to various numbers, I invited him over to my house late one night. I served him Black Label whiskey—the preferred drink of most Pakistani men. We sat on my couch. He was nervous to tell me anything, and I knew I had to win his trust. He knew both Bhutto and Sharif. He liked Bhutto. He did not like Sharif because of a dalliance Sharif allegedly once pursued. According to this military man, the woman was the third most beautiful in the world.

Here was something I could give, a quid pro quo to get this man to trust me, a potentially damaging fact that was not actually damaging.

"I know Sharif. He must like women. He may have once fancied me, at least a little bit."

The man struggled to hold his Black Label without laughing. He swallowed with difficulty.

"You? No. Never."

"I was probably mistaken."

"I mean, you're OK," he said. "But Nawaz Sharif could have any woman he wants. He had the third most beautiful woman in the world. And you come nowhere near that."

"You could be right," I acknowledged.

I decided not to risk anything else. After all, I didn't know whose side he was on. I had learned that much about Pakistan by this point. Someone was always listening, and few things were what they seemed on the surface—except, apparently, for the gift of a brand-new, latest-model iPhone.

CHAPTER 25

YOUNG AMERICANS

I flew to Kabul in a blatant attempt to be relevant. If my newspaper wanted local news, I planned to deliver. I would follow the Illinois National Guard as soldiers attempted to train the Afghan police, which was suddenly seen as critically important. Everyone had realized that the Afghan police were corrupt, incompetent, and often high. And only when they and the Afghan army got their act together could anyone leave.

This was my seventh embed, my seventh time hanging out with U.S. soldiers, my seventh version of the same drill. We met for a briefing in a plywood hut in Camp Phoenix, on the outskirts of Kabul.

"So can we shoot if they have a remote control?" one soldier asked.

"If that remote control looks like a pistol aimed at you, then I would say, light 'em up," replied the first lieutenant in charge, who then listed hot spots for roadside bombs. "Pretty much the whole downtown area."

"Awesome," another soldier replied.

Light 'em up. Awesome. Let's roll. Get some. Over the years, I had learned the lingo of the U.S. military and slipped into it easily, as familiar as a Montana drawl. I had also figured out different categories of U.S. soldiers—the Idealists, the Thinkers, the Workers, the Junkies, and the Critics. This first lieutenant was an Idealist, a true believer who thought that he and America could make a difference here. In a way, I found his situation report—or "sit rep"—funny. They were talking about Kabul, a city I had driven around for years, a downtown I had walked around. I never wore body armor in Kabul. I only worried about my security in Kabul when I saw a military convoy because of suicide blasts, overeager NATO gunners, and Afghan drivers who disobeyed warnings to halt.

So this would be my first time seeing Kabul from a Humvee, my first time seeing Afghans as the other. The first lieutenant warned of a white Toyota Corolla without a license plate—a potential suicide bomber, who by the looks of repeated security warnings I had seen, had been haunting Kabul for three years. It was a running joke with longtimers—highly paid security companies fixated on a potential suicide bomber with a long beard, wearing a turban, and driving a white Toyota Corolla, which described pretty much half the men in Kabul.

Our mission was outlined: Drive through the mean streets of Kabul and north to a rural district to train the police. It seemed like a fairly obvious mission, but more than seven years into the war here, the U.S. military had only recently gotten serious about the Afghan police. And the police were a serious problem. Police chiefs were often illiterate thugs and sometimes drug lords who ran their departments like fiefdoms. Some paid big money for their posts, even $100,000, and they made their money back by being on the take. Most low-level police were paid little money and given little training. They took bribes often because they had no other choice. But the police were crucial to any counterinsurgency. If Afghans did not trust their police, they would naturally turn toward the Taliban. The police were also increasingly on the front lines—more Afghan police had died in Taliban-led attacks than soldiers, Afghan or foreign.

Both the outgoing Bush administration and the incoming Obama one stressed that Afghan police and soldiers were essential to solving the morass here—but clearly not enough troops had yet been devoted to the task. The Illinois National Guard ran three police-mentor teams in Kabul Province with thirty soldiers altogether, responsible for about six thousand police in thirty police districts. The Afghan police faced similar numerical challenges—in the district we were going, Mir Bacha Kot, which meant "collection of boys," eighty-five police were supposed to serve about a hundred and twenty-five thousand people living in thirty-six villages.

A trainer from DynCorp tried to explain what the U.S. soldiers would see with the Afghan National Police (ANP), using an example from Paghman district, in the western part of Kabul Province.

"We talk about how things are," the trainer said. "Yesterday in Paghman we had a situation with a guy. He's a mullah by day, Taliban by night. ANP is not gonna do anything about him. Don't trust a lot of the things that you're seeing and hearing."

We climbed into our Humvees. I sat behind the driver, wearing a helmet and flak vest that made me feel somewhat ridiculous. We put on headsets so we could hear one another and barged into a traffic jam on Jalalabad Road. Through the window, I watched the panic start. The Afghan drivers did not wave or smile at the U.S. soldiers. They tried to get out of the way, fear written on their craggy faces. But sitting in a Humvee instead of out in traffic, I felt nervous for the American soldiers. They saw every Afghan, every car as a potential enemy, even though they had been here only for a few weeks and Kabul was a relatively safe city compared with the south. But little wonder: Days earlier, a bomber had attacked another U.S. military base in Kabul, injuring five soldiers from the Illinois National Guard, one of whom later died. Everyone was on edge.

"This is nothing," the first lieutenant announced as we sat in traffic. "Traffic yesterday, we didn't move for forty-five minutes. Jackknifed fuel truck, leaking fuel. We just had to sit there and wait. But I'll take traffic with a lot of vehicles and cars over being stopped in a crowd of people. I didn't like that at all. A crowd of people can turn ugly."

The gunner agreed, mentioning one crowd that had uglified recently. "You could tell their attitudes have turned negative toward us. You're not getting the smile and a wave."

This was educational. If people in Kabul reacted this way, how did they feel in the provinces? And if U.S. soldiers felt this way, what chance did anyone have to turn this war around? Years into this, I was still hearing the same comments from U.S. soldiers, the same gripes about Afghanistan. We had learned so little. Most of these Illinois soldiers had only found out after arriving here that they would be training police. They had been told they would be doing something else, like briefings, PowerPoint presentations, and administrative work. And much of their training in the States focused not on the police, not even on Afghanistan, but on Iraq.

The soldiers continued to dissect the traffic of the capital.

"All and all, my personal favorite is the left blinker, and then they turn to the right," the first lieutenant said. "Half the people do that."

"Traffic rules don't exist," the gunner agreed. "Just like everything. No laws. I don't care what everybody says. This place never gets old."

The discussion then turned to me.

"So you're normally just out there, without any protection?" the first lieutenant asked.

"Yep. In a white Toyota Corolla," I joked.

"Aren't you nervous?"

"I'm actually more nervous sitting in this Humvee," I admitted.

We pushed through the traffic jam, toward Massoud circle, the ugly monument where I had covered the massive attack on a U.S. convoy more than two years earlier. The first lieutenant started to worry at the circle because the Afghan police had set up a checkpoint. He told the gunner to get his head down. "I don't want my guys to get shot in the head," he said, picking up the radio. "All gunners, get down."

The gunners complied, ducking down as we passed through

the circle. Someone in our Humvee put on the singer George Thorogood, music to get macho to. We drove past fruit markets and Afghans on motorcycles. One nearly fell over in its attempt to get away.

"A white Toyota station wagon with Toyota written in the windshield," the first lieutenant said, looking out the window. "That's nice. I feel safe."

We drove past a donkey, past a dozen white Toyota Corollas, past Soilstone Laboratory, past the beige huts on the outskirts of Kabul, toward our destination: Collection of Boys.

"It's like fourth world here," said the gunner, surveying the bleak countryside. "Dirt walls, blankets for doors. That guy's got one shoe, he's saving up for a second shoe."

The song "Bad to the Bone" came on. The gunner tapped his boot. Within the hour, we pulled up to the police station at Mir Bacha Kot. Two Afghan officers guarded the road into the parking lot. Neither had a weapon or gloves. One had the wrong boots. The American soldiers first took an inventory of the weapons to make sure none had been sold. They had already seen the corruption here—in another district, U.S. military discretionary money had bought a powerful generator for the police station. The district governor then took the generator to his house.

In the parking lot, basically a pile of rocks, the Americans then lined up fourteen Afghan officers. With all their equipment, the Americans looked like superheroes. The Afghans looked pathetic. Six did not have weapons because they were not qualified to have weapons. Of the other eight, only three said they had been to the main police-training center. And one was probably mistaken; he grinned wildly and raised his hand to every question.

The Afghans mimicked the Americans raising their weapons. The Americans ducked.

"They've had training, right?" one soldier asked. "They could have shot everyone."

The police officers without weapons aimed their fingers and laughed hysterically. They leaned back as they pointed their guns and fingers. A U.S. soldier started going apoplectic because an Afghan soldier wouldn't bend his knees. Another police officer stuck his rifle butt between his knees, pointed the weapon at his head, and started yanking on something inside his empty cartridge.

"Tell him, never stick his hand in his weapon," a U.S. soldier said. He turned away and muttered, "Takes every fiber of my being."

One Afghan officer jumped over razor wire, his finger on the trigger. Another, finger also on the trigger, leaned on his loaded weapon, muzzle on his boot—in years past, I knew of at least one Afghan police officer, nicknamed "Crazy Eyes" by U.S. soldiers, who had shot a hole in his foot that way. On a walk through the village, an Afghan police officer waved his gun at a baby. Another held his gun upside down with his finger in the trigger loop.

At one point I had to turn around, I was laughing so hard. The photographer was laughing.

"These guys are the best Afghanistan has to offer?" he asked.

"The Afghan police make me laugh," I admitted.

Probably not the best attitude, but it was true. I also kept a video of the Afghan army trying to do jumping jacks, which resembled a really bad dance or an incurable disease. I often showed the video to Americans who thought we could train the Afghans quickly to take care of their own security and then get out. The Illinois soldiers would visit this police station once every few weeks for a couple of hours at a time. And then, in another nine months, they would leave.

The soldiers gave the police some concertina wire—apparently, they had done a good job—before heading back to Kabul, listening to Metallica's "Ride the Lightning." At a debriefing back at Camp Phoenix, some of the Illinois soldiers were frustrated. Training was inconsistent; none of the fifteen rolls of razor wire donated the last trip had been used; new AK-47s were still in boxes; all the police demanded flashlights. The police officers had to share the district's only pen, that is, the ones who could write.

"What struck me is how these guys are supposed to be trained," one soldier said. "Are you kidding me? These motherfuckers can't even pivot. Don't they all have jobs to do? I know at the last police department, we asked them, 'Do you ever arrest anybody?' 'No.' 'What do you do?' They're like, 'Eating, sleeping, nothing.' I mean, what are they policing? This is another brick wall we're running into. They aren't doing anything."

Everyone griped. Then the first lieutenant made a proposal.

"I was able to talk to the chief. He wanted to take one kilometer of wire up to the cell-phone tower. Then they can have twenty-four-hour electricity."

Everyone looked at him, silent.

"You can't do that," the DynCorp guy finally said. "We're trying to teach them about corruption. You can't help them steal power."

The first lieutenant was unrepentant. "It makes sense. It's an easy thing we can do that will really help them."

"You can't be serious," the DynCorp guy said.

He was. Quick fixes, fast turnarounds, an easy bang for the buck. That pretty much typified the international approach. But the only thing that would make a difference with the Afghan police was a whole lot of training, for a whole lot of years, with a whole lot of money. This was a largely illiterate country wracked by thirty years of war, a place where young men from the provinces didn't know how to lace their boots because they'd never had boots. It's not like Afghans couldn't fight—of course they could. But the only recruits willing to earn so little money to be cannon fodder were not the best and the brightest. Mostly, they were the no-hopes.

While on this embed, I wrote at least one good story for the *Tribune* about local soldiers helping in a foreign land. But I also wrote a few embarrassing clunkers to appeal to my new bosses, including one about the delivery of Chicago-style pizza to the soldiers, just in time for Super Bowl Sunday. The last time I had written anything that so reeked of jingoism and free advertising, I had just entered puberty. Even so, I got mocked by colleagues at the Associated Press and was sent a piece of hate mail because I quoted a soldier who criticized the pizza. I could not win.

Starved for the relative normalcy of Kabul, I soon left the soldiers. A friend who worked as a UN adviser to the Afghan-run Independent Electoral Commission came to town. Over lunch, he described the election fraud he had witnessed in the southeast. Already Afghans were registering to vote for the upcoming presidential election. But my friend had caught Afghan election workers creating thousands of fake registration cards. Women had also registered in unprecedented numbers in the conservative southeast—numbers that were likely inflated. In one province, when asked about registration, a top election official bragged that his province not only was registering a lot of women but was also registering children. My friend reported the suspected fraud; his UN superiors said they would send a committee to investigate but never did. I was not entirely surprised. The previous fall, Karzai had named loyalists to run three ministries—Interior, Education, and Tribal Affairs. Interior ran the police. Education ran the teachers. Both ministries had people everywhere. Tribal Affairs worked with the tribes, crucial to any election. By that point, the fix was in. UN officials and Western diplomats started distancing themselves from the election, referring to it as "an Afghan process" and "Afghan-led." It wasn't too difficult to decipher their meaning—they were absolving themselves of any responsibility, even as the UN put its hat out to raise more than $300 million to foot the bill.

A few weeks later, I flew to southern Helmand Province to watch Illinois soldiers posted there help eradicate poppies. This was part of NATO's new approach to drugs, the first time that any foreign troops had been involved in eradication, even if they only guarded the Afghan police riding tractors that ripped up the poppies. The soldiers' surroundings were stark, and they certainly didn't get any Super Bowl Sunday pizza. Instead, they were attacked almost every time they left the base—by the Taliban, the farmers, the villagers.

Outside the base, fields of newly planted poppies stretched forever, beautiful carpets of green. People in Washington sometimes tried to portray poppy farmers as small guys, eking a living from the land. In Helmand, at least, these were corporate drug farms.

The Afghans and their international guards made a show of clearing a patch of poppies right outside the base gate—a patch they had been saving to show off for the media and top Kabul luminaries, a patch with limited risk of attack. A man from the U.S. embassy, thrilled to be outside, wore a patch on his flak vest: AMERICA, FUCK YEAH, it said, quoting the movie *Team America*. Was there a better description for what we were trying to do here? If so, I had yet to hear it.

CHAPTER 26

WHEN THE MAN COMES AROUND

In some ways, I hoped Obama would be the savior. After he switched the war's focus from Iraq to this region, I thought that maybe everything would turn around, that Afghanistan and Pakistan would suddenly reverse course and miraculously start improving. Selfishly, I figured my job was safe. After all, Obama was from Chicago, as was my newspaper, and if this region was seen as the most important foreign story in the world in the coming years, surely the *Tribune* would need its own correspondent. So I launched my own tactical surge in preparation for the upcoming U.S. surge. I knew the United States could do only so much inside stubbornly sovereign Pakistan; I planned to spend as much time as possible following the Americans in Afghanistan. But I needed to cut my costs. I decided to move from my giant house in Islamabad to a friend's house and use the savings to rent a room in Kabul. I decided to cut my fixer costs, and offer Farouq a take-it-or-leave-it deal of $1,600 a month, regardless of whether I was in Afghanistan. For most Afghans, this was a fine salary. But not for Farouq.

He was already upset with me for a variety of reasons. Given my stress, I had been short with him, not treating him like before. I was treating him like my employee—not like my friend. I was tired of worrying about money and scrimping like a freelancer. I was tired of stacking all my interviews over a few days, so I could pay Farouq for only a few days' work, which meant he was always on call, unable to work for anyone else. I was tired of his occasional macho rants. Given the boom in interest in Afghanistan, Farouq could make much more money anywhere else. Both of us were frustrated.

"You can think about it," I said, after making my offer.

"No, Kim. I can tell you what I think right now. I can't work for that amount of money. I'm sorry."

"I'm sorry, too," I said.

We pledged to stay friends, but I knew we wouldn't talk for a while. We were both raw, mainly over the irony that when the world finally realized that Afghanistan was circling the drain, so were both of our jobs. In slight shock over my bold move, I hired someone else.

I flew back to Pakistan, where Nawaz Sharif again made noise about restoring the judges fired sixteen months earlier by Musharraf. That old story—he was like Musharraf with the miscreants. But President Zardari had just punched himself in the eye by removing Sharif's brother as the head of the Punjab government. A planned march by the long-suffering lawyers—who by this point had been in a monotonous state of protest for almost two years, occasionally staging symbolic three-hour hunger strikes—suddenly had momentum. The Sharifs threw all their significant political weight behind the lawyers. I sent a text message to Sharif, asking him to call.

"I haven't seen you for a long time," he said when he called that Friday evening. "Where have you been?"

"Afghanistan," I replied. It was easier that way.

Nothing was mentioned about the iPhone, or our past meeting, or his offer.

Then Zardari banned the march and put Sharif and various opponents under house arrest—moves that only drew attention to the march and guaranteed its significance. Zardari acted like Musharraf, but he forgot one thing—he didn't have the army behind him. The Sharifs and their key aides plowed out of house arrest in SUVs.

The police were not about to stop them. Their convoy moved out of Lahore, paralyzing the country and forcing Zardari's hand. Diplomats like Hillary Clinton twisted various arms.

And suddenly, surprisingly, stunningly, after midnight we heard that the country's prime minister would soon restore the judges. Unlike many rumors, this one seemed true. I rushed over to the former chief justice's house, where I encountered one of the few true magical unscripted moments I had ever experienced in Pakistan—actual joy, a sense of disbelief, that finally, after so long, the lawyers' movement actually might win. For the past two years, I had been with these lawyers when they were beat up, gassed, arrested, and ignored by the United States, Musharraf, and Zardari. A lawyer friend pulled me inside the former chief justice's house. Iftikhar Mohammed Chaudhry sat in an armchair in a corner of his living room, greeting an endless line of well-wishers. In another room, lawyers crowded around a TV, waiting for the prime minister's speech. I walked outside. People shouted, "Go, Zardari, go!" Small groups of lawyers, in their uniforms of black suits and white shirts, danced and sang.

At daybreak the prime minister finally announced that the judges would be restored. Within days they were, setting up an inevitable showdown between the bench and Zardari. I had a feeling that Zardari's former criminal charges, ranging from corruption to murder, would eventually come back to haunt him. I also had a feeling, lingering in the back of my head, that Chaudhry's megalomania could eventually approach that of Musharraf. But I shook it off. Must have been the lack of sleep.

My request for an actual vacation that month had been ignored, and back in Chicago, it seemed like everything was being ignored. Conference calls were scheduled; rumors flew that would put Pakistan to shame. We received new directions every day. New story formats were developed—we were supposed to file information for "charticles," we were supposed to write new "brights" for the front page. The man in charge of innovation for the company sent subversive "think pieces," stream-of-consciousness rants with random capital letters, confessions like "I've been on a continual road trip" and misspellings like "NOTOCABLE," "INSINCERETY," and "VISABLE." One example of a "think piece": "Check these out. They reflect exactly the kind of POWER that subtle and cerebral can deliver . . . It oozes timeless, all demographic QUALITY." I said yes to everything, happy to be of service, sifting through management "think pieces," trying to find the hidden messages in the capital letters, to figure out why on earth people who flaunted their inability to spell, capitalize, and punctuate would want to run a media company.

Finally, on a Monday night, my boss called just as I walked in the front door.

"Kim, they made a decision, and some tough decisions had to be made," he told me. "And as part of those decisions, they would like you to come home and work for the metro desk."

Ultimate Fight Challenge was done. I hung up the phone and burst into tears. The next day, during the requisite conference call, the paper's editor informed me that the company was unifying the foreign reporting team to serve everybody, which meant "more strategic company-wide use of our expertise." He used words like "partnership" and phrases like "a big chessboard." I felt like we were breaking up. All told, thirteen—or maybe sixteen—correspondents survived from both newspapers, including only two from the *Tribune*, which had once had eleven. (The numbers were unclear, because the company also kept a few *Los Angeles Times* correspondents on contract.)

"There's no right or wrong choice," said the big boss, adding that he thought I could use my expertise covering the war on terror in Chicago. The gangs must have really stepped up their game.

I could hardly blame the company—it was, after all, bankrupt, and foreign news cost a lot of money. My bureau cost about $120,000 a year in expenses alone. The *Tribune* foreign desk was essentially eliminated, almost quietly, just as the newsroom loudly promoted a class for "Advanced Twitter." The *Los Angeles Times* would run the company-wide foreign desk, and the new foreign editor would be the same man who had written the competing *Los Angeles Times* story on *Afghan Star*, the one that had run the same day as mine and put me squarely in Sam Zell's crosshairs. Curses—my nemesis. I felt sad and numb and rejected, almost like a spurned lover, but this rejection felt even more personal. I loved this job, I was this job. If I didn't have this, what would I be?

I was given time to think about the metro offer, and I did think. I knew everything in Afghanistan was increasingly messed up. "America, Fuck Yeah" was the future. Many talented Afghans were leaving, including Farouq, whom I thought had abandoned his dreams of ever studying outside Afghanistan. He sent me an e-mail when he won a prestigious scholarship to a university in the West—to study communications, not medicine. I was not surprised—if Afghanistan ever got rid of the mullahs and warlords, that guy could run it. (Once, Farouq had told me how he would police a traffic roundabout with a hammer, breaking the windows of traffic offenders. "Believe me, people will enjoy my roundabout," he had opined. That was his philosophy of governance in Afghanistan, the necessity of a strong hand.) Back in Pakistan, Samad continued building his life in his mother's tiny apartment, washing his car fifty times a day. His wife was now pregnant, even though he barely had any money. Yet if all Samad ever had in his life was his family and his car, I knew he would be happy.

Afghanistan and Pakistan continued to dominate the news. The day after I was deemed irrelevant, news leaked that the term "war on terror" also was. The Obama administration preferred "Overseas Contingency Operation." Days after that, Obama announced his much anticipated new strategy for Afghanistan and Pakistan. After more than seven years, the region had finally become a situation.

"The situation is increasingly perilous," Obama warned.

An editor e-mailed me that night, asking if I had anything I'd like to add to a story on Obama's speech. I said I was sick, and I kind of was. Within a month, that editor was laid off.

I still didn't know what I would do, but I had to leave Pakistan and Afghanistan for now if I wanted to hold on to my salary. I also knew I had to get out of here if I wanted to get any perspective. Samad, ever the wounded puppy, started to cry when I told him and called me his sister. Large tears pooled in his large brown eyes.

"Stop it," I said. "You're killing me."

Friends in Islamabad decided to throw me a going-away party at the house where I was staying. But that night, as I drew on eyeliner, I heard a distant thud outside. I chose to ignore it and went back to my eyeliner. Samad soon ran inside the house, knocking on my bedroom door.

"Boss, big bomb, maybe Jinnah," he announced, agitated.

"No. No way. Not tonight." I had moved on to mascara.

"Yes, boss. Tonight." He smiled.

Samad still didn't understand my syntax all that well. Jinnah was the giant supermarket closest to this neighborhood, where foreigners always shopped.

"I can't fucking believe this."

Samad looked at me. "Yes, boss?"

"Can you go check it out?" I asked.

"Yes, boss."

He ran off.

A Swiss friend called, panicked. She was hiding with her boyfriend in a closet, the Swiss version of a safe room. She heard shots in all directions.

"I don't think I can make it to your party," she said.

I called Samad, now curious. Maybe I needed just one bomb for the road.

"Come pick me up."

He really didn't need to drive. We could have walked to the bombing, which was not at a supermarket but in a grassy median a couple of blocks away. A man had blown himself up near a tent filled with Pakistani security forces. Eight had died.

More than a hundred journalists were there, scribbling on notebooks, jostling for position. It was like old home week. A friend and I walked near an ambulance. Shots rang out. We dropped to the ground. Pakistani men in cream-colored salwar kameezes threw themselves on top of us and fondled us back across the street, over to the other journalists. I started laughing. This was the perfect going-away party for Pakistan. A senior police officer insisted that the situation was under control, even as shots ricocheted through the neighborhood, an alleged second bomber ran loose, and a group of elite armed soldiers darted in front of the house where the party was supposed to be.

"Should we still have the party?" I asked a friend from the Associated Press.

"Oh yeah," she said. "Otherwise, the terrorists win."

I certainly didn't want that. So we threw the party, and most people came, filled with that need for alcohol and numbness that by now I knew accompanied any terrorist attack. (Tammy stayed home—she was too depressed about Pakistan.) At the end of the night, fueled by booze, socks, and a treacherous marble staircase, I fell. The next morning, I woke up with a knot the size of a golf ball on my forehead. I left Pakistan a few days later with a concussion and slight double vision, and without telling my bosses. And that, I later realized, was how Pakistan should always be left. With a head injury.

Pondering my options on the flight home, I realized I would rather scoop out my eyeballs with a rusty spoon than go back to my life from seven years earlier. This came as a shock. The newspaper industry was hemorrhaging jobs left and right—by the end of that year, more than forty thousand jobs would be cut. I should count myself lucky to hold on to any job at any major newspaper. But after covering these countries, after writing about life and death and chaos and war, I knew I couldn't just write about frenzied families and carefree couples in Chicago, the paper's new target demographic. I couldn't move backward. My heart wouldn't be in it because my heart would still be somewhere halfway around the world, wearing a flak vest.

I decided to do something I had never done before. Quit. And, in a move that many deemed insane, I decided to go back to Afghanistan to have a quiet place to figure out what I wanted to do next. Maybe it was the story, which had burrowed into my bloodstream, or the concussion. And maybe it was the newspaper industry, and the fact that no one was willing to pay for the news anymore. Only a few weeks after I quit, the bare-bones *Tribune* newsroom would be forced to lay off more than fifty people. The same day, the company's bosses would ask the U.S. Bankruptcy Court to pay more than $13 million in bonuses to almost seven hundred people deemed essential to the future of the company. Still, Sam Zell couldn't stop talking about Afghanistan. That same night, he would tell a group of college students: "I'm not going to the *Chicago Tribune* for news about Afghanistan." Of that, I was absolutely certain.

CHAPTER 27
HOTEL CALIFORNIA

Unemployed, with no backing and no concrete purpose, I flew back to a war zone, to Kabul, the closest place I had to home. I moved in with a friend who charged me bargain rent. Some days, I watched entire seasons of TV shows on pirated DVDs. Some nights, I worked as a bartender at my friend's bar. I was burned out, so much so that I lived in a new country, one that contained only my room, or more accurately, my bed, piled with notebooks, ideas, DVDs, and socks. I thought about what I would do next.

The weeks ticked down to the Afghan presidential election, which I viewed with the kind of anticipation that others reserved for cultural events like a new zombie movie. I pretended that I was still part of this world, that I still mattered. I researched freelance stories and a book idea. One night I tagged along with some friends to the Red Hot 'n' Sizzlin' restaurant, a low-slung and low-key steak house on the outskirts of Kabul. Past guests had scrawled graffiti in black marker on the brick arches inside the restaurant, nicknames such as "Mighty Mick," helpful household tips such as "Up UR bum no babies." People came here for meat, for main dishes like Bacon Wrapped Hamburger Steak and Gold Rush Pork Chops, flavored with condiments like Cowboy Butters. The drink list was equally creative. Shooters were called 3 Dollar Hooker, A Kick in Crotch, Hand Job, Monkey Brain, Minty Nipple. Cocktails ran $6.50, with names such as Mexican Sexy Lemonade, Sex on the Boat, Sex on the Sofa, Sex Peak, After Sex, and Gloom Raiser.

Halfway through the Texas-sized Onion Loaf, the trouble started. An American woman known for asking for threesomes as cavalierly as Afghan children demanded "One dollar, lady," stood up from her computer and spotted a security guy at our table whom she blamed for losing her previous job with a USAID subcontractor. She weaved toward us, then toward her husband at the bar. Normally her husband was the problem—he often got so drunk that he could barely walk, and his problems walking on the perilous streets of Kabul were compounded by the fact that he was blind. The woman was angry, and he hugged her and told her to sit down. But she veered back to the security guy sitting next to me.

"Fucking asshole, fucking asshole," the woman shouted, slurring her words. "I am one step away from Obama. Do you know who you're dealing with?"

The entire restaurant did. A restaurant worker rushed toward her, followed by her husband, who tapped over with his cane.

"You don't know who you're messing with," she shouted as they hustled her out the door. "You have no idea."

The song "Highway to Hell" came on. It seemed apt. Why did the West keep getting Afghanistan wrong? Situations like this were as good a reason as any. Most foreigners had created a world where it was possible to rarely deal with the natives, where acceptable behavior included being staggeringly drunk by 8:45 PM on a Tuesday in an Islamic country that banned alcohol, frowned on pork, and certainly would never tolerate a drink named after sex.

Some foreigners wanted to make Afghanistan a better place, viewed Afghanistan as a home rather than a party, and even genuinely liked Afghans. But they were in the minority, and many had left, driven out by the corruption and the inability to accomplish anything. For most, Afghanistan was Kabul High, a way to get your war on, an adrenaline rush, a résumé line, a money factory. It was a place to escape, to run away from marriages and mistakes, a place to forget your age, your responsibilities, your past, a country in which to reinvent yourself. Not that there was anything wrong with that, but the motives of most people were not likely to help a fragile and corrupt country stuck somewhere between the seventh century and Vegas.

I was hardly better than the rest. A life led constantly inside, whether in a house or a car or a burqa, whether by a foreigner or an Afghan, sparked a constant desire for release. But at least the taxpayers weren't paying my salary.

Many diplomats rarely poked their heads outside embassy walls. Many consultants traded places every six months and then promptly repeated all the mistakes of their predecessors. How out of touch were they? Employees of the Department for International Development (DFID), the British equivalent of USAID, decided it would be a good idea to throw a going-away party just before the election, with the dress code specified as "INVADERS—Alexander the Great, Hippies, Brits, Mughals, Russians, and general gratuitous fancy dress. Gorillas welcome." It was unclear if the misspelling of "guerrillas" was intentional. Pictures of the festivities were posted on Facebook, showing one partygoer with her left breast almost hanging out of her white Grecian dress, three pirates, two aliens drinking beer, two men in turbans, a Mughal, a cowboy, a jihadi. Any member of the Afghanistan Network on Facebook—and plenty of Afghans belonged—could see the photos. Well, at least it wasn't the Tarts and Talibs theme party, thrown the year before. Graveyard of Empires, indeed.

Meanwhile the invaders continued their invasion. By August, the month of the presidential election, a record 101,000 international troops had arrived in Afghanistan, including a record 62,000 Americans, each of whom cost up to $1 million a year. In July, not coincidentally, a record number of international troops had been killed, largely by roadside bombs, the weapon of choice of weaker insurgents determined to wait out their enemies. Military spending in Afghanistan was set to exceed Iraq for the first time. The United States was also now spending $200 million a month on civilian governance and development programs—double that under Bush, an amount equal to the nonmilitary spending in Iraq during its heyday. Too bad it was having such a hard time attracting USAID employees to fill those jobs—one USAID official confided that the agency would be lucky to get the C-team of applicants. Almost eight years into this war, mustering new enthusiasm was difficult.

Regardless, significant results needed to be shown in the next year, in time for the 2012 U.S. presidential election. The United States kept reviewing its strategy and redefining success; the goal posts kept shifting. Our partners seemed equally tired—Canada had just reiterated it would pull its 2,830 troops by 2011, and the 84 soldiers promised by Colombia the same week would hardly make up the difference, even if the Germans finally decided to do actual patrols up north. The British lost their two hundredth soldier, and the Brits back home grew increasingly divided about the war; meanwhile, their incoming army chief said they might need to stay forty years to fix Afghanistan. This patchwork quilt seemed unlikely to hold—as one U.S. soldier in Ghazni had complained to me, to request air support he had to ask the Poles, who ran the battle space, had no airplanes, and passed any request for air support up to the U.S. military in Bagram.

The Afghan side of the quilt looked similarly tattered. Karzai led in the polls before the August 2009 election, but with forty opponents and the popularity of swine flu, he did not necessarily have enough votes to win an outright majority. To gain more power, he had made a dangerous gamble, signing various pacts with the same warlords he had once claimed to disdain and promising them future spoils. He had also continually criticized his foreign benefactors, saying that they were the real root of the problems in Afghanistan. In other words, Karzai had publicly cut his strings with the West, and by sewing up the regional strongmen, he managed to outmaneuver the Obama administration's halfhearted attempts to push any other viable presidential candidate. So U.S. officials, who had profoundly alienated Karzai by repeatedly criticizing him privately and publicly, were left with no other likelihood but a very annoyed Karzai. This was amateur hour.

The week before the election, I bluffed my way into a Karzai campaign event, even though I was no longer on the media list. The reclusive Karzai had made only a few campaign appearances with handpicked audiences. I rode with a friend to Kabul University, where we walked up a dusty road to a dusty parking lot. The security guards made us drop our bags for the dogs to sniff. The male journalists were lined up as if facing a firing squad. The women, meanwhile, were marched up the road to a spot behind a white plywood guard box blocked off by green tarps. One by one, each female journalist was taken behind the tarps. Soon it was my turn. I assumed the position, held out my arms, and held in my breath. I looked at the ground, covered in weeds, memorizing the empty milk boxes and candy wrappers. After the usual deep-tissue massage, the guard pulled up the front of my shirt, yanked my belt and pants out from my waist, and looked down. That was a new move in the guard repertoire.

I walked back to my bag. Money spilled out of the open zippers. "No problem," an Afghan soldier said, grinning. Going to see Hamid Karzai always cost something, most often my dignity.

After security clearance and another bag search, we were shuttled inside the large tent with about a thousand women, all teachers let out of school and forced to come see Karzai speak, more proof of how government employees were confused as to whether they would keep their jobs if someone besides Karzai won. The tent magnified the heat somewhat like a sauna, and the women dripped sweat and fanned themselves, including one woman who looked like she was trying to take flight with a Hello Kitty fan. Large posters of Karzai hung behind the podium, along with a banner proclaiming OUR WAY IS THE WAY OF PEACE. Afghan anthems played over tinny loudspeakers, with lyrics such as "We're really happy to stay in Afghanistan."

"How is Dr. Farouq?" an Afghan friend asked me.

"I think he left the country," I said.

I had heard that Farouq might still be in Afghanistan, or maybe he had left for graduate school, but I had not heard from him in months. Plans of dinner at his house, of getting together, had never materialized. Our friendship had just gone silent. My fault as much as his.

Helicopters rumbled in the distance. I asked if Karzai was coming by helicopter, which would be further evidence of bad security and Karzai's isolation.

"What do you want?" his campaign spokesman said. "He's not coming here by helicopter. He's driving. Come on."

Ten minutes later, the sound of helicopters grew louder.

"So is he coming by helicopter?" I asked.

"No, he's coming by road," the spokesman said.

"But those are helicopters."

"What do you want, they're just patrolling."

The helicopters landed. Karzai strode into the building, waving, shaking hands with the women. He was polished as always—wearing his peaked hat made from the hair of a slain newborn goat, a gray suit jacket over his pressed cream-colored traditional long shirt and pants. He pumped his hands in the air, put his hand over his heart. Women gave speeches, praising Karzai for naming a lone female governor, for letting them work in the ministries.

Karzai spoke for more than half an hour, acknowledging that some people felt he had not done enough in his first term.

"I saw a lot of improvements on my way from the presidential palace to here, beautiful houses and big buildings," said Karzai, neglecting to mention that many were built by profits from the drug trade and corruption. "If I win the election again, I will ask the Taliban to work hand in hand with their Afghan brothers, so they can help each other to make a peaceful and secure Afghanistan in the future."

Oh, great. Them again. Now, after making deals to win the support of the country's most powerful warlords, Karzai wanted to make a deal with the Taliban, who clearly would balk at women being teachers, let alone governors. Regardless, as Karzai finished his speech, the women rushed toward him, handing him pieces of paper, favors they wanted, or shaking his hand and crying. He called me "ma'am," pushed his way toward the door, and as he did so, a loudspeaker burst into flames, creating a hysterical logjam of headscarves and burqas. Caught in the middle, I shoved the tiny Afghan women to the side like Godzilla, but still, one rammed into my right knee. I limped outside and watched Karzai run toward one of the helicopters and climb inside, to fly the lonely three and a half miles back to the presidential palace.

The signs were growing that it was time to pull out—for me, at least. I went to the Nova beauty salon, where an Afghan beautician sliced open the bottom of my foot with a razor before plucking more than half my eyebrows, leaving me looking permanently frightened, a line of tiny scabs above my right eye. (The eyebrow, sadly, would never grow back quite right.) I opened the refrigerator at the house and found a tenement-sized rat, nonchalantly sitting on the middle shelf and gnawing chorizo. I suffered two bouts of food poisoning in three weeks. I ran into my ex-boyfriend Dave, who got mad when I wouldn't look at his photographs of his various embeds. I attended my new driver's brother's wedding, where an Afghan woman wearing hair extensions, heavy makeup, $70,000 worth of gold, and an occasionally see-through dress featuring tiger and leopard prints looked at me disapprovingly and offered to get me a new hairdo. A friend's fixer sneaked into our house to steal a Heineken.

The security company Edinburgh International put out an extremely helpful warning of a possible suicide bomber to its clients. "He is described as having a long beard and is wearing a white or green head covering (turban). Potential targets are not known." I spotted an Afghan bus with a red sticker of a buxom longhaired naked woman lounging in a martini glass. Finally, Abdul Rashid Dostum, the chest-thumping, King Kong–channeling warlord who had gone to Turkey after winning his confrontation with my onetime shooting buddy and Afghan grandpa Abdul Jabar Sabit, returned from Turkey to endorse Karzai, the fifth horseman of the warlord apocalypse.

The explosions started.

On the Saturday before the August 20 election, I woke up about 4 AM, sick with food poisoning. The bomb shook the house a few hours later. We had been expecting a spectacular attack for months, and a photographer friend, Paula, and I rushed to the scene, right in front of NATO headquarters, right where the Afghan kids sold gum and bracelets, just down the road from the U.S. embassy. This attack was particularly audacious, designed to show that the Taliban could strike anywhere. Seven people died. At least ninety were injured. We stood behind a barrier of red-and-white tape, and all we could see were emergency vehicles, tree limbs and leaves on the ground, a car with its windows blown out and its lights on. An Afghan man in a peach button-up shirt and tan pants wandered around aimlessly, covered in blood. The journalists were all there, mostly young freelancers, hungry, new to Afghanistan, here for the election, for the excitement, talking about who got there first, who snapped the car still on fire, who saw the bodies. They were eager, like I had once been. One demanded that Peach Button-up Shirt answer his questions for the TV camera in English, please. I stood back from the tape. I felt almost done. I didn't need to see any more bodies, didn't want to stick my hand in any more human flesh, didn't want to scrub any more people off the bottom of my shoes.

But I still wanted to see the election, a different kind of tragedy. On Election Day, Paula and I drove to various polling stations. Most were quiet, although I could hardly blame Afghans. Why risk voting when no candidate seemed particularly inspiring, when Karzai's victory seemed assured? Compared to the first presidential election five years earlier, when people had lined up for hours for the privilege of voting, this day was just depressing. At one point, we hurried to a report of a shoot-out. The cops had shot one alleged terrorist— another may have escaped. We walked past the pickup truck with the terrorist's body slung in the back like a side of beef and over to the crumbling building where police still searched for evidence. More and more kids and young men surrounded us, more and more journalists showed up, until finally, I decided I'd feel safer in the car. Soon after, I heard shouting and looked up—Paula was sprinting toward the car, flanked by four other huffing photographers. A gaggle of police ran behind them. I popped the back door open— photographers and cameras dove inside. Then we locked the doors. The police surrounded us, brandishing their guns. Apparently they had been told to seize all the cameras of the photographers and maybe the photographers themselves—the Afghan government had earlier banned publicity of Election Day attacks in another dramatic victory for freedom of speech here.

"They're going to kill us!" one photographer shouted.

"Drive, just drive!" another screamed.

They were new. I felt strangely calm. I knew Afghanistan's finest would never shoot. If they did, they'd never hit us. Paula, who had jumped in the passenger side of the car, stretched her foot across to the driver's side and punched the gas. Once the car hopped forward, the police scattered. We roared down the road.

That was enough excitement for my day. Within minutes of the polls closing, Karzai's people claimed victory. It was soon clear why. The fraud had been epic, the kind of fraud that would make dead voters in Chicago sit up and applaud. Ultimately as many as one in three votes would be deemed suspect. Karzai's supporters would bear the most of the blame.

The fallout would smother and choke everything anyone was trying to do here. Karzai would eventually be declared the winner. But if this election was seen as crucial, then it was a crucial failure. Over the following weeks, the UN mission here would fracture. The Obama administration would waver on whether to send more troops to back a corrupt Karzai government and quibble over how best to solve the Afghan morass and nibble at the edges of the more critical threat, Pakistan. Obama's base would split over his eventual decision to send more troops and support, at least for a little while. There would be more talk of a truce with the Taliban, of a political solution, and more demand for building a functioning government. Then more violence, more spectacular attacks, more demands for Karzai to shape up or else. Or else what? We had no stick. Our carrots were limp after almost eight years of waggling around.

I could see the stories that stretched for years into the future, much like the ones that stretched back years into the past. More bombs, more sudden death, more adrenaline. Never had I felt as alive as in Pakistan and Afghanistan, so close to chaos, so constantly reminded of how precious, temporary, and fragile life was. I had certainly grown here. I knew how to find money in a war zone, how to flatter a warlord, how to cover a suicide bombing, how to jumpstart a car using a cord and a metal ladder, how to do the Taliban shuffle between conflict zones. I knew how to be alone. I knew I did not need a man, unless that man was my fixer. But also, I knew I had turned into this almost drowning caricature of a war hack, working, swearing, and drinking my way through life and relationships. My brother now described me as 100 Percent Id, an epitaph I didn't want. Maybe having these four months of unemployment in Kabul helped me figure it out.

After the running, the bombs, the death, the downward spiral, I had a choice—I could choose life, or I could choose to keep hop-ping from one tragedy to the next. Like any junkie, I needed to quit. I decided to go home, knowing full well that this decision was a lot tougher than staying in the warm bath of Kabul. I decided to get out while I could, to graduate from Kabul High. At this point, at least, the party was over. The disastrous election of Karzai was last call. The foreign community's clumsy efforts to save this region so late in the day were like trying to recover from the Afghan rapper DJ Besho deciding to do an impromptu rap show at a Halloween party at 2:30 AM. There was no recovery from that, only the likelihood of some Afghan in his entourage stealing a cell phone on the way out the door.

Tom, my fellow journalist and former housemate at the Fun House, also decided to leave. We planned a going-away party, our last Thursday night throwdown before checking out of the Hotel California. That afternoon, a friend and I drove over to Tom's house to drop off a dozen cases of illegal and therefore expensive wine and beer. As we unloaded, Tom's phone rang.

"Oh, hey Farouq," he said.

I looked at Tom.

"Yes, please come," Tom said. "Yes, yes, it's for her as well."

"Is that my Farouq?" I asked.

Tom nodded. He hung up.

"Why hasn't he called me?" I said. "Is he mad at me?"

Kabul High. Then my phone started ringing. Farouq.

"Hey you!" I said, extremely enthusiastically.

"How are you?" he asked.

I had figured that he had already left Afghanistan on his scholarship. He had figured that I was upset with him, or that I had fled the country when my job did. But after everything we had been through together, any hurt over money, over macho aggression, over perceived anti-Afghan slights simply fell away.

"You're coming tonight, right?" I said.

"Of course."

This was an old-school party, circa 2006. Tom and I decided against having a guest list. We invited our Afghan friends. The garden filled up quickly—predictably, about one-third of the people stumbling around knew neither Tom nor me, various random foreigners who heard about the party from the rumor mill at L'Atmosphère. But Farouq and my Afghan journalist friends showed up, along with various Afghan officials. And I ended up spending most of the party hanging out with the man who had really mattered here more than any other: Farouq. We danced in an oddly shaped hallway, filled with mostly women, a few straight men, a few gay men, and a few tactile British security contractors who were apparently on Ecstasy. Farouq used a scarf as a dancing implement, pulling it behind his neck, pumping his hands in the air. For hours we danced, that is, until Farouq jumped toward me suddenly. His dancing implement had attracted attention.

"Kim!" he whispered. "I think that man is a gay." He nodded toward an American guy.

"Yep," I said, slipping into Farouq lingo. "He is a gay."

We danced a little more. Farouq, the macho Pashtun, then leaned forward again.

"Kim!" he whispered sharply. "The gay just pinched me."

"OK, let's get you out of here."

I walked him outside, and soon he left for home. We always covered each other's backs. Within weeks, Farouq would be on a plane out of Kabul.

Over the next four days, I said my goodbyes, the painful ones, the easy ones, the ones I had put off for years. I visited my embittered Afghan grandpa, Sabit, the country's former attorney general and failed presidential candidate, who sat in his almost empty seven-bedroom eyesore, complaining about the election.

"There was so much fraud, so much fraud," he said, after berating me for disappearing for years. "I tell you, if this was a fair election, I would have won. I was the most popular candidate, everywhere

I went, crowds of people, thousands of them, would come on the streets."

Oh, Sabit, who still had no idea how his popularity had plummeted, who lived in his own Sabit universe. Officially, he won only 5,791 votes, placing nineteenth. Before I left, he asked me whether I knew any foreigners who would rent his house for $5,000 a month.

I packed up my belongings and got ready to fly home. The day I planned to execute my exit strategy, my phone rang. And the caller was the other eccentric older man who had dominated my time, from the other side of the border. Nawaz Sharif. His timing was always impeccable.

"Is this Kim?" he asked.

"Yes," I said, shoving Afghan tourism guides from the 1970s into a suitcase. I was hesitant, unsure of what he wanted.

"So. It's been a long time," he said, awkwardly. "What are your plans to come to Pakistan?"

"Actually, I'm moving back to the U.S. New York, in fact. I'm leaving in a few hours."

"Oh, congratulations. I will have to come see you when I'm in New York," he said.

"That would be great," I replied.

"We're still friends, right?" he asked, tentatively.

"Always," I said.

"We'll stay friends, right?" he said.

"Sure."

We said goodbye. I had about the same level of intention of being friends with Nawaz Sharif as I did with Sam Zell. But I figured I could just end our relationship through the inevitable ennui of distance and time, and through the likelihood that he would never get his hands on my U.S. number. (He was more resourceful than I thought.)

I soon finished packing. Then I looked around my bedroom, grabbed my backpack and two large suitcases, shut off the lights, and walked away, closing the door behind me. In the corner, I left a gray plastic trunk crammed with the things I needed only in Afghanistan. My long-sleeved, pajama-like shirts. A dozen scarves given to me over the years. Packets of wet wipes and a camouflage water bottle for embeds. Maps of Ghazni and Helmand, random electrical cords, and even the T-shirt proclaiming TURKIYE. A sleeping bag. Books on Pashtun tribes and the Taliban. Unused notebooks and ballpoint pens proclaiming AFGHAN PEN on their sides, as if that were some mark of pride and quality, as if Afghanistan were known for its ballpoint pens. I left all of it behind, waiting for me, gathering dust almost as soon as I shut the lid, in a house filled with similar boxes in different rooms, forgotten by people like me, foreigners unwilling to fully commit to leaving Afghanistan but unable to figure out how to stay.

TAKE IT OR LEAVE IT

I n December 2009, President Obama decided to send thirty thousand more U.S. troops to Afghanistan. At the same time, he announced that he would start pulling those troops out by July 2011. In other words, the West continued to send mixed signals to Afghanistan and Pakistan: We love you, we love you not. America's ambivalence was likely because of its amorphous goal—with Al-Qaeda long on the run from Afghanistan and now being picked off by drones in Pakistan, the new focus was on creating some kind of perception of success in the region as quickly as possible so that the U.S. could leave. The strategy seemed to be this: Overwhelm the enemy with superior military force, train some Afghan mopes as police and army, make a political deal with members of the Taliban (who would for some unknown reason make a deal despite the fact that they seemed to be holding all the cards), call it stability, and get the heck out.

In the minds of many in Pakistan and Afghanistan, who were by necessity playing a much longer game, the Americans' endgame was an interval of stability instead of actual stability, and the interval would surely be followed by a civil war, with Pakistan starring as evil puppet master in the background. In this environment, with the West halfway out the door, the Taliban could be seen as peacemakers, as the suitor who would actually commit.

So it was hardly a surprise when U.S. and NATO progress was much slower than anticipated. Attempts to manipulate tribes, as had been done in Iraq, were frustrated by the complicated Afghan tribal system and by competing loyalties. U.S. troops still managed to win hand-to-hand battles—if they couldn't beat a bunch of guys with Kalashnikovs and sandals, the military had much bigger problems than anyone suspected—but a highly publicized Marine offensive in the obscure Helmand district of Marja ended up a draw because of poor follow-through. The planned U.S.-led offensive in Kandahar, Afghanistan's second-largest city, was amended and postponed until it appeared to be more of a playdate. Civilian casualties and corruption continued to alienate the countryside. Roadside bombs and guerrilla attacks continued to pick off NATO troops and Afghan officials. And even as the military drove out the Taliban from various communities, there were still not enough troops to make a permanent stand and no credible Afghan government to fill the gaps. The West's civilian effort was even less effective than the military one. More than eight years into this war, no single agency coordinated all the Western aid or development, least of all the UN.

Karzai, meanwhile, imploded. He allegedly threatened to join the Taliban, pushed out several competent top officials, and consolidated power among his family members and closest allies, the ones who never said no. A particularly loud-mouthed former UN official publicly accused Karzai—now often described as "erratic" in news reports—of being on drugs. I was convinced that wasn't the problem, and that certain drugs might helpfully silence Karzai's demons. But regardless, the gulf between Kabul and the West widened, to the point that Karzai and his backers actually suspected the United States of sponsoring terrorist attacks in Afghanistan. His public courting of the Taliban—apparently he had found an address, even if most of his entreaties were ignored—needed to be seen through his anti-Western lens. Convinced the United States was against him, convinced the United States was leaving, Karzai started planning for his own future. That's likely the major reason he wanted to make a deal with elements of the Taliban—he saw their Pashtun base as the only way to ensure his own survival. His suspicions spread like a contagion through the government. Foreign consultants practically had to submit to colostomies to get visas; restaurants that served alcohol were frequently raided and even shut down; police at checkpoints spent more time shaking down foreigners than they did on hinky Toyota Corollas.

As Afghanistan skidded off the rails, Pakistan was close behind. The Pakistani army launched new offensives against militants in the tribal areas, but as usual, targeted only those groups fighting the Pakistani government or whoever had the misfortune to be the number-three member of Al-Qaeda at the time. The Pakistani Taliban grew bolder, attacking at the heart of the Pakistani army, at national headquarters and the mosque where top military officials prayed on Fridays. Anti-American sentiment reached a kind of zenith. The State Department had a very hard time finding Pakistani police officials willing to travel to the States for training because of ISI warnings to stay home. After all, the ISI asked while strongarming the police, whose side were they on? America's or Pakistan's?

At some point, I realized the horrible truth—the United States and its allies could win every single battle in Afghanistan and blow up every single alleged top militant in Pakistan, but still lose this war.

In my new position, as a press fellow at the Council on Foreign Relations, I was often asked what I thought should be done about the mess in South Asia. I was sure of two things: that a deal among governments and militants would never hold in that harsh environment, and that our current plan with its expiration date was doomed to failure. The United States would be better off bringing everyone home than sticking to a compromise, to the impassable middle road. The only workable solution to the region's many problems was a long-term commitment from the world, with no end date in sight, focused on building actual governance systems rather than prop-ping up various personalities. Only a long-term plan would prevent the region from falling into further chaos, allowing a potpourri of militants, including the largely diminished Al-Qaeda, from eventually creeping back to Afghanistan and claiming a major propaganda victory.

C oming back to the States was an experience similar to having my spleen removed while on laughing gas. Parts of reentry were pleasant. Others were like being cut open without anesthetic. At one point Sean called, concerned about how I was adjusting. He was in Africa on a project, his first time traveling on a story after leaving the Taliban's clutches in Pakistan.

"So, are you finding yourself spending too much time at home, by yourself?" he asked.

"Definitely."

"And you're drinking too much?"

"Possibly."

"And you're dancing around your apartment a lot, listening to loud music, doing a lot of cocaine?"

"Um, no. Perhaps that was you."

But he was right. It was no picnic coming off the adrenaline of a war zone cold turkey, or losing that sense of importance that infused even the most banal activities in Pakistan and Afghanistan. I felt like I was trudging through life, waiting for the "what next," craving airports and a fix. I constantly felt uneasy, like I should be doing something else. Out to dinner with friends, I sensed some unknown deadline hanging over my head. I angered easily. I could not relax. I could not sit still. I could not connect. I had more in common with many U.S. soldiers than I did with my family. I talked often to Farouq, who earned straight A's in his first semester of a master's degree. Eventually his family was able to join him in his new Western home. He wanted to return eventually to Afghanistan to help lead the country; he worried that it wouldn't be safe for his children.

With the passage of time the pull lessened slightly, and the adrenaline monkey on my back shrank to more of a sea monkey. The longer I was in the States, the farther away the war seemed. Maybe it was the loft party in Brooklyn with a misshapen-apple mirrored disco ball dangling from the ceiling and a giant inflatable rat in the corner, but New York started to feel more like home.

Still, the region wouldn't let me go that easily. An amateurish bomb was planted in an SUV in Times Square, just blocks from my apartment, and for hours, my neighborhood was shut down. The wannabe bomber clearly had attended the jihadi short course in Pakistan as opposed to summer camp; he used the wrong kind of fertilizer and left his keys in the car. Improbably, the Pakistani Taliban—a group that was very skilled at bombing, much more so than the Afghan Taliban—was blamed for the botched effort. The Taliban was stalking me! Even if I was moving on, clearly they could not.

Then, in May 2010, with my fellowship almost over and unemployment looming, the call came. It was a major news organization. Would I go back to Kabul? My first thought was, Hell yes! Yes to Kabul, yes to bombs, yes to that electrical jolt I got just thinking about Kabul. Yes to chaos and crazy, yes to toga parties, yes to Kabul High, yes to *insh'Allah,* yes to endless cups of tea, just yes. I thought about it seriously for a few days, before waking up one morning and realizing—no. Just like I couldn't go back to Chicago, I couldn't go back to Kabul. I had already graduated, after all, and everyone knows you can't go back to high school. Especially when that high school is a war zone, especially when that war zone is falling apart. I rationalized my decision: I could always go back for the class reunion, which if the past was any guide would be in another ten or twelve years, when history would probably repeat itself, when all the same players or their latest incarnations would start the dance again.

ACKNOWLEDGMENTS

This book started out as comic relief, as an antidote to all that was falling apart. I would never have been able to write it without the help of Farouq and my other Afghan friends—they're some of the funniest people I know, even if I still don't get the Mullah Nasruddin jokes. Credit also goes to my friends in Pakistan, especially to my unnamed translator. You know who you are. If comedy is tragedy plus time, time has been compressed into minutes in that part of the world.

For their insightful comments on early drafts, a DJ Besho–like shout-out to Lisa Cowan, Nicole Ruder, Bay Fang, Katherine Brown, MP Nunan, Dorothy Parvaz, Jasmin Shah, Ronan McDermott, and Rebekah Grindlay.

Although most of the journalists in Afghanistan and Pakistan are more like my extended family, special thanks are due to Soraya Sarhaddi Nelson for handing me that shot of whiskey at 9 AM, Jason Straziuso for talking books and teaching me to play poker, and Aryn Baker for running around three countries with me. Thanks also to Tom Coghlan, Jeremy Foster, Tammy Haq, and especially Sean Langan for their collective sense of humor and fact-checking. For late nights and unwavering support, I owe countless favors to Nurith Aizenman, Sophie Barry, Belinda Bowling, Paula Bronstein, Carlotta

Gall, Joanna Nathan, Rachel Reid, Candace Rondeaux, Mary Louise Vitelli, and Frauke De Weijer.

For obvious reasons, I'd be remiss if I didn't thank the *Chicago Tribune* and my editors, who gambled and sent a unilingual green reporter overseas. The *Tribune* is still home to some of the best journalists I've ever worked alongside.

Back in the United States, I'm also extremely grateful to my agent, Larry Weissman, who understood this book as soon as I pitched the idea, and to my editor at Doubleday, Kristine Puopolo, who believed in my absurd vision.

I'm indebted to the Council on Foreign Relations for rescuing me, supporting me, and reminding me which fork to use. And to ProPublica—thanks for keeping me grounded and giving me new challenges.

Last, but never least, much love and gratitude to my family. To my brother, Todd Barker, for pushing me to jump. And to Gary Barker and Connie Collier for putting up with my disappearing act. It's almost too much to ask of parents, even former hippies.

ABOUT THE AUTHOR

Kim Barker grew up in Montana, Wyoming, and Oregon, and graduated from Northwestern University with a degree in journalism. She worked at the *Spokesman-Review* in Spokane, Washington, for four years, and the *Seattle Times* for two years, winning awards for her investigative reporting. In 2001, at age thirty, she joined the *Chicago Tribune* and began making reporting trips to Afghanistan and Pakistan the next year. Barker was the *Tribune*'s South Asia bureau chief from 2004 to 2009. She was then awarded the Council on Foreign Relations' Edward R. Murrow press fellowship to study Afghanistan and Pakistan. She now lives in New York City, where she works as a reporter at ProPublica.